Queering Colonial Natal

*Indigeneity and the Violence of
Belonging in Southern Africa*

T.J. Tallie

UNIVERSITY OF MINNESOTA PRESS

MINNEAPOLIS LONDON

An earlier version of chapter 1 was published as "Queering Natal: Settler Logics and the Disruptive Challenge of Zulu Polygamy," *GLQ: A Journal of Lesbian and Gay Studies* 19, no. 2 (2013): 167–89. An earlier version of chapter 3 was published as "Shifting Alliances: Social Order and the Politics of Friendship in Colonial Natal, 1850–1910," in *Ties That Bind: Race and the Politics of Friendship in South Africa*, edited by Jon Soske and Shannon Walsh (Johannesburg, South Africa: Wits University Press, 2016). An earlier version of chapter 4 was published as "Sartorial Settlement: The Mission Field and Transformation in Colonial Natal, 1850–1897," *Journal of World History* 27, no. 3 (2016): 389–410.

Published by the University of Minnesota Press
111 Third Avenue South, Suite 290
Minneapolis, MN 55401-2520
http://www.upress.umn.edu

Printed in the United States of America on acid-free paper

The University of Minnesota is an equal-opportunity educator and employer.

Library of Congress Cataloging-in-Publication Data
Names: Tallie, T.J., author.
Title: Queering colonial Natal : indigeneity and the violence of belonging in southern Africa / T.J. Tallie.
Description: Minneapolis : University of Minnesota Press, 2019. | Includes bibliographical references and index. |
Identifiers: LCCN 2018058232 (print) | ISBN 978-1-5179-0517-0 (hc) | ISBN 978-1-5179-0518-7 (pb)
Subjects: LCSH: Colonists—South Africa—KwaZulu-Natal. | Zulu (African people)—South Africa—KwaZulu-Natal—Social life and customs—19th century. | KwaZulu-Natal (South Africa)—Colonial influence. | KwaZulu-Natal (South Africa)—Race relations. | KwaZulu-Natal (South Africa)—History—1843–1893. | KwaZulu-Natal (South Africa)—History—1893–1910.
Classification: LCC DT2223.Z85 T35 2019 (print) | DDC 968.4004963986—dc23
LC record available at https://lccn.loc.gov/2018058232

Contents

Ukuphazama iNatali

Queerness, Indigeneity, and the
Politics of an African Settler Colony

Natal, the focus of this book, was a nineteenth-century settler colony on the southeastern corner of the African continent. The British government established Natal in 1843 after forcibly annexing the then five-year-old polity of Natalia, a space carved out by land-hungry Dutch-speaking farmers from the lands of Nguni language speakers[1] recently under the hegemony of the Zulu royal house led by Shaka kaSenzan-gakhona (r. 1816–1828) and later his brothers, Dingane (r. 1828–1840) and Mpande (r. 1840–1872). Unlike many other settler colonies in the British Empire, which experienced a disproportionate increase in white settler population in relation to indigenous peoples, the European population in Natal remained a distinct minority throughout the nineteenth century, outnumbered by indigenous Africans by nearly ten to one.[2] The racial demographics of Natal force us to significantly reexamine the ways in which settler societies make claims over indigenous bodies and spaces.

For much of the nineteenth century, Natal was somewhat neglected by imperial officials in London and served as a space of intense contestation between a tiny settler minority and a far larger indigenous population.[3] Imitating the practices of earlier settler societies across the globe, Natal's new government sought to cordon off indigenous land reserves and enshrine African custom in a static and separate legal code. With the arrival of the Byrne settlers in 1850, Natal's first major immigration scheme, and continuing throughout the century, Natal's nascent white population sought to increase their numbers to legitimate their political claim to the colonial territory.

British settlers and colonial officials alike envisioned Natal as part of a global nineteenth-century Anglophone settler project, predicated upon the dispossession and marginalization of indigenous peoples in order to claim access to their lands and labor. By 1879, Natal's settler society appeared to be relatively secure. The independent Zulu kingdom to the northeast had been defeated by British troops and their king, Cetshwayo kaMpande, had been exiled to the Cape. In addition, the colony had secured a sustainable and profitable industry in sugar planting, depending primarily on the labor of Indian migrant workers, who labored largely on the coastal regions of the colony, south of the bourgeoning port city of Durban. Yet as the nineteenth century wore on, Natal's settler population faced a discomfiting realization: they had failed to surpass indigenous people in numbers, and a rising Indian population also threatened to overtake them as the largest exogenous community within the colony. Outnumbered by African peoples they desired to supplant and Indian immigrants they viewed as threats, the colony's European settler population worked to achieve autonomy from the imperial government and legitimize their claim to sole control in Natal. The *legitimacy of logistics*—the gradual establishment of a settler majority in the colony through external migration and anti-indigenous violence—that occurred in other settler societies like Australia, New Zealand, and Canada continued to elude Natal. As Lady Barker, the wife of the colony's governor, opined in 1877, "There is no doubt about it, Natal will never be an attractive country to European immigrants, and if it is not to be fairly crowded out of the list of progressive English colonies by its black population, we must devise some scheme for bringing them into the great brotherhood of civilization."[4] This left Natal's settler population (largely concentrated in the cities of Durban and Pietermaritzburg and in pockets of farmlands in the midlands) without a demographic justification for their claims to sovereignty over the region, and weakened their claims to speak for and know what was best for the indigenous peoples of the colony, at least in the eyes of British administrators.

Achieving political and military dominance over the independent Zulu kingdom did not bring the demographic security desired by Natal's settler population. Immigration continued to be slow, and the predominant numbers of indigenous peoples never shrank like they did in most other British settler colonies in this period. Slowly but surely, Europeans in Natal began to agree with the assessments of men like H. Rider Haggard, who first observed in 1882:

> To suppose that the emigrant would go to Natal when he came to understand that it was an independent settlement of a few white men, living in the midst of a mass of warlike Kafirs, when Australia, New Zealand, Canada, and the United States, are all holding out their arms to him, is to suppose him a bigger fool than he is. At the best of times Natal is not likely to attract many desirable emigrants.[5]

As a consequence, in the 1880s and 1890s Natal's settler elites sought to solidify their control over the reins of political power in the colony, and worked to limit the legal, social, and political options of indigenous Africans and Indian migrants. The last decades of the nineteenth century witnessed an intense contestation between peoples as settlers attempted to consolidate power, Africans and Indians challenged these actions, and a paternalist imperial government tried to pursue multiple prerogatives. All groups in Natal utilized language of race and conceptions of gender and race to make claims to sovereignty and autonomy in the colony.

As a settler society with a relatively unique demographic formulation and geographic position, Natal provides an ideal vantage point from which to study the uneven realities of British imperial sovereignty in the nineteenth century. Natal's history implicitly challenges the official claims of a unidirectional imperial project of expanding civilization and indigenous acculturation. In fact, parliamentary papers, newspaper editorials, and personal letters reveal an anxious colonial state that worried that emigrant men and women would fail to create a properly ordered territory. In light of these sources we are in need of an interpretation of settler societies like Natal that takes into account the concomitant nature of race and gender production in the colony amid fears of contamination from indigenous influence. Indeed, throughout the empire, indigenous peoples did not meekly submit to the pulls of capitalist economic processes or Christian acculturation.[6] They could—and often did—selectively appropriate ideological or cultural ideas for their own use, forging links across trans-imperial spaces as distant as New Zealand, India, and North America.[7]

What follows is a recounting of the history of Natal in the second half of the nineteenth century that pays careful attention to the intertwined nature of the discursive and the material while studying the refracting, mutable connections of a settler outpost with the larger empire. *Queering Colonial Natal* analyzes social relations within the colony while keeping its messy, multisided histories at the fore. I do this through a methodology that combines queer theoretical approaches with critical indigenous studies.

I was first drawn to the destabilizing potential of queer theory as a graduate student at the University of Illinois, where I began interrogating the shared stakes of settler colonialism, indigeneity, and claims of belonging. A queer theoretical read of a subject can seek to understand just *how* the norms that underpin structures of power are created, and to peer beyond the claims of hegemonic groups to see how these norms are made and unmade through daily actions. In thinking through queer theory and its application in colonial Natal, I am critical of the ways in which institutions like marriage, the family, the church, the military, or the colony more generally depend upon assumptions of normativity, heterosexual reproduction, and proper behavior. To do this involves examining intersectional, relational forms of gender identity, from thinking through precolonial African women's roles to the forms of bricolage created by the collision of colonial missionaries and indigenous social norms.

Indeed, queer theoretical texts are invaluable in analyzing institutions within colonial Natal. Judith Butler's insistence on gender as performative and of heterosexuality as a project always on the brink of failure offers immediate insights into the understanding of settler colonialism in Natal.[8] Such analysis reveals much about the lives and aspirations of European settlers, particularly in contexts like Natal's white male boarding schools, where race and gender were identities that had to be inculcated through quotidian acts of violence, as Robert Morrell attests.[9] This theoretical analysis also can reveal the ways in which patriarchy structures the self-conception and strategies of indigenous Africans in response to settler pressure. Thinking of the ways in which gendered claims to authority and autonomy are constantly made and unmade in a relational context illuminates much about Zulu masculinity.[10] Similarly, the investigations of Michel Foucault into knowledge, power, and the body have done much to further understanding of colonial contexts, particularly in its elaborations by Ann Laura Stoler.[11] Stoler and Foucault, along with theorist Anne McClintock, have insisted that gender and sexuality are core components for understanding colonial interactions.[12] They point to the idea that all hegemonic structures of power require forms of embodied discipline and control. This is apparent in instances ranging from Shaka's shaping of male and female age ranks to the attempts of the settler state in Natal to enforce laws around proper marriage, family, and reproduction. Queer theory, then, has much to offer in thinking through and with structures of power and domination in colonial Natal.

Likewise, *Queering Colonial Natal* connects southern Africa to the larger contemporary world of nineteenth-century settler colonialism, something that has been profoundly missing in academic work on the colony. The critical study of settler colonialism has enjoyed a new prominence in histories of North America and Australasia as a means of understanding the relations that structured the lives of both colonists and previous inhabitants of these lands.[13] Yet, with few exceptions, this framework has not been widely applied to southern Africa in general and Natal in particular.[14] Settler colonial studies situates the inherent conflict between indigeneity and settler nationalist claims to belonging within a larger framework of marginalization and appropriation, foregrounding the historic violence that structures these nationalist assertions of autochthony[15] in sites of recent European settlement. "Settler colonialism destroys to replace," as the late anthropologist Patrick Wolfe has bluntly stated. "Settler colonizers come to stay: invasion is a structure not an event."[16] For Wolfe, settler colonies differ from colonies of extraction (or nonsettlement) in that the colonizer literally comes to stay;

unlike in other colonial societies where the colonizer eventually returns to the metropole, the nature of occupation is naturalized and daily enacted in an emergent national form.

Recognition of the inherently genocidal attitude of settlers toward the indigenous population remains critical to understanding settler colonialism as a social and political formation. Such a claim has been debated by scholars of settler colonialism, most notably Wolfe himself, but Natal (as well as the Cape) possesses a lengthy history of imperial genocidal logics. In 1851, British politician J. A. Roebuck argued before Parliament that "English colonists could not be placed [in South Africa] without the inevitable consequence of annihilating the aborigines. That was what had been done in New Zealand, in Australia, in North America, in all our colonies, and that was what would be done in South Africa if the present system were continued."[17] Roebuck (who spent his childhood in British India and Canada) argued in favor of a global policy of elimination, maintaining that "we should dispossess them of their land, and the poor wretches would be driven back and exterminated." This view appeared to have purchase on the ground in settler circles as well. Natal settler Charles Barter stated unequivocally in 1852 that Africans, as in the examples of indigenous peoples in North America and Australasia, must follow "the mysterious law which has ordained that the brown men should disappear before the white, as the snow melts beneath the rays of an April sun."[18] While its demographic realities differed considerably from other, non-African settler colonies, Natal certain fits within the genocidal logics espoused by their settler contemporaries.

An indigenous studies–centered approach within a settler colonial framework allows room for reading forms of resistance and challenge while foregrounding the significant power disparities that operated in European settler relations with indigenous Africans (as well as Indian migrants) in Natal. As theorist Aileen Moreton-Robinson has noted, historic settler violence has resulted in the privileging of European claims to authority in systems of knowledge production throughout (post)imperial spaces.[19] As a result, settler colonial spaces like Natal were not merely sites of intense negotiation, but locations shaped profoundly by a quotidian and violent Eurocentrism that presumed superiority.

A queer theoretical approach has allowed scholars to analyze not only instances in which subjects evince a sexual identification that is not explicitly heterosexual, but also the ways in which actions or positions can challenge larger normative systems. A *queer* reading, then, can offer an exploration of how lines of assumed order are skewed by ideas, actions, or formations. If settler colonialism itself is presented as a form of orientation, of making a recognizable and inhabitable home space for European arrivals on indigenous land, then native peoples and their continued resistance can serve to "queer" these attempted forms of order.[20] In such circumstances, the customs, practices, and potentially the very bodies of indigenous peoples can become *queer* despite remaining ostensibly heterosexual in their orientation and practice, as their existence constantly undermines the desired order of an emergent settler state.[21] Following this line of inquiry, queer theorists have questioned the theoretically normative underpinnings of settler occupation and orientation of indigenous bodies (and lands). This has the potential for producing forms of decolonizing praxis in contemporary settler societies and providing a powerful means of critically engaging with established normative frameworks in a wide range of settler states.[22] Scott Morgensen has combined an indigenous reading of settler naturalization with a queer challenge to normative formations: "[S]ettlers practice settlement by turning Native land and culture into an inheritance granting them knowledge and ownership of *themselves*."[23] Indeed, a queer read of settler colonialism can allow for theorizing about the genocidal, acquisitive *desire* inherent within the efforts to remove and replace indigenous peoples. What would it look like to exist in a space where the reproduction of one group of people was encouraged directly at the expense of another? In the context of colonial Natal, this included using the specter of indigenous African social and sexual formations, such as polygamy, to denote threats to European dominance as well as to define what constituted "proper" and "civilized" settler behavior.

An approach that combines queer theory with indigenous critique has the potential to *unsettle* the presumptions of a settler state to lay claim to the bodies and lands of indigenous peoples. The logics of settlement, which presuppose a demographic legerdemain whereupon new

European immigrants must replace the indigenous peoples whose lands they hope to usurp, require a determined emphasis on reproduction, both physical and social, in the contested colonial space. With the bodies of the indigenous peoples deemed queer by settlers for resisting their attempts at cultural and social hegemony, sexuality and heteronormative reproduction become paramount in a settler colonial context. And while indigenous practices may themselves be read as heterosexual by European observers, the very existence of alternative social and sexual formations presents a queer threat to a potential settler state. The continuance of indigenous social formations like polygamy and the problem of limited European population growth reveal the anxieties surrounding reproductive futurity that operated at the heart of colonial Natal. By deeming the bodies of the indigenous peoples queer for resisting their attempts to enforce European mores, settlers underlined the centrality of sexuality and heteronormative reproduction in colonial society. The reproductive futurity established in settler states, to borrow from Lee Edelman, constitutes a privileging of the figure of the white colonial child as the hope for securing the occupation and legitimacy of the next generation of settlers.[24] While settlers may have viewed indigenous social and sexual formations as queer threats to the reproductive regimes they hoped to establish in Natal, indigenous people clearly did not see themselves in this fashion. Rather, these very formations had the potential to enact their own normative regimes of behavior, both to resist settler co-optation and to maintain internal hierarchies of power within indigenous African societies.[25] As a consequence, *Queering Colonial Natal* also pushes queer theory beyond a normative/transgressive paradigm, instead emphasizing that indigenous and settler practices (such as marriage) could be normative and still potentially quite queer.

Combining queer theory with indigenous studies in studying the history of colonial Natal offers two significant results. First, such a theoretical approach produces a powerful critical synthesis. Thinking through the colonial record with an eye for both structures of power as well as the norms that enabled them destabilizes visions of settler colonial society in the archival record. In doing so, issues like indigenous polygamy and *ilobolo*, the ceremonial offering of cattle from one family to another at marriage, become intensely contested sites between European legislators, missionaries, and African peoples. African men and women challenged settler claims that they possessed a monopoly on social and sexual order, undermining the imperial project. As a theoretical framework, a queer and indigenous approach to Natal not only allows for a subversive read of settler claims but also opens up the possibility of privileging indigenous thought and intervention in colonial society, a particularly difficult task.

Second, a queer indigenous studies reading in Natal's colonial history puts pressure on queer theory more generally. Much has been written about the limits of queer theory, particularly in light of its colonialist, Western framework. Most notably, Nigerian anthropologist Ifi Amadiume has taken to task Western readings of indigenous sexual and social practices under a larger universal queerness as a form of cultural imperialism.[26] Indeed, by extrapolating theoretical understandings of gendered and sexual norms from Western perspectives, queer theory can run the risk of reinscribing imperialist identifications on the lives and identities of African peoples. One crucial way of avoiding this pitfall lies in identifying queer identifications as relational; as a consequence, for peoples or practices to be labeled queer, such targets need not be nonheterosexual, a claim advanced by scholars like Cathy Cohen and Mark Rifkin.[27] Such an innovation can, therefore, draw upon such diverse sources as Gayle Rubin's hierarchies of appropriate sexualities and Frantz Fanon's invocation of the profoundly othered black subject in order to show the ways in which a queer subjectivity can exist as an external label rather than an internalized identity.[28] An indigenous-centered approach also challenges us to think of the ways in which notions of troubling sexuality and gender may still involve universalizing Western epistemologies or categories in relation to indigenous peoples, a position that should be constantly, critically assessed.[29]

Thus, doing the work of queer indigenous work in Natal allows us to both *queer* settlement and *indigenize* queerness. "Queering settlement" refers to the work of destabilizing, challenging, and critically reviewing the normative structures of power that enabled the world of settler colonialism in Natal, while paying particular attention to moments of challenge and resistance. "Indigenizing queerness" connotes the difficult task

of thinking through queerness as more than an external intellectual project that can be merely mapped onto exotic and different contexts. This
work involves constant, critical analysis that looks at sexual and gender
norms within indigenous African culture in Natal and examines the
ways in which these norms could subvert or resist heteronormative
settler order.[30] This is why I have titled this introduction *Ukuphazama
iNatali* rather than "Queering Natal." *Ukuphazama* means "to disturb,
interrupt, or distract." (Indeed, the noun form *isiphazamisa* has been
claimed as the root of the common word *spaza* for the local home-based
shops designed to disrupt the regular capitalist pattern of patronizing
white-owned businesses during the apartheid era.)[31] Although I have
found very few references to what Westerners would have termed nonheterosexual practices among indigenous Africans in nineteenth-century
Natal, traces are available in the archival record. Fleeting references exist
in English-Zulu dictionaries prepared by missionaries that describe
forms of sexual socialization among African men. In addition, Zackie
Achmat's study of the Ninevites at the turn of the century reveals the
potential of recovery and analysis of divergent African sexualities in the
contemporary period.[32]

     With that spirit of *ukuphakazama* in mind, each chapter follows a
queer indigenous analysis of colonial Natal. Chapter 1 examines how the
Zulu practices of *ilobolo* (the ritual exchange of cattle from the groom's
family to the wife's upon marriage) and polygamy became critical sites
for the demarcation (at least in settler eyes) of "proper behavior," resulting in the creation and negotiation of claims of legitimate occupation of
the land. I argue that discourses of civilization and "proper" family structures mapped onto emergent categories of racial difference in nineteenth-
century Natal. Consequently, Natal's legislators attempted to shore up
discursive difference through the creation and implementation of Native
Law, a formation through which the settler state sought to quarantine
threatening indigenous difference from the European population. Simultaneously, however, settler legislators worked to render their own sexual and social practices as effectively normative, a process visible in the
debates over sororate marriage in Natal. Zulu articulations of polygamy
and *ilobolo* further complicated the interplay between indigenous and

emigrant, resulting in a colony where race and gender could be mobilized by multiple actors in pursuit of sovereign claims in a highly contested space.

Chapter 2 explores settler claims to self-control and sobriety with the subsequent attempts of the settler state to legislate racial difference by restricting intoxicant consumption only to Europeans. By legally restricting alcohol use to whites, settlers in Natal linked citizenship, camaraderie, and sociability to specific bodies within the colony while purposefully denying access to populations of color, actions other settler colonies, such as British Columbia and New Zealand, also simultaneously attempted. The attempts of the Natal legislature to establish racial distinctions in alcohol consumption throughout the nineteenth century reveal similar limitations and complexities in the creation of settler colonial power. Africans continued to find access to European-produced alcoholic beverages through a variety of channels, and the brewing of *umqombothi*, a traditional beer made from grain, could not easily be eliminated by a disapproving government. Likewise, Indians in Natal found themselves the focus of widespread settler displeasure for consuming intoxicants. However, they successfully managed to evade legislative limitations throughout most of the century, often by making claims to higher civilization or to being citizens of the empire rather than subjects, like Africans. The attempts of a settler state to legislate "proper" consumption demonstrate the links between colonial civilizational discourses and the subsequent attempts to legislate racial hierarchies.

Chapter 3 begins with the 1854 arrival of Anglican bishop John Colenso in Natal, and his first encounters with African peoples. Recalling that settler administrators had discouraged familiarity with indigenous peoples, Colenso found himself reluctantly performing a show of self-possessed indifference in front of the first African peoples he countered. This moment of interrupted friendship provides a profound and intriguing site of rupture in the colonial record. Focusing on the constitutive and constructed nature of raced and gendered hierarchies in colonial Natal, I propose a reading of friendly encounters that underscores their protean nature. Friendship and various forms of sociability across gendered or raced lines could work to either reinforce or unsettle

European power in the nineteenth century, and the legislative record is rife with concerns over "improper" forms of socialization. By isolating certain moments of broad social consensus (available in newspapers, settler legislative debates, or isiZulu periodicals), this chapter studies the ways in which friendship could either support or trouble quotidian relations in Natal.

Chapter 4 studies the dynamics of the Christian mission, and the ways that developing categories of race and gender could be affected by discourses of spiritual transformation espoused by European and American missionaries. These transformations, however, were dependent upon observable physical changes—most notably in dress, domestic lifeways, and family organization that signaled a move toward civilization. As with polygamy and intoxicants, the settler state sought in a piecemeal fashion to legislate racial distinctions, particularly in its attempt to pass the Clothing of the Natives Bill in 1880. This bill attempted to shore up claims of white civilization as symbolized by "appropriate" sartorial display within the colony, and built upon previous legislation that tried to compel Africans to wear suitable clothing. The spaces of the mission station, then, reveal the limits of settlement and civilization in the colony as the legal apparatus of the state attempted to enforce raced and gendered mores in the latter nineteenth century.

The final chapter analyzes the rise of educational institutions within colonial Natal. As indigenous Africans, Indian migrants, and British settlers all clamored for access to education, the state attempted to develop institutions that forced various peoples into roles most amenable for an emerging colonial hierarchy. The messy, collisionary creation of educational institutions in Natal from the 1870s to 1910 offers a unique vantage point with which to understand the creation and development of raced and gendered markers within the colony, and the ways in which people sought to use these markers to push for their own claims of belonging. This chapter, unlike the others, focuses on the development of a larger institution in Natal to see how a variety of actors made claims and counterclaims to be rightful members of the colony.

A queer and indigenous studies–centered reading of southern African history is a difficult, uneven task. It has been a particular challenge throughout *Queering Colonial Natal* to prioritize statistical normalities or consistent finds in the archival records with theoretical analysis of settler colonialism, indigeneity, and "queerness." Such an analysis, however, foregrounds indigenous agency, challenges the normalizing efforts of settlement, and addresses the complex intersections of race, gender, and class in nineteenth-century colonial Natal. *Ukuphazama iNatali*, then, is an ever-unfinished project, one that consistently attempts to read and disrupt historic structures of power and domination in a region claimed by many differing peoples.

CHAPTER ONE

"That Shameful Trade in a Person"

Ilobolo *and Polygamy*

Soon after arrival in colonial Natal, European men and women artic-ulated their claims to belong there as proper citizens, a process supported by the creation and use of marriage law, which rested upon constitutively developed concepts of race and gender. In this context, indigenous practices both within Natal and in the powerful Zulu kingdom on the colony's northeastern border of *isithembu* (polygynous marriage, rendered nearly universally in contemporary documents as "polygamy") and *ilobolo* (the traditional offering of cattle from the groom to the bride's family)[1] became sites of intense contestation where settlers could make civilizational claims of advancement against improper native formula-tions. Yet African peoples frequently viewed their practices as normative, resisting and reframing European attempts to mark them as aberrant, thus shaping the contours of settler colonialism in Natal.

This is not to deny the immense power inequities between European settlers and indigenous Africans (as well as Indian migrants) in Natal. Theorist Aileen Moreton-Robinson has crucially noted that the systems of knowledge production throughout (post)imperial spaces have been stamped resolutely by a European claim of authority, insidiously eras-ing indigenous work through the naturalizations of settler violence.[2] As a result, settler colonial spaces like Natal were not merely sites of intense negotiation, but locations shaped profoundly by a quotidian and violent Eurocentricism that presumed superiority. Newspaper editorials and legislative debates indicate that polygamy and *ilobolo* offered con-tinuous reassurance of European claims to civilization and moral author-ity in the face of "uncivilized" Africans. Polygamy and *ilobolo* also served to discipline potentially aberrant marital and social practices among white Natalians. These contestations over indigenous social practices reveal the limits of settlement in colonial Natal, as settler claims to legit-imacy through the moral superiority offered by their ostensibly more enlightened gender roles and marriage practices ran headlong into the persistent and powerful logics of the indigenous peoples that outnum-bered them ten to one.

In this chapter I specifically engage with indigenous studies and queer theory to destabilize the presumed norms of settler colonialism and push against the interpretations offered in previous South African and British historiography. An approach that combines queer theory with indigenous critique has the potential to profoundly unsettle the presumptions of a settler state to lay claim to the bodies and lands of indigenous peoples. Queer theory has enabled scholars to analyze not only nonheterosexual sexuality, but also actions or ideas that challenge larger normative systems. Following this line of inquiry, queer theorists have questioned the theoretically normative underpinnings of settler occupation and orientation of indigenous bodies (and lands).[3] A queer reading, then, of colonial Natal explores how the customs, practices, and potentially the very bodies of indigenous peoples can become *queer* despite remaining ostensibly heterosexual in orientation and practice, as their existence constantly undermines the desired order of an emergent settler state.[4] In a colonial context, this may also mean using the specter of indigenous social and sexual formations, such as polygamy and *ilobolo*, to more clearly denote what is proper and civilized settler behavior.

By deeming the bodies of the indigenous peoples queer for resisting their attempts to enforce European mores, settlers underlined the cen-trality of sexuality and heteronormative reproduction in colonial society. And while indigenous peoples may not themselves be nonheterosexual, their very existence, and the existence of alternative social and sexual formations present a queer threat to imagined reproductive futurity.[5] Although the genocidal rhetoric of settlement diminished considerably in Natal in the last years of the nineteenth century, the 1850s–1870s undoubtedly featured triumphalist narratives of indigenous disappearance and settler inheritance. But the indigenous peoples did not disappear, and nor did their social practices, while at the same time European settlement lagged. These demographic realities underlie the anxieties surrounding reproductive futurity that operated at the heart of colonial Natal.

The purposes of this chapter, then, are twofold. First, I wish to examine how *ilobolo* and polygamy became critical sites for the demarcation (at least in settler eyes) of proper behavior, for both settlers and indigenous peoples in the colony. Throughout the latter half of the nineteenth century these indigenous marital and social practices served as a significant battleground where settlers and indigenous observers both offered profoundly raced and gendered claims to legitimately occupy the contested spaces of Natal. For settlers, the remaking and reorienting of African bodies away from savagery into civilization took a visible form in the fight over polygamy. Secondly, I argue that a resultant legal compromise evolved over the course of the nineteenth century where settlers reserved civil law unto themselves and relegated indigenous practices to a codified sphere of management named Native Law. This legal and social maneuver attempted to both bolster (while simultaneously defining) standard settler practice as the norm against indigenous practices while also working to quarantine polygamy and *ilobolo* in an "invented tradition" described by historians like Terence Ranger.[6] This compromise, however, was an imagined solution to the inherent problems of settler colonialism. In everyday interactions, settlers and Africans created ideas of race, gender, and sexuality that the legal apparatus of the colonial law attempted to domesticate and control. Yet the settler state in Natal could not be secured by legal legerdemain. Rather, the legal and moral wrangling demonstrated the slipperiness of colonial social formations, and the ways in which race and gender could be marshaled on all sides in changing contexts to press claims for belonging, control, or legitimacy.

The Stakes of Theorizing *Ilobolo* and Polygamy in Colonial Natal

Why did indigenous social and sexual practices like polygamy and *ilobolo* offer such a challenge to the settler project in Natal? Ultimately, the two practices became flashpoints in a broader struggle over significance in the settler colony, both for their role in indigenous economic processes and in colonial discussions of propriety throughout the century. Polygamy and *ilobolo* existed as discrete yet deeply interlinked concepts— although most marriages among Nguni-speaking peoples in the pre-colonial era involved some form of contractual acknowledgment through the exchange of cattle, certainly not all marriages were polygamous in nature. Yet in the nineteenth century, both processes became even more deeply enmeshed as a result of two long-term developments in colonial Natal.

First, colonial economic coercion led to a transformation of the pre-existing socioeconomic processes that governed much of indigenous African life, from gendered divisions of labor to social hierarchies within local communities. Secondly, polygamy and *ilobolo* were linked more tightly through racialized and gendered discourses of morality articulated by British settlers who struggled to render such practices comprehensible on their own, normative terms. As British settlers attempted to understand, demarcate, and reshape the colonial spaces they occupied, social formations like polygamy and *ilobolo* became more than means of ensuring economic and social reproduction for Africans. Rather, as an emergent settler state sought to codify legal systems and straighten disorder through colonial governance, polygamy and *ilobolo* became part of a raced and gendered means of interpreting indigenous peoples and societies, a process Renisa Mawani has termed juridical truth-building.[7] This juridical process is essential to understand the colonial project in Natal, yet its implementation occurred directly as a result of a *discursive* truth-making, as nonlegislative observers penned critical views of polygamy and *ilobolo* and demanded governmental recourse to the problems of indigenous social formations. This discursive environment facilitated and fueled the machinery of settler governmentality, which culminated in the establishment of a separate Native Law and the legal recognition of customary polygamy under Law 1 of 1869.

For indigenous Africans, both immediately before and during the advent of colonial rule in Natal, polygamous relationships served several functions. For men in power, they acted as a means of controlling

access to women of marriageable age, reinscribing hierarchical relationships between older and younger generations.[8] They also allowed for
forms of economic and social production well adapted to the veldt of
Natal through the combined labors of wives and husband in an *umuzi*
(pl. imizi), or homestead-based agricultural/pastoral economy. In addition, *ilobolo* functioned as an investment in the labor and productivity of
the household, allowing for new opportunities for economic growth while
further connecting kin in links of obligation that increased a sense of
commitment to the success of the *umuzi*.[9] A vigorous debate exists in
South African historiography surrounding the power and position of
women in precolonial indigenous African societies, despite the diffi-
culty of accessing the interior voices and opinions of indigenous women
in the mid-nineteenth century.[10] While the precolonial labor and political aspects of *umuzi* system depended upon the extraction of women's
agricultural and domestic labor power by men, the daily reality involved
a considerably complex set of power relationships between indigenous
men and women prior to the arrival of British settlers. It is far less certain that women were completely constrained by these gendered relations
or viewed their own normative marriage and social formations as inherently oppressive.

Whether or not indigenous African women themselves saw polygamy
as a means of negotiating their position in an agrarian society mattered
very little to settlers. In newsprint, missionary pamphlets, and travel literature, Natal's settlers consistently depicted women as oppressed by the
barbarism of their men—particularly through *ilobolo* and polygamous
marriages.[11] The majority of settlers read indigenous gendered systems
of labor as institutionalized female drudgery and depicted *ilobolo* to the
simple purchase of a wife (or multiple wives, in the case of polygamy).
Settler authors painted a picture of indigenous social formations as both
deviant and degrading to proper gender order. As an editorial in the
Durban-based *Natal Mercury* put it succinctly, the primary problem in
the colony was "woman-slavery, inducing indolent habits in the men."[12]
Polygamy and *ilobolo*, then, challenged European attempts to control
indigenous peoples to support both normative discourses of gender and
the economic needs of an emergent settler state.

Indeed, the continued practice of polygamy among African men and women exposed the limits of European social control and authority. With both a minimal settler population and military presence in its first decades, colonial Natal frequently demonstrated the limits of European hegemony over sexual practices and mores. Like other frontier settlements of the British Empire in the mid-nineteenth century (such as British Columbia and New Zealand), Natal was host to a number of white men who themselves engaged in interracial, polygamous, same-sex, or other non-normative social/sexual formations.[13] By making polygamy and *ilobolo* the main focus of their attacks, settler authors could obliquely attempt to police their own polities or at least render them more legibly heteronormative by comparison. These practices were abominable in settler eyes largely because of a presumed moral inferiority that manifested in a gender inequality that settlers claimed that they themselves lacked. However, moralist attempts to legitimate occupation due to the proper social practices of Europeans were not as monolithic as some Natalians may have imagined. The moral attacks on these formations also served to discipline settler behavior, as the legal cases of unorthodox settler marriages and press depictions of degenerate British men demonstrate.[14] Natal was not alone in its project of demarcating indigenous social projects along raced and gendered lines of propriety; indeed, much of the Anglophone settler world of the nineteenth century expressed similar settler fears of indigenous degeneracy, acknowledging the precarious and constructed nature of settler claims to the lands they occupied.[15]

Contemporary rhetoric that attempted to categorize polygamy and *ilobolo* as disturbing, degrading social practices revealed considerable anxiety over the viability of settler social reproduction. As an editorial writer in the *Natal Mercury* in 1863 argued, "the atrocities of Native Law . . . [and] the so-called 'successful management' of the Kafirs was fraught with untold danger in the future to our posterity if not to our ourselves; and . . . upon the moral and social system of the colony."[16] When settlers argued that polygamy and *ilobolo* made African men brutish attackers of women, they implicitly disciplined their own masculinist behavior, but they also demonstrated their fears for settler futurity. How would a white settler in Natal remain secure from contagion for the sake of his unborn children and grandchildren, wondered many members of the settler community, if the degradation caused by these indigenous practices persevered? These fears manifested within a variety of legal and political interventions in the colony throughout the nineteenth century, from the constantly revised body of traditional Native Law (through which the colony recognized polygamy and fixed *ilobolo* at a set number of cattle) to the reformation of settler marriage practices to shore up colonial claims to respectability.

The linked concepts of polygamy and *ilobolo* offered a consistent reference point for settler anxieties over social reproduction in an intensely contested colonial space. By marking these concepts as aberrant, white settlers used the social formations as a means of constructing a raced identity that bolstered their claims to belonging in the colony. Yet African men and women certainly did not see themselves or their social formations as aberrant or *queer*; indeed, both polygamy and *ilobolo* were entirely normative for indigenous peoples, and deeply woven into the fabric of everyday life. As a consequence, the debates surrounding these formations offer a significant source of study for Natal, and more generally for settler colonialism and imperial history. Polygamy and *ilobolo* represented the worst fears of Natal's settlers (about themselves and indigenous peoples), a means of potential resistance for Africans, and proof that the raced and gendered contours of the colony were not mere window-dressing for the more important economic, political, and social questions at the time. Rather, the discourses that circulated around the concepts of polygamy and *ilobolo* in nineteenth-century Natal had direct legal, economic, and social implications for the wider colony. These indigenous formations and the many responses to them in colonial Natal demonstrate that race and particularly gender are wholly constitutive in comprehending nineteenth-century attempts of settler capital to manipulate African labor in Natal as well as simultaneous indigenous resistance to these actions.

Quarantining the Colony: Space, Contagion, and Legal Solutions

Following the annexation of Natal by the British in 1843, a nascent colonial government attempted to bring political and social order to bodies—

both citizen and subject—under its ostensible authority. Faced with an increasing confusion over the status of the varied Boer, British, and indigenous populations, Natal's Legislative Council enacted Ordinance 3 of 1849, which reserved ultimate authority over the indigenous population for the lieutenant-governor and authorized the institutionalization of customary or Native Law for indigenous peoples, separate from civil law for white settlers.[17] Although ambiguous in its early implementation, Ordinance 3 gradually evolved through the 1850s, enshrining cultural practices like polygamy and *ilobolo* under the aegis of native custom. This followed the previous establishment of indigenous land reserves in the late 1840s, which created both a legal and physical space apart for Natal's African population, out of the immediate reach of labor-hungry colonists. Although the colonial government in Natal wished to exert more totalizing power in order to compel Africans to labor for white farmers (and establish a sustainable economy for the nascent and struggling colony), they were constrained by the practical realities of controlling an indigenous population that outnumbered them many times over.

Consequently, in 1852, the colonial government in Natal authorized a Commission of Inquiry into the state of indigenous life and practice. Tellingly, white farmers comprised the majority of the commission's respondents; no evidence was taken from Africans themselves.[18] The commission produced a narrative profoundly hostile to the paternalistic approach to indigenous control offered by Secretary for Native Affairs Theophilus Shepstone.[19] In particular, the majority of those surveyed by the commission argued that indigenous land tenure was a danger and that social customs like chieftainship, polygamy, and *ilobolo* needed to be eliminated post-haste in order to provide for both the advancement of settler civilization and the demands for African labor in the colonial economy. In its final report, the commission merged these two concerns, arguing that polygamy and *ilobolo* allowed for a threatening competition with white farmers for economic viability, a condition, "drawn from the forced labour of females . . . [and] evidence of the increasing means of sensual indulgence available to the males."[20]

The act of physically reserving land separately for the sole use of Africans in Natal occurred concomitantly with the work to reserve a legal subject status separate from the civil status of settlers. As a result, both African bodies and lands were marked as inherently separate from Europeans, both for the benefit of white settler society. Former special commissioner Henry Cloete announced before the 1852 Native Commission that the creation of land reserves had been a "great and fatal mistake," offering African men "the strongest inducement possible to look to their herds for their sole support, and, instead of devoting one single hour to habits of industry or agriculture, to leave their rude state of cultivating the soil to their unfortunate women as drudges if not as slaves, and themselves to continue a life of listless apathy, indolence and sensuality."[21] Discursively and materially, the twin threats of polygamy and *ilobolo* offered an ideal means of encapsulating a variety of issues that challenged the nascent settler state. Indigenous autonomy, economic compulsion, questions of civilizational progress, and the dictates of Christian morality each factored in the debates that flashed across government proceedings, local newspapers, mass-produced missionary pamphlets, and personal correspondence. The body of the Zulu woman—and the debates over what should be *done* to her, whether by Zulu men or the paternalist interventions of settler society—became crucial to debates over the survival of a settler society in Natal.

It is here, in the midst of the cacophony of differing voices, that a pattern surrounding indigeneity, control, and quarantine becomes clearly audible. The continued existence of both polygamy and *ilobolo* in the face of settler opposition ran headlong into the rough and shifting consensus that linked settler society in early colonial Natal. The disparate voices of multinational and multidenominational clergy, farmers, and colonial officers coalesced around the threat of Zulu contamination to colonial society. Despite their many differences, settlers generally could agree upon the idea of a social order that required whites to be the only ones to set the terms of encounter with indigenous Africans. As settler power and population expanded in Natal in the 1850s, the ever-present question of indigenous formations like polygamy increased in urgency in the settler press. Settler newspapers like the *Natal Witness* and the *Natal Mercury* contained frequent editorials debating what should be done to the moral and social scourge of wife-selling or woman-slavery among the native peoples of the colony.

In settler eyes, the existence of polygamy among Africans threatened the very gendered and raced dynamics of the colonial order they hoped to establish. Writing back to potential emigrants in the metropole, Natal settler James Methley discussed the dangers inherent in Zulu polygamy. In his popular text (which went through multiple printings in London in 1850 alone), Methley included a section from fellow emigrant George Duff, stating:

> It is to be deplored, on every account, that the systematic practice of idleness in the men, superinduced by the degradation of women, by the allowed purchase of a plurality of wives for oppressive and continual drudgery, has not also been abolished. No good will be done with the Fingoes, the Kaffirs, or Zulus, until polygamy is entirely set aside. It brings on idleness in the men; idleness favours thieving; thieving creates wars, and all their attendant evils.[22]

Duff's reading of the social realities of Natal in 1850 is telling. He asserts that *ilobolo* and polygamy are despotic forms of masculine authority that allow Zulu men to enslave and degrade women in order to pursue lives of idleness. By exercising such arbitrary power, Zulu men fail to enact what can be deemed appropriate forms of masculine behavior in Duff's eyes (and ostensibly the British audience). These allegations against Zulu masculinity can also be read as means of warning *white* settler men about their own appropriate sexual behavior. If Zulu men were locked into retrograde cycles of hypermasculinizing oppression of women through their polygamy, then British men—inferred to be monogamous—must control their own power relationships with their wives in order to enact an expected and proper demonstration of masculinity. It is this aberrant social formation—and at its heart the perceived regressive male authority of Zulu men—that lies at the heart of the "attendant evils" that threatened the existence of the settler state in colonial

Natal. Duff created a slippery-slope logic chain that lists the steps in which Zulu men, steeped in debasing sensuality, and then further failing at proper masculinity by their enjoyment of idleness, would turn to crime and eventually war and rebellion.

Although they operated both within and outside of settler society, the many missionaries present in Natal frequently opined on polygamy and *ilobolo*. Natal's missionaries were a diverse group, representing a variety of largely Protestant faiths[23] and a sizeable number of countries, with representatives from Britain, Germany, the United States, and Norway among others; by the mid-nineteenth century they had made Natal one of the most densely missionized places on the globe.[24] Whether they stated it expressly or not, missionaries were keenly invested in the reorientation and reframing of their indigenous charges into modern social, sexual, and economic formations. The practice of polygamous marriage offered one of the most visible forms of incorrect indigenous behavior in missionary eyes, and mission periodicals, settler newspapers, and even legislative committees saw frequent condemnation of the practice.

Most missionaries were, perhaps unsurprisingly, resolutely opposed to Zulu polygamy and disavowed it as a viable social formation. The most notable exception to this view was posed by John Colenso, the Anglican bishop of Natal from 1855 to 1883,[25] who advocated a missionary policy that sanctioned polygamy on a limited basis. While he was not in favor of the continuance of polygamy indefinitely, Colenso advocated a gradualist path of social change, arguing that both polygamy and *ilobolo* were culturally coherent formations that supported family life in indigenous African society:

> In compelling a Kafir husband to put away his wives, we are doing a positive 'wrong,' perhaps to the man himself, but certainly to the woman, whom he is compelled to divorce. We do wrong to the man's own moral principle—his sense of right and justice—his feelings as a husband and a man. . . . For a Kafir has a feeling of family and home. It is an outrageous slander upon the character of these poor natives, to say that they are void of affection—that their wives are merely their slaves, their children so many conveniences, for raising money by

the labour of the one sex, and accumulating cattle by the sale of the other. . . . [W]hat right have we to assume that the practice of polygamy has degraded and debased our own poor Zulus beneath the level of the brute?[26]

Relying on the same tropes of family responsibility, normative masculinity, and attachment as colonial opponents, Colenso argued that abolishing indigenous polygamy and *ilobolo* would undermine both the viability of evangelism and the unity of the family.

Colenso's views, both as a missionary and more broadly in white Natal society, were certainly in the minority. Multiple pamphlets were printed in Durban and Pietermaritzburg to challenge the dangerous theology the officially sanctioned bishop of Natal seemed to be offering in support of polygamy and *ilobolo*. Missionary Hyman Wilder was hardly alone in his refutation of Colenso's claims, arguing that for the Zulus, "the holy institution of matrimony is in ruins" as polygamy caused a husband to "blunt his moral feelings, and in sensuality place him on a level with a brute."[27] This charge on Zulu men served to reinforce the idea that polygamy as a sexual and social formation was not only unmanly, it was subhuman. Wilder's formulation served then to mark the subhumanity of Zulu men by their overindulgence in sensuality.

Yet Wilder's deployment of an ostensibly universal state of marriage threatened with ruin simultaneously worked to delimit appropriate raced and gendered behavior for white settler men. Wilder's pamphlet offered, in effect, a denouncement and a threat at once. While he marked polygamy as the process that engendered a barbaric masculinity in African men, its very continuance threatened moral structures of behavior in the colony's white male population. "If [anyone] denies what we have proved," charged Wilder, "*that the only true marriage which is a Divine Institution, is the union of two persons of different sexes for life*, and asserts that this union in certain circumstances may consist of more than '*they twain*,' then we ask why it may not exist in England as well as in Natal? Why not among white men as well as black men?"[28] This allegation illustrates several points on which the normative framework of settler logic pivots. Wilder's rhetoric underscores settler fears that the inability of Europeans to control the actual bodies and social formations of Africans will result in the unraveling of social connections back home.

The regulation of bodies and their attendant raced and gendered identifications—themselves formulated directly from the collisionary encounters of colonialism—thus sustains the settlement project and provides an impetus for logics of occupation. Indeed, at the height of the polygamy debates, *Natal Witness* editor David Dale Buchanan penned an anxious plea to the larger community:

> If the Church's pure bosom is to open to the admission of male polygamists, why not lay down the doctrine as fairly for female delinquents? By what principle of morality, or common sense or dictate of Scripture, should the prostitute be excluded? . . . Come ye chaste Christian mothers, with your daughters come and sit down to the communion, in company with the new members of the new sect which is to spring up—an offshoot of Mormonism.[29]

Like Wilder's, Buchanan's fears of polygamy are not merely for what lies in wait out there, but for what transformations could occur internally within settler society. If Natal's ostensibly Christian society is to make room for the sexual degeneracy of Zulu men, what is to stop the assumption of tolerance or encouragement for fallen women, be they British or Zulu? Continuing this, Buchanan offers a specter of white women converted to polygamy in a form of "Mormonism"—in effect arguing that Zulu social customs ran the risk of spreading corruption to settlers and to their normalizing institutions, like the Christian church.[30]

For observers like Buchanan and Wilder, polygamy and *ilobolo* had to be disavowed in Natal, or the very hierarchical structures that sustained a gendered order and enabled a civilized/savage divide between settler and indigene would crumble. Wilder argued that to allow indigenous peoples to practice polygamy was "to throw away our old standards of right and wrong taught us by the Bible, and the experience of nearly six thousand years, and adopt those of a degraded heathen, who has . . . lived in a state of debasing sensuality."[31] He posited that if indigenous polygamy was not abolished forthwith, it would be more than a simple spiritual/moral failing; rather, the ostensible unilateral direction of colonialism—the movement of power, vitality, and civilization from Europe to Natal—ran the risk of profound disruption. If the logics of settler colonialism sought to render the colony both properly accessible only for bodies perceived as white and straight/heteronormative, then polygamy—as a profoundly nonwhite and an inherently non-normative practice—needed to be abolished at all costs.

If European descriptions of sexual normality are based in a constellation of practices that identify a properly white, bourgeois, nuclear family model, then both native and nonheterosexual populations can be seen as being "queer" in a sense of deviation from healthy, ostensibly real social reproduction.[32] Wilder's distinction, that Zulu polygamy is a threat to the definition of marriage as a dual-sex, family-oriented union, emphasizes the nature of the settler project as directed toward forms of white bourgeois (re)production within the new colony. The continued presence of Zulu polygamy, of enduring indigenous social/sexual formations marked as queer and disruptive by colonists and missionaries alike, served to demonstrate the *limits* of settler hegemony that undergirded Natal's very legitimacy. Zulu men could then be seen as rendered dangerously oversensuous by the lustful lures of polygamy and the dehumanizing aspects of *ilobolo*. As a result, they could be read as a template for an excessive heterosexuality, ironically being rendered "hyper-straight" through settler processes of queering indigenous sexuality.[33]

The rhetorical attack on polygamy drew significant strength from a near-axiomatic equation of the practice with female slavery. By deploying this strategy, settler observers could redirect any discussion onto safer ground—rather than enter into religious debates over the humanity of Zulus or their ability to create social formations on their own terms, the slavery argument immediately marked polygamy as illegitimate, retrograde, and destructive in the discourse of post-abolition Britain. An angry letter printed in the *Natal Witness* demonstrates both the vulnerabilities of the settler project as well as the ways in which the 'slave turn' could render the argument on amenable terms for colonists:

Whether the Government can sanction, by taxation or law, the crime of bigamy, is not likely long to remain a matter of doubt. We heard a few days since of a white man purchasing a Caffer wife, and if by paying a couple of cows he may be allowed to carry on this species of slave and bigamy trade . . . we shall soon arrive at a very high state of moral excellence as a community.[34]

This letter reiterates Wilder's fears of contamination, of the corruption of the settler project's supposed unilateral lines of direction toward a future of reproducing white, British society within Natal. The figure of the nativized white man shows a rejection of these lines of reproductive desire. Yet this fear is quickly followed by the axiomatic depiction of polygamy as slavery. This man purchased his wife through *ilobolo*, the exchange of cattle for the right to marry, and a ritual rendered as a simple commercial exchange that does not allow for the possibility of alternative social formulations. Rather, the indigenous wife is immediately understood as being made into a slave. This discourse of slavery offered an understanding of indigenous social formulations as exotic and depraved, ultimately challenging British claims of liberalism and rule of law. These settler and missionary writings do more than simply critique offensive African marriage practices. They also speak to larger race and gender norms at stake within the colony. From Wilder's fears of transplanted Mormonism to the sarcastic condemnation of Natal's "very high state of moral excellence," these publications make clear that the ability to define proper masculine norms extended not only to Africans, but also back to white men within Natal.

The direct equation of polygamy with enslavement allowed for multiple rhetorical actions to occur simultaneously. First, by marking an alternate social formation as morally illegitimate, this equation erased the implicit threat that its very existence posed to the power that the settler state claimed for itself, namely to define what constitutes heteronormativity in marriage. Secondly, it allowed for a discourse of British exceptionalism by claiming the spread of liberality and freedom through their benign rule. In so doing, Natal's settlers could assert a superior, British morality that differed from other European colonial enterprises

and indeed from native men themselves, who are seen as the source of
female oppression. A writer to the *Natal Witness* asserted that

> Our swarthy neighbours should be informed that they are living under
> English law, and . . . tell the wives already held in bondage, that England
> will have no slaves residing on her soil, and that the English law, under
> which she is living, gives her the right, if her lord will take another
> wife, to enter an action against him for so doing.[35]

In this iteration, the British settler state in Natal became a bulwark
of defense against the predations of African enslavement. This discursive shift cast Zulu social practices of *ilobolo* and polygamy as "queer"
or inherently destructive social formations. The axiomatic definition of
polygamy as slavery attempted to obscure the challenges rendered to the
very legitimacy of the settler state by the continued existence of alternate
forms of sociality.

While the 1850s and 1860s saw critical discussion of the very nature
and practice of indigenous polygamous formations and their potential
effects on the settler state, one letter to the *Natal Witness* keenly summed
up the true stakes of the colonial project:

> We may talk till doomsday about the location, polygamy, and appren-
> ticeship, or labor questions; but, to my mind, it is pretty clear that we
> can do nothing until, by the presence of a larger European population,
> we are become more nearly equal with the Kafir in point of number, and
> are able to command without the fear of being disobeyed and laughed
> at into the bargain; to say nothing of more disagreeable, yet, perhaps
> not improbable, consequences.[36]

White settler colonialism in southern Africa, much like its other contemporary iterations across the globe, consisted of a series of different
attempts to reorder, reframe, and redirect the physical spaces and indigenous peoples of territories newly claimed by Europeans. This published
letter best illustrates both the similarities that linked Natal (and South
Africa at large) to contemporary settler colonies and the specific differences

that placed the colony on a very different historic trajectory. Settlers in Natal shared with their global compatriots plans to dominate and occupy their newly colonial homeland, reinscribing themselves as the new natives and enacting biopolitical controls over the remaining indigenous populations. Yet, the demographic evening of population never materialized in the case of Natal; indigenous people, even at their lowest ebb, outnumbered settlers by more than eight to one.

The Law of 1869, Institutionalization, and Settler Backlash

The difference between discursive and juridical truth-building reached an apex in 1869, when the legislative actions of the settler state veered decidedly out of line with general discursive discussions and fears surrounding polygamy and *ilobolo*. Despite having quarantined the practice of polygamy and *ilobolo* in the realm of customary law, settlers continued to decry it as an aberrant and threatening social formation. General settler antipathy toward polygamy and *ilobolo* continued to simmer throughout the 1860s, only to experience a form of government co-optation following the passage of Law 1 of 1869, which significantly attempted to alter some indigenous marital and social practices while retaining and strengthening others. The law was passed largely at the behest and upon the authority of Theophilus Shepstone, Natal's long-serving secretary of native affairs. Feeling pressured between the increasingly strident demands of settlers who viewed native land reserves as barriers to their expansion while simultaneously resenting what they perceived as uneven public expenditure that benefitted indigenous peoples at their expense, and the task of maintaining native compliance with the veneer of authority Natalians claimed over the colony, Shepstone sought to cobble together a compromise measure by passing the marriage law.[37] In the latter half of the 1860s the colony was mired in an economic slump brought on by real estate overspeculation combined with catastrophic weather and a decline in British emigrants. Feeling the economic pinch, settlers voiced even more strongly their habitual grievances, seeing the native reserves in particular as frustrating checks on economic growth and decrying the significantly taxed indigenous population (who received very little return on hut taxes from the colonial state) as too lightly taxed in comparison to their own fiscal burdens. To satisfy the rapacious demands of settlers, Shepstone increased a tax on indigenous marriages while resisting the marked increase in hut taxes settlers sought.[38] Law 1 of 1869 officially fixed the average price of *ilobolo* at ten cattle for a non-noble bride and placed an additional £5 registration tax on any marriage carried out under Native Law.[39]

In so doing, Shepstone attempted to effect a complicated legal feat: by offering marked increases on the taxes collected per marriage, Shepstone could claim to offset the rising cost of Natal's colonial maintenance while seeking to gradually discourage polygamy among indigenous Africans.[40] Shepstone argued that the law would "favour the operation of natural causes to achieve the extinction of polygamy."[41] Secondly, the law would officially establish the correct amount to be offered to a bride's family for *ilobolo*. By setting the number at a considerably high number (ten cattle), Shepstone could argue that his plan would induce African men to enter the wage economy on settler terms in order to obtain the cattle they needed to contract marriages. Finally, Law 1 offered a moral sop to missionaries and settlers alike—all marriages required the oral consent of the woman in question, consent that must be corroborated by a witness. Unsurprisingly, this compromise satisfied no one. In particular, it stirred up profound disgust on the side of settlers, who now equated Shepstone with amoral plotting for personal power at the expense of indigenous morality, the security of African women, and their own material interests.[42]

Following the passage of the marriage law, settler criticism of the continued existence of polygamy and *ilobolo* sharpened in Natal's periodicals, where settlers pressed what they perceived as the causal link between governmental failure and dangerously persistent indigenous immorality. "Government action is necessarily circumscribed in one way," admitted settler H. E. Stainbank in 1869. "It cannot Christianise the kafirs. But it can prepare them for the influence of Christianity, or at all events remove many obstacles from the way."[43] For Stainbank and other incensed letter writers, Natal's government, while certainly not omnipotent when it came to controlling the lives and practices of indigenous peoples, was obviously remiss in enshrining polygamy and *ilobolo* in Native Law. Such an action was no less than an implicit endorsement of a practice they

deemed both nefarious and damaging to native society and more importantly to settler security. Stainbank argued specifically that polygamy
and "its attendant female slavery" worked jointly in order to enact the
oppression of African women:

> Compare the case with that of other countries, and we shall find that
> the social treatment of the woman has a practical effect on the race,
> and that where polygamy is most rampant, there, surely, the race dete
> riorates. Here we have both in full swing, sanctioned by the laws—
> Polygamy and slavery.[44]

The rhetoric of deterioration played directly into settler scripts of the vanishing indigenous population. In this configuration, polygamy becomes
shorthand for savagery that cannot continue to exist in the face of settler
civilization. By linking polygamy and *ilobolo* to slavery, Stainbank repeats
discourse that situated these indigenous formations as a moral challenge
that necessitated humanitarian occupation by white settlers.

Spurning the compromises in the 1869 marriage law, the editor of the
Natal Mercury despaired that "these two things, Tribal Titles, involving
large locations, and woman-slavery, inducing indolent habits in the men,
have been, are now, and probably ever will be, the curse of this colony."
He went on to link the continued existence of this colonial curse to a
fault of Natal's government, openly wondering

> whether it was possible for the Government of Natal, consistently with
> its duty to the 'native' races, to have so influenced the minds of these
> children of nature, as to have made them regard their facilities for
> enriching themselves, by honest labour for the white man, as a privi
> lege highly to be valued, instead of a burden to be ungraciously borne,
> or systematically avoided.[45]

The editorial cannily listed the central problem facing Natal as an economic one, brought about by an inability to compel indigenous labor to
meet the demands of settler capital. Yet key to this failure was the persistence of social formations like polygamy and *ilobolo* that did not line up

with the economic needs and moral strictures of settlers. Consequently, settler rhetoric marked polygamy and *ilobolo* as emblematic of continued indigenous civilizational *failure* simultaneous with the failure of government to properly reproduce social propriety and economic prosperity through the manipulation of indigenous bodies and practices.

Ultimately, as part of a series of hasty compromises surrounding revenue, government authority, and indigenous autonomy, Law 1 of 1869 officially enshrined the legal status of polygamy and *ilobolo* as a part of Native Law. While the law did enact a cordon sanitaire of sorts as a means of protecting settlers from the perceived contamination to their institutions and way of life, it did *not* eliminate the non-normative practice as many settlers had hoped. The angry tirades of 1869 demonstrate a divide between the discourses of instability created by polygamy and *ilobolo* and the legal responses to these discourses offered by settler legislators and the imperial government officials who claimed to represent them in the name of civilization and good order. In particular, Shepstone was deeply savaged by a colonial press that felt he had made a Faustian bargain, perpetuating the moral quandary of enslavement in order to continue to enact indigenous governmentality on the cheap. The resultant divide between these two groups would have profound implications for Natal history—an isolated Shepstone turned to increasingly autocratic measures to shore up his authority in the 1870s. This resulted not in a coherent and insidious "Shepstonian system" of native management, as argued by David Welsh and Mahmood Mamdani. Rather, Shepstone's attempts to maintain power as an indigenous interlocutor and imperial administrator without settler support resulted in an ad hoc realpolitik that relied far more heavily on the stick than the carrot for his African subjects. The resultant post-1869 authoritarian approach by Shepstone is visible most clearly in the harassment and pursuit of Langalibalele in 1873, the ostentatious coronation of Cetshwayo that same year, and the disastrous land concessions to the Transvaal that eventually sparked the Anglo-Zulu War of 1879.[46] While the passage of 1869's marriage law may have initially secured an imagined colonial hegemony in the Shepstonian mold where immoral practices were segregated in native legal codes away from whites, the decision would have profound ramifications in the decades to come. Law 1 demonstrated a division between settler discourses, in which indigenous social formations were mapped along raced and gendered lines as threats to colonial authority, and the juridical responses of the colonial state, which operated within and responded to those very discourses. Law 1, then, demonstrated an extension of legislative maneuvers to quarantine indigenous formations in legal and physical reserves, a move which clashed with the original discourses that gave rise to these juridical choices. While settler discourses sought a full abolition of polygamy and *ilobolo*, the state established a formal division between indigenous and European legal practice. And European marital formations continued to be somewhat suspect themselves, as late nineteenth-century debates suggest.

Zulu Voices in Natal's Polygamy Debates

In the cacophony of voices, actions, and motivations, missionaries sought to harmonize African opinion on *isithembu* and *ilobolo* with their own, attempting to create a consensus among the *amakholwa* (singular: *kholwa*), or newly converted. In 1863, Ira Adams, a missionary at the Amazimtoti mission station, addressed the *amakholwa* in *Ikwezi*, the station's Zulu-language newspaper, seeking to create a Christian indigenous response to polygamy and *ilobolo*:

> U kona o wa ti, ku bonisa utando lokutanda umfazi. Mina ngi ya pika, ngi ti a ku njalo, uma ku njalo, ku ya ngani ukuti uma intombazana i tanda umuntu o nge nayo inkomo, kwaliwe, ku tiwe si funa ukudhla tina, a ti noma ku yindoda i tanda intombazana, kwaliwe ngokuba i nge nazo izinkomo, noma i se i yile kuye, ku fike omunye nje o nezinkomo, ku vunywe yena noma inga m tandi intombazana. Futi ni pikellani ukuti intengo? Make ni tyo a ku mangalwa na ngako? Futi e file a zi kitywa na? uma kungeko omunye umtwana wokukok o fileyo na? ku pi ukumtanda kwake na? Uma wa be m tanda, nga ye enga ku buli into pela e ya be i bonisa utando njalo.

> [You have heard it said, that *ukulobola* shows a man's love for a woman. I disagree, I say that it is not so; when a woman loves a man but he

does not have cattle, the family will refuse him, saying that they want to eat, or if a man loves a woman but does not have cattle, they will refuse, but if a man comes with cattle they will let him have the woman even if she does not love him. Why do you disagree that this is a form of trade? Are you all still not surprised? If the one you pay *ilobolo* for dies, is that a misfortune? Or will you acquire another wife to replace the one who has died? If he loved her, where is the proof shown of that love?][47]

Adams repeats the common assertion by missionaries that *ilobolo* was a simple market exchange of women to the detriment of all involved, but his argument goes further here. By phrasing his work in Zulu and making appeals to notions of love, value, and affection, Adams seeks to indigenize Western conceptions of social relationships, particularly the form of companionate marriage, while rendering them as natural and intrinsic to Zulu culture. In short, Adams attempts to naturalize his willful separation of Zulu social obligations from expressions of affection; by presenting extreme examples of *ilobolo* as distinct from "love" and arguing in a Zulu idiom, Adams works to erase his outsider status in critiquing Zulu gendered social conventions. Indeed, Adams furthers his point by appealing to "the ways of the elders . . . they would have stopped such a thing, saying that *ilobolo* appears to be that shameful trade in a person."[48] The *Ikwezi* article in effect argues that *ilobolo* works to perpetuate an enslaving/dehumanizing logic of commodification that exists apart from affection, and subsequently elides the externality of this assertion by rendering it in Zulu idiom as an *internal* assessment rather than a form of religious reorientation.

Adams was not the only missionary to attempt to harmonize Zulu voices in order to create a sense of order in the debates surrounding *ilobolo*. M. W. Pinkerton argued in 1879 that "Native Christians, on some older and larger stations, gave me great help by urging my people to stand by me and keep Ukulobolisa out of the Church."[49] Pinkerton based part of his resistance to *ilobolo* in part on his understanding of the Zulu-language terms for the practice:

Ukulobolisa is, by the natives, very often unmistakably called a sale. The word ukuthengisa is very generally used instead of ukulobolisa, and ukuthenga instead of ukulobola, in speaking of this exchange of women for commodities. . . . The truth appears to be that ukuthenga is a generic word, meaning to purchase for a price, while ukulobolisa is a specific word meaning to purchase a wife for cattle. The easy, economic and social usages which modified the transaction when the Kafirs had no money, and no commercial relations with the world abroad, have now given place to the severe standards of cash, and the hard laws which govern commercial transactions; so that, now the generic word best applies. In accordance with this view, after full discussion, the native preachers and pastors of the American Mission, in June 1876, declared that under the English rule, ukulobolisa has become strictly a sale, and that it ought to be abolished.[50]

By positioning himself as the interlocutor between Zulu language and English reader, Pinkerton sought to harmonize discordant voices in the debate over *ilobolo*. Pinkerton could claim, therefore, to speak paternalistically *for* Zulu speakers by using their own words. Thus, like Adams, Pinkerton attempted to naturalize external critiques of indigenous practice as originating within changing Zulu cultural frameworks and erasing his own position as an observer.

Yet despite these efforts to create a sense of indigenous agreement, Zulu people seemed far more ambivalent regarding *ilobolo* and *isithembu* than settlers wished to admit. Zulu women "do not, as a whole, condemn polygamy, or wish it done away from among them," missionary Aldin Grout reluctantly conceded. "The evils resulting from it they would call excrescences, and if those were palliated the whole thing would be *tolerable*."[51] Zulu men and women consistently demonstrated their own autonomy in deciding whether or not they approved of or supported *ilobolo* and *isithembu*.

In addition to the persistent Zulu women that Grout encountered, two *kholwa* catechists trained by the controversial Anglican bishop John Colenso frustrated European attempts to render *isithembu* as a resolutely

anti-Christian practice. Missionary Josiah Tyler evinced bitter disappointment that William Ngidi, "the bishop's interpreter and principal preacher,
laid aside all his civilized clothing, married four wives, and is now living
in a kraal to all appearance a besotted heathen." When Tyler attempted
to reassert a religious and moral sense of order by "reminding him of
his accountability to God," Ngidi "replied, with a derisive laugh, 'I was
taught otherwise.'"[52] Ngidi's response demonstrates one form of Zulu
resistance to complicity in missionary efforts to indigenize external critiques of *ilobolo* and polygamy. Despite Tyler's insistence that Ngidi had
"regressed," Ngidi deployed his own relationship to Colenso and his
patriarchal position as the head of an *umuzi* to counter Tyler's claims.

Likewise, Magema Fuze, *kholwa* intellectual and future author,
asserted his own independent understanding of *isithembu*'s relationship
to Christianity and civilization. Magistrate James Stuart noted that Fuze
"considers it is not in conflict with Christianity to have more than [one]
wife; that one may be a good Christian and yet have more wives than
one."[53] Writing in 1891, after larger numbers of Zulus had begun to convert to Christianity, and amid increased questioning of the propriety of
ilobolo for *amakholwa*, Fuze wrote to his fellow countrymen, saying:

Ukulobola kambe ngumkuba nje wobuhlobo owemiswa kuqala yilabo
abangapambili. Uma bekungalotsholwanga kambe, izwe lakithi nga-
likade lapenduka onondindwa.

[*Ilobolo*, of course, is first and foremost about joining two families
together. If *ilobolo* had not been paid, our nation would long ago have
become wanderers].[54]

Fuze's statement is significant here; he rejects arguments propagated
by missionaries, settlers, and later by *amakholwa* that assert that *ilobolo*
perpetuates slavery. Rather, he seeks to articulate *ilobolo* within a relevant and useful cultural tradition, asserting Zulu autonomy in a social
formation that challenged settler claims. However, his articulations are
not without their own provocative claims to masculinist authority; specifically, Fuze asserts that without *ilobolo* the Zulu nation would have become

onondindwa. While this literally means "wanderers," the term itself is applied almost exclusively for female prostitutes, who were deemed women who inappropriately wandered about without sanction.[55] Fuze's writing points to a particularly thorny issue within indigenous articulations of tradition in the face of settler biopolitical controls: frequently they could be coupled with patriarchal appeals that advanced male autonomy at the expense of women's movement. Fuze and Ngidi resisted efforts to be complicit in missionary efforts to indigenize external critiques of *ilobolo* and *isithembu*. These acts of resistance and autonomy demonstrate the clashing and contradictory motivations and conversations that surrounded Zulu custom as settler society tried to impose its will over indigenous lands and bodies.

Assessing the Quarantine:
Patriarchy, Legality, and the 1881 Natal Commission

In 1881, Natal's Legislative Council sought to assess the effectiveness of government intervention in Zulu polygamy, more than a decade after establishing polygamy as a fundamental part of Native Law, an act that simultaneously enshrined its practice in legal form while attempting to quarantine the practice from potentially challenging settler society. The 1881 Natal Native Commission offers a particularly important glimpse into the change in governmental practice in the decade following the controversial Law 1 of 1869. While settlers continued to voice disapproval of the existence of polygamy and *ilobolo*, the rhetoric focused less on the threat that these formations offered to settler norms and more on the idea of reforming Zulu society. The commission made apparent that despite the initial vitriol against Law 1 a decade previously, most white observers considered the division between Native Law and English civil law an effective social and discursive barrier between indigenous social practices and settler society. After a decade of wars and upheaval, public opinion seemed to have shifted. The 1881 Commission revealed a new settler consensus that coalesced around the idea that polygamy and *ilobolo* no longer posed a threat to settler identity per se, but that indigenous Africans still required transformation and uplift through white civilizational contact.

Although the 1881 Commission demonstrated a marked decline in settler fears of contamination from indigenous practices, this does not mean that Natal's Legislative Council was supportive of the continued existence of such practices. Indeed, many of the questions asked by the 1881 Commission still concerned the possibility of eliminating *ilobolo* outright. However, one particular fear settler legislators frequently repeated was of the possibility of indigenous women losing their sense of value as a result of the removal of the practice; frequent mentions, both oblique and explicit, were made about the virtue of such "devalued" women. While interviewing James Allsopp, the missionary leader of the African Christian settlement at Edendale, the commissioners asked openly if "the abolition of *ukulobola* would tend to prostitution amongst Native girls from the less sense of value which may seem to be involved in the practice."⁵⁶ Allsopp, perhaps predictably, asserted that "because the girls are beginning to see that they are not mere chattels, and they object to being sold," that *ilobolo* on the mission stations, particularly Edendale, was dying out rapidly, particularly as the town's residents were interested primarily in "living like Englishmen."⁵⁷

This opinion was not shared, however, by other self-acknowledged experts on indigenous custom. Theophilus Shepstone, the then-retired secretary of native affairs, and his brother John W. Shepstone (who now held the position) both asserted that eliminating *ilobolo* rapidly would result in immediate social instability that would lead to increased sexual immorality among Zulu women. J. W. Shepstone took pains to assert *ilobolo*'s workings as a moral system deeply structured in family hierarchies; "at present the girls are looked after and narrowly watched; the parents have a decided object in looking after their morals. I consider that at present it is the best of two evils."⁵⁸ While it is perhaps unsurprising that the Shepstone brothers offered an impassioned defense of the system they had helped to create in its present legal form, it is worth nothing in particular the basis by which they claimed the structural morality of *ilobolo*. Ultimately, the Shepstones offered an administrative assessment of *ilobolo*, describing it as a social mechanism that drew from contemporary patriarchal systems in order to enact controls over the bodies of African women. Such an articulation echoes both Jeff Guy's and Benedict Carton's arguments that the settler colonial state (or at least its official functionaries) sought to maintain order through an investment in collaborative, patriarchal male authority between the state and African men while capitalizing on the claims of older generations of African families to dictate the choices of the younger.[59]

Unlike the 1852–53 Commission, the 1881 Commission included several indigenous African voices, translated and saved in the official record, although as in the previous commission, all respondents were male. The questions asked of African men showed a consistent preoccupation of Natal's settler government with securing control over the bodies of indigenous women for the sake of preserving morality. Ultimately, the questions posed reveal that in the wake of ostensibly quarantining polygamy and *ilobolo*, Natal's settler government sought to measure and contain the effects of indigenous social practices by means of patriarchal alliance-building with Zulu men. The Zulu men surveyed provided an array of responses to the particularly leading questions asked by settler observers. Although some Christian Zulu respondents were quick to assert that *ilobolo* was practiced and desired by those living "in darkness," others seemed to indicate a large-scale interest in the continuation of the custom, urged on by both Zulu men and women. Two of the respondents, Jacobus Matiwane and John Kumalo, vehemently asserted that *ilobolo* was both inappropriate and dehumanizing, while William Ngidi, Magema Fuze, and Nambula all asserted that the practice was still both significant and value-laden for Zulu men and women.[60] As Nambula announced before the commission, *ilobolo* "creates relationship" between a husband, wife, and their respective families, challenging the idea of the practice as merely enslavement or barbarism.[61]

The continued stability of Africans as both a labor force and a subject population within Natal became an important point of investigation by the commission, which feared larger social disturbances resulting from any hasty government action to quash polygamy or *ilobolo*. The male Zulu informants on record offered differing suggestions for the resolution of the social questions created by the continuance of practices like polygamy and *ilobolo*. Some men urged for the practices to be eliminated immediately on the grounds of Christianization and civilizational uplift for their people, while others argued for the practices in terms of preserving the value of women within the larger society. As William Ngidi lamented before the commission, the abolition of *ilobolo* would make Zulu women "prostitutes and wanderers."[62] Similarly, Umnini, chief of the Amafala, testified before the commission that the marital regulations of Law 1 of 1869 had eroded patriarchal controls through an emphasis on female consent to the marriage. While the law had enshrined *ilobolo* and polygamy as legitimately protected and recognized institutions, they had also been altered through legal codification—both consent and divorce standardization by the settler state had directly impacted these practices. "I may pay *ukulobola* for a girl, and bring her home, and may have reason to complain of her conduct," asserted Umnini. "If I speak to her she says 'Dare you say this to me,' and goes and gets a divorce. She may commit adultery with my own sons at the kraal. . . . It is the bad women who get divorces."[63] For Umnini, the marital reform enacted by Law 1 of 1869 had undermined patriarchal control over women's bodies; in his estimation women were no longer subject to male discipline or confrontation because they now had recourse to divorce. The testimony of men like Ngidi and Umnini demonstrate a gendered response to the colonial fact-gathering of the 1881 Commission. Rather than accept the benefits of the 1869 Law as a safeguard and quarantine as settlers did, the Zulu observers described the law either in terms of a loss or a threatened loss of male patriarchal control; while *ilobolo* and polygamy continued as indigenous traditions, multiple male informants challenged the celebration of legal quarantine that characterized much of the settler response.

Ultimately, the 1881 Commission reflected the changes in settler approaches to polygamy and *ilobolo*. Although the practices still drew disdain from settler observers, who continued to use them as a means of differentiating indigenous "barbarism" from settler "civilization," the crystallizing of these practices in legal form had the effect of redirecting settler energies away from fears of contamination and more toward reform of a "foreign" population. The pages of the commission reveal an attempt by the Natal government to obtain male patriarchal cooperation in pursuit of a form of colonial hegemony. Yet indigenous men challenged and potentially reshaped the conversation away from settler desires for reform and more toward the everyday social relations in which they lived. Thus, the 1881 Commission remains important because it demonstrates not just a shift in settler attitudes but also an increasing rapprochement with and reliance upon the separate Native Law system championed by men like Theophilus Shepstone.

Alternative Formations:
European and Indian Marriages and Respectability

The constant debates over the continued "problem" of indigenous polygamy and *ilobolo* in the colonial record underscore the co-constitutive nature of race and gender construction in Natal. As settlers decried the demoralizing and barbaric practices of polygamy and *ilobolo* in comparison with their own, they worked to shore up their own matrimonial and social formations in contradistinction to the indigenous peoples who surrounded them. Despite separating colonial civil law from Native Law, creating a legal reserve that simultaneously preserved indigenous social customs and yet quarantined them, lest they negatively impact white society, Natal's settler community had their own matrimonial irregularities that needed policing. Natal's settler government set up civil laws on marriage that resembled those of the Cape and other colonies throughout the empire. However, a significant number of early settler/traders, including Henry Francis Fynn, later an administrator, engaged in polygamous relationships with local Nguni women prior to the colony's formal establishment in the early 1840s. These men attempted to "straighten" their aberrant marital relationships in order to improve their standing in the new colony; after leaving their African wives, they married suitable white women upon the increased arrival of the latter in the 1850s.

Yet another simultaneous crisis loomed for the settlers who wished to construct their sense of civic inclusion in Natal along raced and gendered lines: that of sororate marriage, the union of a widowed husband and his late wife's sister. The question of sororate marriage in Natal echoed larger concerns about proper forms of marriage throughout the British Empire, as legislators in the Australian colonies and in the metropole itself debated the legality of such a measure throughout the nineteenth century. In

Natal, the day-to-day realities of settlement amid a larger indigenous population significantly colored the dimensions of the marital discussions. As Nafisa Essop Sheik has asserted, the Deceased Wife's Sister Bill (later the Colonial Marriages Act) became a central preoccupation for colonial legislators and newspaper writers throughout the final quarter of the nineteenth century.[64] Sororate marriage ran counter to the religious underpinnings of English civil marriage, falling within the prohibited degrees of affinity of the Anglican Church. Yet the minority of British settlers in Natal that found themselves in this awkward familial configuration discovered they had very few options for remedying their irregular matrimonial condition, as Sheik's research attests.

Until the law's passing in 1897 (ten years before the British Parliament followed suit), clergy, legislators, and colonial officials contested the legitimacy of absorbing such a seemingly unorthodox practice into civil law. Civil law was, after all, held up as a defining means of difference that provided the critical civilizational marker that applied to all whites in Natal and only a minimal number of exempted Africans. The crisis generated by the discussions over the bill demonstrated the frequently co-constitutive nature of gendered and raced norms in colonial Natal. Preexisting, indigenous practices like polygamy, *ilobolo*, and *ukungena* (levirate marriage, or the marrying of a widow to her deceased husband's brother) could be consigned to the world of tribalized Native Law, while settler practices needed to be seen as sophisticated, set apart, and advanced. Ultimately, the nineteenth-century conversations that took place over sororate marriage for white settlers revealed the anxieties present over determining appropriate raced and gendered behavior in a colony that depended upon markers of difference between citizen and subject. "Society is not eager for such marriages," admitted an editorial in the *Natal Witness* in 1877, while still asserting that "every man moving in society knows that public opinion is by no means opposed to marriages with a deceased wife's sister. No woman loses caste by entering into such a marriage."[65] While acknowledging the heterodox nature of such marriages in British society, the *Natal Witness* writer argued tellingly that those who contracted such marriage would not suffer in settler estimation and, even more tellingly, would not "lose caste." The acknowledgment of racial *castes* clearly references the still unspoken presence of the Indian (and also African) other whose labor and marked difference underpinned the very nature of the settler project in Natal.

Thus, the cries of moral collapse or decline that echoed throughout nineteenth-century settler consternation over indigenous moral decay sound somewhat different when contrasted with the realities of internal anxiety that surrounded the aberrance of their own marital practices. The shoring up, so to speak, of settler matrimonial respectability remains an integral part of the story of the raced and gendered logics of settle-ment in Natal. Certainly, the white marital "crises" of the last quarter of the nineteenth century contributed to the larger construction of proper (white) civic inclusion within the colony. For Sheik, the colonial world of Natal offered British men and women the opportunity for social mobil-ity through the establishment of other, lesser classes through racialized labor (namely Africans as well as Indian migrants). While this is certainly the case, this social mobility was dependent upon an idea of securing the proper future for settlers in the midst of these racialized competitors. For white men and women in Natal to claim a social mobility in and through the occupied spaces of the colony they needed to police both labor and matrimonial systems in order secure their own settler futurity, embod-ied in the next generation they hoped to secure. Indeed, the *Natal Wit-ness* article continued to argue in favor of the passage of the Deceased Wife's Sister Marriage Bill, stating that the law would eliminate the "sin-gular ingenuity of injustice [that] makes the children suffer for what is regarded as no fault on the part of the parents."[66] Such an argument takes its force from a deep vault of reproductive futurity that the settler state was attempting to establish. The work of maintaining a colonial soci-ety in occupied land while greatly outnumbered by an indigenous popu-lation produced a profound anxiety, visible in settler writing, surrounding the viability of such a project. As a result, the figure of the settler child, the material manifestation of the desire for social reproduction in a contested space, developed a particularly powerful valence within Natal's colonial discourses.

As settler legislators worked to increase the racial stratifications that underpinned the political, economic, and social realities of the colony, the white settler child increasingly came to be invoked in newspapers and speeches as a means of ensuring a real future in the face of over-bearing numbers of indigenous and Indian competitors. "Observer," a settler writing to the *Natal Witness* in 1878, revisited the sororate marriage debate, arguing that it was unimportant "whether a man marries his wife's sister or not, but what we want is that the bachelors of the Colony should marry someone." Observer continued, arguing that marriages, sororate or more traditional, between European colonists should be en-couraged by the government with a grant of 1,000 acres of Natal land:

> This would tend to free our towns of many a worthless spendthrift, and be a means at least of encouraging them to till the land and become useful members of society. What is the use of our Crown lands to us if they are reserved as a breeding warren for Kafirs? Down with polyg-amy, which is nothing else than slavery! A man takes as many wives as he thinks proper; the woman is bought for a price, and if she should neglect or refuse to work, the purchaser applies the rod.[67]

In this passage, the stakes of settler respectability are revealed anew. Observer directly links the debate over sororate marriage to larger con-cerns about settler reproduction. Allowing the Deceased Wife's Sister Bill to become law ostensibly legitimates the matrimonial practices of settlers, who imagine their own relationships in contradistinction to indigenous Africans. The act of broadening the social acceptability of settler matrimonial practice by assimilating it into preexisting civil law allowed settlers to continue to claim moral distinction and superior-ity over Africans who operated initially as subjects of separate, inferior Native Law.

In addition, sororate marriage could increase the number of legiti-mate, state-recognized marital formations that could potentially produce more white settlers who could fill the land and legitimate their occu-pation of the colony. As the first *Natal Witness* letter makes clear, the justification for such marriages could therefore be predicated upon a mission to protect the white settler child and therefore the security of the settler project, which depended on constant repetition of norms as well as the constant re-creation of entitled populations. Yet as Observer's letter indicates, the sacralization of the white settler child (and with it the imagined security of a reproductive colonial futurism in Natal) depended upon the simultaneous construction of the indigenous matrimonial formations (and resultant children) as aberrant, antinormative, and in a manner of speaking, *queer* to European eyes.[68] Thus, in the minds of settlers, the legal sanction of sororate marriage would further the establishment of colonial legitimacy over bodies deemed non-normative and supersede the threatening claims of indigenous peoples to the land that settlers desired. These late nineteenth-century debates concerning white sororate marriage offer moments where settler articulations of distinctiveness and respectability vis-à-vis an indigenous population whose labor and claims to the land colonists seek to acquire can be directly observed. These articulations, in turn, are made possible through a co-constitutive creation of a heteronormative settler social order in Natal that maintains that indigenous social formations like polygamy and *ilobolo* are inherently destabilizing and non-normative and must be sacrificed in order to secure the economic, political, and social hegemony envisioned for the yet-unborn colonial generations to come.

Like Africans and Europeans, Indian men and women were impacted by both discursive and juridical developments surrounding marriage in Natal. The state's acknowledgment of Indian marriages operated primarily along religious lines. If Indian men and women professed a Christian faith, then their marriages were contracted and regulated under the same rules as European Christians or African *amakholwa* in Natal. However, non-Christian marriages, which constituted the majority of marriages for Indian men and women, were handled separately.[69] Indian men and women who wished to marry by non-Christian rites were required to declare their intention to marry to either their local magistrate or the protector of Indian immigrants. These marriages would then be solemnized in the presence of two witnesses by the magistrate or protector, and the names, races, and religions of the married couple would be entered into an "Indian Immigrants' Marriage Register."[70] The immigration numbers of the couple would be entered as well, or if colonial-born, those of their parents. Thus, Natal's legislature enacted a separate juridical mechanism to enact, define, and regulate marriage for peoples deemed to be Indian. These records themselves served as an orientation device not only to mark the heteronormative practices of marriage, but also to reproduce and patrol the racial and religious boundaries of peoples in Natal. Matrimony laws—and the ambiguities that surrounded them—demonstrated both the desire of an emergent settler state to categorize its population and the limits on its power to do so.

Marriage laws pertaining to Indian men and women also shifted over time, reflecting the ambiguous legal and political status of these people within colonial Natal. Under Law 12 of 1872, all polygamous marriages of Indian migrants, if registered with the protector of Indian immigrants, were deemed legally valid by the colony.[71] As a consequence, Natal's legal system had created three varied systems of legal marriage recognition based on race: Europeans were forbidden to practice polygamy, African customary law sanctioned it, and an Indian exception existed within settler civil law. Yet this condition did not last indefinitely. In 1891, Natal's Legislative Assembly voted to cease legal recognition of polygamous marriages among Indian migrants.[72] Law 25 of 1891 specifically denied recognition to any second or subsequent marriage among Indian peoples, a move that brought juridical discipline of Indian subjects more in line with European restrictions.

The limits of this decision were put to the test in 1899, when an Indian woman, Tulukauem, sued her husband Munsami for an annulment on the grounds of polygamy. Munsami had married Tulukauem as well as another woman, Thayi, prior to their departure for Natal from Madras in 1895, and these marriages had been recorded by the immigration agent. Upon arrival in Natal, their marriages were duly recognized by the protector, despite the change in recognition as governed by the 1891 law. Indeed, Tulukauem maintained that she did not know that polygamous marriages were not recognized in the colony, and the protector "admitted that he did not tell the parties that such was the case."[73] In the protector's view, polygamous marriages that had been recognized in India by way of a proper certificate from the immigration agent should be respected as equally valid marriages in the eyes of Natal's law. The protector subsequently acknowledged that he had approved twelve such polygamous marriages. The case ultimately seemed to test whether or not the protector had the authority to circumvent the authority of the legislature, whose act in 1891 appeared to ban all forms of plural marriage for Indian peoples. Despite the protector's insistence, Judge W. Broome ruled that while polygamous unions "would be valid in India or any other country where no special enactment to the contrary had been passed, terms of section 66 of their law prevented such marriage from being registered and considered valid here" and granted Tulukauem her annulment as well as custody of her young children.[74]

This case is significant for several reasons. First, it reveals the discrepancy between legal mandate and actual practice in colonial Natal on the subject of polygamous marriages for Indian peoples. While the legislature had moved to repeal the allowance of 1872 in the 1891 law, its wording was sufficiently ambiguous to allow the protector to feel that some plural marriages were still legally recognizable. Indeed, the legal status of Indian polygamous unions continued to differ from those of Africans or potentially for Europeans. Europeans were banned from such marriages under risk of imprisonment and hard labor, and Africans were legally allowed to contract them if they remained under customary law, but Indian polygamous unions were simply unrecognized by the state. Such distinctions led lawyer George Hulett to grouse in 1904 that while Indian polygamous marriages were disallowed by law, they were hardly prohibited, as no punishment came for participating in such unions.[75]

Second, the annulment trial reveals the moment in which colonial discourses and legal systems intersect around polygamy. At the trial, questions over whether or not Indian marital practice would be allowable in the colony, the role of the legislature versus that of the protector, and the future of Natal as a colony, all rose to the surface. When Tulukauem argued that her marriage was not a viable one in Natal, she challenged one set of hierarchical authority (the protector) by using another (the colonial legislature). The legislature's decisions, in turn, had been created through colonial discourses that not only argued in favor of European civilization over Indian semi-barbarism, but also advocated for greater centralized control over the bodies of all peoples within the colony. At its heart, the case revealed the continued ambiguous status of Indian peoples within Natal. Indian peoples were non-native to the colony, yet they could not call upon the same civilizational discourses as the European settlers in power. As such, they occupied an ambivalent space between settler and indigenous, a position reflected in legal statuses from marriage to suffrage to alcohol consumption. Indian men and women pushed for inclusion in Natal's settler polity, and secured profoundly uneven gains—settlers reinforced Indians' distinct status vis-à-vis Africans, but did not include them in the same position as Europeans. In the particular issue of polygamy, Indians were subject to a similar legal quarantine as Europeans, yet they were ambiguously allowed to practice their polygamous unions without legal punishment, just a lack of civil recognition.

Thus, by the 1890s, as settlers pushed for and eventually received the recognition of Responsible Government,[76] Natal's legislature attempted to "straighten" the multiplicity of marriages that existed within the colony. To do so offered a demonstration of the strength of settler colonial ambition; yet these attempts also demonstrated the limits of settler power. As Natal's legislators attempted to fix the irregularity of European sororate marriage and eliminate the legal recognition of Indian polygamy, they revealed the constant failures of the settler project to guarantee hegemony and secure futurity within the colony. Likewise, as the case of Tulukauem makes clear, Indian men and women could utilize these new restrictive laws to their own purposes in the colony, and make claims to autonomy even as the settler state attempted to eliminate legal ambiguities surrounding marriage, sex, and reproduction. Sororate marriage and the de-recognition of Indian polygamy demonstrate how heteronormative discourses translated into juridical truths in turn-of-the-century Natal. These truths continuously developed in relation to fears over African reproduction and marital practices, underlining the co-constitutive nature of race and gender in colonial Natal.

As British settlers sought to establish themselves as the new natives of a colonial landscape they wished to render familiar and accessible, they simultaneously asserted claims over indigenous peoples and their lands by attacking social formations like *isithembu* and *ilobolo*. Settlement, as a fragile, constitutive project, required the sublimation of indigenous social and sexual formations. In particular, colonial officials, missionaries, and settlers viewed the practices of polygamy and *ilobolo* as destabilizing because they threatened the political and economic supremacy of white settlers. Settler discourses throughout the 1850s and 1860s focused primarily on the idea of eliminating the threatening formation from the colony for good.

As settlers and indigenous peoples continued to interact, the figure of the Zulu woman as singularly oppressed and the African man as despotically brutish produced gendered and raced realities in the colony. The settler state attempted to respond to these discursive truths through juridical maneuvers, mainly through the quarantining of polygamy and *ilobolo* into legal and physical reservations. Yet the ultimate extension of this quarantine, the establishment of Law 1 of 1869, alienated settlers, who felt that the juridical solutions differed dramatically from the discursive world in which these legal maneuvers had emerged. These quarantines did not provide hegemonic security for Natal's settlers. Beset by their own gendered and raced concerns, the settler state attempted to offer juridical responses for white society as well in response to the discourses of polygamy, *ilobolo*, and savagery. The shoring up of sororate marriage and attempts to regulate Indian polygamy revealed the vulnerability of white settler formations despite the legal quarantine of Native Law. By the 1880s, after a decade of warfare, instability, and sororate squabbles, Natal's settler population still disdained polygamy and *ilobolo*, but had become increasingly invested in a Shepstone-initiated system of quarantine. Yet the few indigenous voices that appear in archival sources—from the 1881 Commission to indignant missionary reports—demonstrated that African men and women remained autonomous actors in these clashes between discursive and juridical truth-building. The continued existence of polygamy and *ilobolo* by the end of the colonial period demonstrates not merely the resilience of indigenous formations, but also the failure of settlers at attaining the discursive worlds that they imagined. As legislators and editors argued back and forth, attempting to bring a settler society into fruition that would safeguard the future they imagined for their children, African and Indian peoples stubbornly challenged, subverted, and remade these legal maneuvers at every turn. Thus, marriage law in Natal offers more than a study in conjugal commandments; they reveal for us the constant failures of settler ambition and the continued resistance of indigenous and Indian voices to colonial control.

CHAPTER TWO

Sobriety and Settlement

The Politics of Alcohol

For people living in Natal, alcohol was not merely a highly desired commodity and a mood-altering substance that facilitated sociability. As people imagined the future of the colony, alcohol provided a critical lens through which people comprehended, contested, and challenged ideas about gender and race. Settler legislators, newspaper writers, missionaries, Zulu converts, Indian migrants, and British officials maintained widely differing views on alcohol consumption within Natal, yet moments of rough consensus arose among disparate groups around the topic in the late nineteenth century. By privileging moments of temporary alliance between groups, we can understand the ways in which alcohol—as both material product and discursive subject—mapped onto the larger goals of white settler colonists in Natal and how others sought to resist, change, or advance these assertions.

Nineteenth-century British settlers in Natal attempted to create a colony where only white inhabitants possessed full claims to citizenship and inclusion. Consequently, white settlers attempted to restrict the access to alcohol to both Africans and Indians. Restricting non-European consumption of alcohol reflected the idea that full inclusion within the colonial state fell along racial lines. Europeans imagined themselves as possessing unique civilizational traits; these same traits rendered them the only ones able to handle the dangerous effects of liquor. Attempts by Europeans to proscribe alcohol consumption by Africans and partially

for Indians reveal the creation of these racial identities and their relationship to hierarchies of power in the nineteenth century. However,
this logic also placed restrictions on Europeans, who had to demonstrate
restraint in relation to alcohol to prove their lauded civilizational fitness.
Alcohol consumption served to demarcate for settlers the limits between
acceptable sociability in a colony they hoped to dominate and in the process, to create and consolidate social respectability along racial lines.
Yet people refused alcohol under Natal's emergent legal system found
multiple means of challenging these legal restrictions. In addition, alcohol became a marker for understanding the dynamics of how men and
women understood themselves in relationship to each other as well as to
race within the colony.

As with polygamy and *ilobolo*, responses to alcohol use in nineteenth-
century Natal reveal the inchoate nature of race and gender categories in
this period. Such identities were contingent, created through the collisions of differing peoples in the colony and structured through juridical
attempts at control and interpretation. These legal efforts reached their
peak in 1890, when Natal's Legislative Council debated both the Definition of Natives Bill and the 1890 Liquor Law, which sought not only to
further entrench legal restrictions to alcohol access, but also to define
just who belonged to these restricted groups. If the 1890 Liquor Law
became the immediate framework for racial distinction, firmly limiting access to liquor in accordance to hierarchies of inclusion within the
colonial state, then the Definition of Natives Bill represented the sorting
mechanism by which a ruling white settler minority sought to assign
whites, Africans, and Indians proper roles within Natal. This chapter,
then, examines how discourses within settler society surrounding alcohol use interacted with a developing legal administration in the colony, in
the process granting power to emergent hierarchies within Natal. These
legal entrenchments of raced and gendered discourse among settlers ironically reveal the limits of settlement in Natal; namely, the failure of white
settlers to create and maintain what they viewed as respectable order
among themselves and over the colony's peoples more broadly.

Beginning in 1856, Natal's Legislative Council constantly attempted
to control African (and later Indian) drinking throughout the century,

to little success. Why was this the case? What did alcoh
with racial politics of empire? Alcohol—and the sociabili
signified both inclusion and legitimacy within the confines of white settler society in Natal. The specter of the drunken African haunted the
imagination of Natal's settlers, demonstrating both a lack of white control over indigenous bodies as well as the threat of overfamiliarity with
privileges that Europeans believed they alone possessed. However, the
European inebriate also threatened the security of the settler regime.
The idea that white men, whose very claims to a monopoly on drinking
were predicated on their supposed superior ability to handle intoxicants,
could also fall prey to drunkenness threatened the racial hierarchies that
supported Natal society. Therefore, legislators, missionaries, and colonial
officials worked to draw wide boundaries around the socially inappropriate behavior of drunkenness, in order to uphold the racialized logics of
settlement that underpinned the colony.

While a significant amount of literature exists on alcohol production
and consumption in twentieth-century South Africa, comparatively little
has been written about alcohol use in nineteenth-century Natal.[1] Much
has been written, however, by southern African scholars on the contested
meanings, symbols, and opportunities presented in alcohol consumption in the twentieth century.[2] In particular, Paul La Hausse's study of the
Durban system of municipal beer halls remains a compelling and critical
reading of state ambition, African resistance, and the politics of colonial
labor. Anne Mager's work on masculinity and sociability in apartheid-era
South Africa highlights the competing attractions, meanings, and benefits alcohol consumption held for African workers, white South African
students, and shebeen owners, among others. Mager and La Hausse both
assert that alcohol acted as more than a mere commodity whose distri-
bution and consumption settlers frequently attempted to monopolize;
rather, alcohol became a cogent site of contestation between the colonial
state, African workers, and the labor regimes that enmeshed them all.
When alcohol has featured in nineteenth-century histories of Natal, it
has been in passing, subsumed by larger analyses of intergenerational
conflict, ethnic identity formation, or African labor systems.[3] Yet alcohol
certainly offered sociability, threatened colonial order, and potentially

enabled resistance well before a confluence of factors led to intensified labor procurement and indigenous urbanization in the twentieth century. Indeed, the destabilizing potential for drunken sociability in colonial Natal resulted in a flurry of legal attempts to shore up emergent forms of racial and gender supremacy that typified nineteenth-century settler colonialism.

As in settler colonies in North America and Australasia, British authorities sought to restrict alcohol access to indigenous peoples for their own "protection." By declaring Africans (and later Indians) as morally impressionable and unfit for alcohol consumption, Natal's settler elite attempted to grant themselves privileges that legitimated their sense of inherent superiority while justifying their claim to rule over nonwhite bodies (and their labor) in a contested colonial space. Yet, for white settler men to make good on their claims to proper control over colonial bodies and spaces, they themselves had to perform correctly in relationship to alcohol. By demanding proper forms of alcohol use that privileged sobriety and specifically denied indigenous moral agency in resisting drunkenness, settlers in Natal policed their own raced and gendered behavior as well as that of Africans and Indians. These limits of settlement reveal the intersections of imperial and settler ambitions as well as indigenous African and Indian attempts to subvert, respond to, or redirect racialized hierarchies of power.

Although this chapter is arranged largely chronologically, it takes as its fulcrum two major legislative debates in 1890—the Definition of Natives Bill and the 1890 Liquor Law. The period following the Anglo-Zulu War of 1879 until the annexation of the formerly independent Zululand to the northeast (1880–1897) marked a shift in the state of the colony, which saw a boost in settler confidence, population, and increasing attempts to subordinate labor supply through mobilizing raced and gendered conceptions of intoxicant usage. The reducing of the once-threatening Zulu Kingdom to only nominal independence and eventual annexation tipped balances of political, economic, and social dominance more in favor of Natal's settler classes. The 1890 Liquor Law and the Definition of Natives Bill emerged during this post-1879 moment, as Natal's legislature began to act more aggressively to close loopholes that allowed for deviant drinking and smoking practices. In so doing, the state's socio-legal apparatuses built upon previous discursive linkages between race and citizenship by attempting uphold a white monopoly on alcohol (and by extension civic inclusion) within the colony. Subsequently, Africans and Indians found themselves increasingly constrained (although not entirely) by settler attempts to draw them into labor markets on their own terms. Intoxicants, which offered destabilizing forms of sociability that jeopardized both the racialized hierarchy and labor systems that under-girded Natal's settler society, increasingly became a target of legislators, newspaper reporters, and missionaries after 1880.

In the post–Anglo-Zulu War period, the settler colonial state developed considerably in Natal. For its first thirty-five years of existence, Natal was a thinly populated frontier colony, bordering a much larger indigenous Zulu polity. As in other contemporary colonies such as British Columbia, New Zealand, and Western Australia, the inhabitants of Natal resolutely believed that, with hard work and generous immigration enticements, they would become numerically predominant by the end of the century. This did happen in the other three colonies, but not in Natal. By 1880, Zululand had been defeated by the British and existed as a semi-independent satellite of Natal, swelling an indigenous population that already greatly outnumbered settler society. As a result, Natal embarked on a markedly different course by the last years of the nineteenth century as the realization slowly began to dawn upon settlers that they would never have the demographic legitimacy they saw in other contemporary colonial societies. Consequently, predominant settler attitudes toward indigenous peoples began to transform. Viewing indigenous Africans as childlike, willful, and in need of indeterminate paternalistic guidance from white society, Natal's settler government worked to harden pre-existing divisions between white citizens and nonwhite subjects, strength-ening their status as a minority-ruled colony. The increase in settler state power, bolstered by an increase in population, power, and autonomy from the home country (Natal obtained Responsible Government status in 1893) allowed Natal's settlers to demarcate boundaries between white and indigenous society more firmly. Debates over the significance and nature of alcohol consumption throughout the 1880s and 1890s attest to the rise in settler power and a renewed drive to subordinate Africans and Indians to racialized and gendered hierarchies of power in order to provide both the sense of social stability and the compelled labor that colonial Natal required. Invigorated by its new political position after the war, and concerned with maintaining minority hegemony, Natal's Legislative Council extensively debated three problematic instances of nonwhite drinking: traditional beer parties, Indian access to liquor, and the eligibility of exempted natives to consume alcohol.

From Discourse to Debate:
Alcohol, Racial Coding, and Self-Control in Natal

The instability of new constellations of raced and gendered categories, created by the collision of settlers, migrants, and indigenous peoples in the spaces of Natal, predated legal attempts to rein in the potential colonial disorder. Instances where alcohol upset the ostensible order of the colony can be found in print culture, which archived a whole series of challenges to racial distinction—distinction that was threatened by white drunken behavior. The archbishop of Cape Town, Robert Gray, upon visiting the new colony of Natal in the early 1850s, decried the drunken state of its white population:

> Already the natives are becoming educated, in a certain sense, by dwelling among those, many of whom are practically living in worse than heathenism. Three years ago I saw the finger of a Zulu pointed with scorn at a drunken Englishman in the streets of Durban. . . . There will follow an almost total loss of respect and reverence for the white man.[4]

Gray's warning says much about the stakes of alcohol consumption and social behavior in the colony. The whiteness of settler men was dependent upon proper behavior that stressed self-control and restraint over wanton consumption and disorder. As Gray was quick to note, white male self-control was understood chiefly in relationship to rule over indigenous Africans. By failing to demonstrate sobriety or restraint, white men would not exemplify the virtues of white masculine control, employed to justify colonial occupation, which threatened the long-term viability of a settler minority state.

As a result, settler men who drank to excess were called to account for having betrayed the racial underpinnings that supported the very settler project. Such was the case for Martin Swindells, a young colonist who had been arrested following an incident of public drunkenness in the colonial capital of Pietermaritzburg in 1865. Swindells subsequently sent an apology to the attorney general, recognizing his social infraction but attempting to explain his actions, so as to lessen the social embarrassment and collective disgrace he had received. On the night in question, Swindells alleged that he had visited a local canteen and enjoyed two glasses of gin, before desiring a third:

> Unfortunately the gin was just finished, and instead thereof I was unwise enough to take brandy. Directly after I had taken it, I felt the effects of my indiscretion, and on my way homewards, I had the misfortune to drop my stick, and in looking for it, I lost my cap also. I continued sometime upon my hands and knees feeling, for the night was very dark, for my lost property. My impression is that with staying so long with my head downwards together with the brandy I had just drunk, combined to make me helpless, as many attempts that I made to rise were utterly futile. That I was not drunk is proved by the fact that while lying on my back, I wound up my watch, and was perfectly conscious of where I was, and also remonstrated strongly with the Policemen who took me up against conveying me to the Police Station.[5]

The episode is somewhat farcical as Swindells simultaneously attempts to confess and yet contextualize his actions. He was careful to mention his articles of social standing—his walking stick, cap, and watch—and in fact, blames them for the actions that led to his being identified as a drunkard. In emphasizing his attire, Swindells worked to reaffirm a responsible white male status now threatened by his public drunkenness: the stick, cap, and watch became indicators of his class (and race) status. Finally, Swindells attempted to defend his maligned sobriety by making claims to control (over his watch) and knowledge (of his location).

Swindells's testimony is more than a mere example of an apologetic letter in colonial print culture; in it, one can perceive the stakes of maintaining a particular form of gendered and raced hierarchy in Natal's settler colonial society. Closing his letter, Swindells took care to emphasize his intentions to reform: "I beg to express sincere regret that such a thing should have occurred, and I hope that you will be pleased to receive the explanation I have given with the assurance that such disgrace shall not again be attached to my name."[6] Swindells's apology recognized his criminal infraction through drunkenness, and also worked to reinstate his legitimacy as a settler man by writing a controlled letter of remorse to the attorney general. The apology also underscored the idea that Swindells's drunkenness was an aberration, rather than a regular habit, in effect, shoring up his identity as a controlled settler who suffered an occasional lapse rather than an inherent moral failing.

Despite bans on indigenous drinking and public drunkenness, illegal forms of alcohol consumption continued to present a problem for settlers as whites and newly arrived Indians drank to excess (and Africans continued to drink at all). Newspaper trial reports from the 1860s and 1870s show regular reports of drunkenness for Europeans, Indians, and Africans in the colony.[7]

On November 30, 1887, postal clerk Dawson Stransham submitted an application for a promotion within the Natal civil service. After a year and a half of work for the Durban post office, the twenty-nine-year-old Stransham felt he was qualified for the increase in salary and status, and his application was processed accordingly. However, correspondence between colonial officials soon made clear that Stransham's record was far from exemplary. Rather, his history with the post office revealed frequent allegations of drunkenness, irregular behavior, and unexplained absences that confused his superiors and exasperated his colleagues.

"Mr. Stransham is so very unreliable that I could not recommend him for promotion," confessed J. Chadwick, Natal's postmaster general, in response to the application. "Indeed I only refrain from asking that he should be dismissed in view of Mr. Coleman's desire to try him again."[8] John Coleman, Chadwick's subordinate and the postmaster in charge of the bustling port city, was two years younger than Stransham but already an experienced and British-trained administrator who continued to press for additional opportunities for the young man, even as Stransham grew particularly unreliable.

Although Dawson Stransham would regularly put in the hours of labor required at the Durban post office, he had periods that were euphemistically referred to by his supervisors as "not being altogether himself." These problems appear to have reached their highest recorded point in the spring months of 1887, as reports of Stransham's irregularities peaked in September and October of that year. Coleman reported to the postmaster general that one night,

> Mr. Stransham was not by any means sober. I was compelled to send him away at 7pm. After he had left the sorted letters were checked and some 30 mis-sorts were discovered . . . but for the fact of a check having been made this mis-sorted correspondence would have sustained a week's delay in Durban.[9]

In light of increasing complaints in the spring of 1887, it would appear that Stransham's application for a promotion[10] was also a means to get away from his increasingly frustrated colleagues, who were tiring of his behavior. Yet, as 1888 dawned, things rapidly grew worse. In February, Stransham had more drunkenness reports and failed to show up to work, and to alienate even his most ardent supporters like John Coleman by September. And yet, Stransham was *still* not dismissed for his irregularities on the job. His supervisors may have been exasperated, but they either interpreted his continuous lapses as mere aberrations or they felt the need to protect him as a white male settler in the hopes of straightening out his behavior, which threatened white dominance in a racially stratified colony.

Finally, in October of 1888, after a particularly eventful two weeks that included sleeping in the office, being arrested for public drunkenness, and fabricating a stay in the local Addington Hospital for an ostensible "overdose of laudanum," Chadwick and Coleman both came to the decision that Stransham's behavior could no longer be justified, and instead had to be rejected, as it destabilized the racial order of Natal. Stransham was terminated, although he continued an ultimately futile struggle with the Colonial Office to have his dismissal recognized as a resignation instead. Claiming he had "resigned," Stransham and his wife left the colony in November for the brighter pastures of Johannesburg, then the largest city in the independent Boer Republic of the Transvaal near a newly discovered goldfield.[11]

The Stransham affair illustrates the lengths to which colonial officials would go to protect the monopoly of white drinking and sociability even when confronted with antisocial behavior like public drunkenness and missed work. Discussing the situation with the colonial secretary, Natal Postmaster Chadwick mobilized understandings of race and masculinity in order to make his reluctant pronouncement in favor of Stransham's dismissal:

> Mr. Stransham has recently married, and it might be a serious thing for him to be thrown out of employment—though he would, of course have no one to blame but himself—and I would therefore suggest that he be given a trial in some other dept. But for his weakness as regards drink he would not be a bad officer. In some other office, where his hours would always be regular he might be able to time his periods of indulgence so as to avoid their interfering with his duties.[12]

Chadwick's analysis is particularly telling in light of Stransham's two-year employment history with the postal service. He had routinely suffered irregularities after periods of acceptable service. Yet, Stransham's alcohol-related incidents were treated simply as lapses and indiscretions, rather than inherent moral failings. Additionally, Chadwick's mention of Stransham's marital status indicates the raced and gendered expectations of Natal's settlers. As a married man, Natal society demanded that Stransham fulfill his patriarchal obligations in order to perform as responsible, white, male colonist. As a consequence, Stransham's superiors interpreted his drunkenness as occasional lapses in proper white behavior rather than as proof of moral deficiency.

The Stransham case demonstrates the role of alcohol in race and gender making in colonial Natal. Not unlike Swindells, Stransham was expected to demonstrate self-control in relation to the intoxicant, an expectation of white men in the colony. Yet, his repeated failures were not interpreted as indicative of inherent degradation; rather, they were interpreted as lapses from the proper state of things. Thus, it is unsurprising that even the sympathetic Chadwick would write after Stransham's dismissal that it was unfortunate that his employee could not find work that would allow him to pursue his immoderate drinking at more "amenable periods." These amenable periods were to occur out of public view, lest fellow settlers—and even more dangerously, Zulu subjects—view a servant of Crown and colony failing at performing white, male, patriarchal control because of his undisciplined drinking.

A very different case occurred with the attempted promotion of Solomon Kumalo. In 1891, Kumalo, a Zulu *kholwa*, or Christian convert, applied for a position within the colony's civil service, most likely within the Department of Native Affairs in Pietermaritzburg. Like Stransham, Kumalo was employed as a low-level clerk in the office of the resident magistrate in Estcourt, then a rural farming town about sixty miles northeast of Pietermartizburg.[13] Yet, unlike Stransham, Kumalo had earned the confidence and approval of Peter Paterson, his superior. Solomon Kumalo's application for permanent employment, or as the Victorian officers themselves termed it, a "situation," however, resulted in a disastrous charge against him.

Natal colonial officials responded to Kumalo's application by writing to his former educator and religious instructor, the Reverend Frederick Greene, in order to obtain a character reference. While Greene at first appeared to paint a positive picture of the *kholwa*'s character for colonial officials, he soon afterward offered a damning, if spurious piece of evidence. According to Greene, he reluctantly had cause to report that another *kholwa* had told him that he had heard from another man that Solomon Kumalo had been publicly drunk in Pietermaritzburg in the past. With no further concrete information than the third-hand report of an unnamed witness, Greene passed on the information, and John Shepstone, the secretary of native affairs, duly rejected Kumalo's application outright. Solomon Kumalo did not take this rejection passively. With the help of a sympathetic lawyer, Thomas Carter, Kumalo wrote to the secretary of native affairs, the colonial governor, and to his erstwhile accuser, the Reverend Greene.

The resultant official inquiry revealed both the profound injustice and the institutional prejudice that Kumalo in particular and Africans in general faced in relation to alcohol consumption. In a sworn statement to the colonial governor, Kumalo alleged:

> I have endeavoured to ascertain from the said Reverend Greene who his informant was but he refuses to tell me and I am thereby precluded from bringing an action against the slanderer. And I swear that the statement that I was ever drunk in the streets of Pietermaritzburg or elsewhere is false and totally devoid of any foundation whatsoever but has been made maliciously and untruthfully with the object of injuring me.[14]

Kumalo was careful not to cast aspersion on the European clergyman, but made the focus of his critique specifically the informant who had slanderously claimed that he had been drunk, costing him a permanent position. The response of all official parties, however, was to turn to the Reverend Greene, and ask for his information on the matter. Greene outright refused to assist, and the Colonial Office refused to intervene, leaving Kumalo without a job or reputation.

The exchange between Kumalo, Greene, and colonial officials offers a valuable insight into the politics of native drinking in colonial Natal. In response to official requests for information, Greene doubled down on his allegation while simultaneously claiming to be a mere observer to the malicious gossip that had destroyed Kumalo's nascent and promising career. Greene declined to release the names of Kumalo's first- and second-hand accusers, and in response to Kumalo's personal request, condescended to write to his former student:

> My dear Kumalo, I am very sorry to hear that you have been refused a situation with the Government service. . . . I was asked some time ago from the SNA Office whether I knew you to be unsteady. I answered that I had never seen you drunk and that I did not think you had been.

Afterwards I was told that you had been seen drunk in the streets and I was exceedingly sorry to hear it. I have tried to get you a clerkship saying that even had you been drunk, a place in some good office would keep you straight; but the Governor is very strict and if you hope to enter the service at any time you must take good care by working in one place and doing your best, to give no occasion for evil talk. If you have not been intoxicated at any time you can easily prove it.[15]

In this message Greene attempts to paint himself as a passive observer while simultaneously blaming Kumalo for his own accusation. He insists that he worked as Kumalo's advocate, even if offering the most tepid support to the beleaguered *kholwa*. Inexplicably, Greene insists that if Kumalo was not *actually* drunk, then he could easily prove it, a logical contortion that must have puzzled Kumalo as certainly as it baffles contemporary historians.

Greene's letter and the subsequent government response reveals that the fundamental difference between Kumalo's and Stransham's cases is one of normativity and power. Greene asserts that "even had you been drunk, a place in some good office would keep you straight," a perfectly apt description of the ultimately unsuccessful attempts to resolve the Stransham affair. "Straightness" was presumed as the default for men like Devon Stransham, even if they constantly failed to perform it. Yet unlike Stransham, Kumalo was never allowed the benefit of being "kept straight," and immediately denied employment. Indeed, such "straightness" appeared impossible for any African so accused. Men like Kumalo were always already conceived as unfit, as falling out of the normative line of self-mastery with regard to consuming alcohol. In short, Kumalo was always positioned as "queer" in relation to proper masculine controls over intoxication. As Cathy Cohen has observed, the bodies, practices, and very existences of people of color can be deemed as essentially non-normative in societies structured around white supremacy.[16] In the eyes of a settler state that sought to assert control and domination through enshrining certain behaviors as normative and assigning them to emergent raced and gendered hierarchies, the category of "African" became inextricable from that of "drunkard." That Kumalo presented himself as a teetotaler was irrelevant to the colonial government that denied him his employment; he was already inherently degraded in regards to drink, a category that simultaneously served to reify ideas of white civilizational fitness.

Natal's settlers worked specifically to deny Africans the right to drinking in order to maintain a white monopoly over a form of socialization as well as to restrict a potential hindrance to African labor. As Kumalo's case makes clear, settlers appear to have been primarily concerned with the specter of African drinking, rather than that of Europeans; it was through this lens that other racialized forms of consumption were evaluated. The majority of cases described within the *Natal Witness* and *Natal Mercury*, despite some instances of behavior policing for white men, commonly report and decry instances of nonwhite drinking. Scholars differ in their assessment as to why this may have been the case. Leigh Anderson has asserted that "African drunkenness was perceived by whites as a far greater social problem than was white drunkenness. This was because African drunks appeared to pose a threat to the peace and security of the colonists, whereas a white drunk was seen as having fallen from society, and as such did not seem to threaten that society."[17] I agree that generally white settlers appear to have viewed African drunkenness as a far greater social problem than its white counterpart, but not because white drinking did not threaten settler society. If that were the case, men like Swindells would not have to publicly apologize so profusely, nor would men like Grey render such stringent reprimands on drink. While white settler drunkenness could and did threaten white society precisely by undermining raced notions of propriety and order that undergirded settlement, the act of indigenous drinking exposed the limits of a settler state at compelling indigenous actions. White drinking was viewed primarily as a regrettable aberration from the norm, while settler rhetoric served to queer African social practices by rendering them inherently degraded and dangerous to the normative order. Thus, both white male drinking and indigenous consumption were viewed as constitutive challenges to colonial order, although the far larger African population revealed the fragility of colonial power more readily.

Throughout Natal's first two decades, African drinking remained a fearful prognostication of disorder and a threat to be guarded against.

An editorial in the *Natal Mercury* in 1868 bemoaned the constant scourge of African drinking, making explicit comparisons to the problem of indigenous drinking in other settler societies:

> Upon the coastlands Kafirs seem thoroughly infected with the craving for strong drink. Nothing tempts them so much as ardent spirits. Even money is in many instances only valued as a means of buying rum. The Zulus appear to yield just as completely to this acquired vice as did the Indians of America. It bids fair to be a far more potent agent in fashioning the future of this people than any system of political treatment, or any kind of social or education influence.[18]

This editorial marshaled contemporary discourses of a transnational settler project that placed Europeans in direct conflict with indigenous peoples around the globe.[19] The author underlined the imagined moral susceptibility of Zulu peoples by their yielding to the "acquired vice" of alcohol, an act that made them readable as benighted indigenes resembling the "Indians of America."[20] The discursive power of such statements linked settlement on a global scale by presenting drinking as a problem that must be addressed by any settler state, justifying its claims to intervention in the lives of indigenous peoples, even if the state lacked the coercive power imagined in the *Natal Mercury* at this point.

Nearly every year prior to joining the Union of South Africa in 1910, Natal's legislators debated multiple bills to monitor, correct, and control alcoholic consumption and safeguard properly social behavior. Having regarded Africans as inherently degraded in relation to European civilizational fitness, legislators sought to curb the queer drinking habits of the indigenous population through legal maneuvering. In 1890, Henry Bale maintained before the Legislative Assembly that Africans, unlike Europeans, were less likely to resist alcohol's temptations, an assertion not disputed by his fellow legislators.[21] For Bale, the moral inadequacy of Africans, which led to drunkenness, served to present an immediate threat to the white population of Natal as well as to reinforce settler self-policing of behavior. If Africans were inherently more likely to be degraded by drink, then the habits of both an overwhelming

indigenous population as well as ostensibly disciplined European settlers must be managed by a colonial state, lest the fragile weir of racial
order supporting the colonial project be broken by a flood of beer and
spirits.

Throughout the 1880s, settlers raised considerable debate over the
appropriateness of allowing Africans to consume *utshwala*, or "native
beer," which was far lower in alcohol content and used as part of a regular diet. As a result, Natal's settler legislators debated whether to dis-
mantle African traditional drinking customs.[22] As Michael Mahoney has
asserted, African drinking parties were "quite simply the main form of
entertainment and leisure-time socializing (in all the senses of that word)
in rural Natal during this period."[23] The drinking party served as an integral marker for most major social occasions in indigenous societies, and
constituted a means of maintaining and strengthening community ties
in Natal. Yet, for many of Natal's leaders, African drinking was an indication of disorder that threatened an unreliable labor supply. In a language of paternalism mixed with crass self-interest, they sought to limit
the damaging effects of indigenous drinking parties. Sir John Robinson,
the future first prime minister of Natal, thundered in 1886:

> Beer drinkings are in every sense of the term demoralizing and perni-
> cious. In the first place they breed habits of idleness in the Natives.
> They accustom the Natives to a mode of life which is wholly opposed
> to the life of an industrious being. They encourage a constant flow
> of domestic dissipation which is the parent of all sorts of disorders in
> the country districts. No one desires to interfere with the liberty of the
> subject less than I do, but I do not hesitate to say that had the Natives
> white skins these beer drinkings would have been put down with a
> stern hand.[24]

Robinson declared that African alcohol-based sociability was inherently
disordered and raucous, in effect, antisocial qualities specifically forbidden to settlers; its continued existence would threaten an ostensible divide
between white access to ordered alcohol sociability and the paternalist
prohibitions meted out to people of color. Most importantly, Robinson's

denunciation of *utshwala* consumption lay primarily in the fact that it bred "idleness" and opposed industry. Robinson's speech was, in effect, an elegant rhetorical defense of racialized hierarchies for the sake of maintaining African labor for white settler needs.

Some Zulu elders had their own concerns about the nature of drinking parties as well. While these parties continued to be predominant events in African society, recent changes brought on by the wage labor introduced by settlers had begun to alter the parties themselves. Previously, drinking parties served to reflect certain patriarchal forms of order, by paying respect to the rank and privilege of elder men.[25] Women, if allowed to be present, were strictly segregated, and younger men were expected to give pride of place to their elders. Yet younger men, emboldened by independent access to wealth through the colonial economy, and with a decreased sense of obedience to chiefs and elders undercut by colonial authorities, began to rebel, rejecting patriarchal rules of deference, making sexual advances at women in attendance, and even mixing the *utshwala* with *isishimiyana*, a new and extremely potent alcohol made from sugar cane molasses.[26]

Other African observers emphatically linked *utshwala* and *isishimiyana* as socially destructive beverages. In 1902, African Christian J. D. Mzamo wrote to the district magistrate in Verulam, who in turn forwarded Mzamo's message to the secretary of native affairs. Mzamo alleged that *isishimiyana* and other sugar-based liquors were fundamentally destructive; as a result "our people on the coast here are fast being demoralized, socially and morally." For Mzamo, *ishishimiyana* created a general alcoholic dependency that caused severe social disruption, announcing that "Natives have lost their status as a race from this treacle and sugar."[27] Mzamo explicitly linked *utshwala* consumption to this more dangerous liquor, stating that African women sold the indigenous beer specifically to obtain money with which to buy the dreaded molasses. While the magistrate doubted the connection between beer and sugar purchase, he concurred that drinking was causing general havoc among the African population of Durban and played a role in the bulk of crimes in the region. These overlapping concerns over indigenous drinking between Mzamo and colonial officials functioned in part as what Jeff Guy has termed "an accommodation of patriarchs," a conditional understanding between white settler legislators and African elders that decried the potential destabilizing power of African youth subverting traditional order in the colony.[28] In this moment, African leaders could make common cause (of a limited nature) with Natal's legislators, and form a fragile consensus on the need to limit the excess of African drinking parties or illicit liquors. While elders would not have agreed as vehemently with Robinson about the inherent degradation of beer parties, brewing intergenerational conflict would appear to demonstrate that moments of consensus were reached between the two disparate groups of African elders and settler officials.

Debating Drink: Alcohol Legislation and Racial Designation in Natal

In 1888, the unthinkable happened—Africans who were exempted from Native Law were legally allowed to purchase and consume European liquor. The Natal Legislative Council had inadvertently allowed a legal redefinition of the term "native." This act had the legal consequence of allowing Africans who applied for exemption from Native Law to be exempt from *all* inherent restrictions for natives—in effect, treating them as Europeans under the Natal legal system.[29] While exemption from Native Law theoretically allowed Africans to exit a legal system designed for their separate development and steeped in an "invented tradition" (to use Terrence Ranger's evocative phrase), the reality was far different. Prior to the 1888 redefinition, exempted Africans (the *amazimtoti* in isiZulu) were indeed placed on the same legal footing as Europeans (and also forbidden from partaking in polygamy, thereby sealing the limits between indigenous social formations and colonial civilization), but they were not allowed three rights that whites possessed—the right to alcohol consumption, the right to purchase firearms, and the right of the franchise. These divisions assured white settlers that even if Africans could acculturate, they would never be offered full equality with the settlers they outnumbered nearly eight to one. While both the firearms and franchise aspects of the laws had already been corrected, the alcohol portion had been allowed to stand for nearly two years. Realizing the enormous consequences of their inattention, Natal's white legislators quickly worked to define the unruly category of native in order to better control indigenous bodies and restrict their access to rights that they believed only settlers should legitimately possess.

The debate over the Definition of Natives Bill of 1890 centered over whether or not to return Africans to their legal status before the debacle of 1888—exempted Africans would still come under European law, although their access to alcohol would be removed. Natal's legislators did not find themselves in agreement over whether or not the legal restrictions should be reestablished. Some legislators were not in favor of restoring the ban for the minority of exempted Africans. John Bainbridge argued:

> this measure, if carried, will confer a very great hardship upon a num-
> ber of Natives who are loyal and who are highly civilized, and have
> adopted our civilization, much more so than you find many whites
> practicing in different parts of the Colony. They have all the Europe-
> an's customs, they have civilized food, and it is a very natural thing
> when they are sick that they should want a little pontac or spirit.[30]

In this instance, desires for the maintenance of Natal's racial hierarchy ran headlong into notions of paternalist caretaking. Legislators against the restoration of the restriction supported the idea that a minority of elite Africans granted full European privileges could culturally assimi-late. To allow a fraction of *amazimtoti* the drink would not overwhelm-ingly change settler hegemony, and could serve to channel frustration with inequality by granting rights to a tiny few who could demonstrate they had reached a point of civilizational equity with their colonial rulers. In addition, according to Bainbridge and other colonists, the *amazimtoti*, provided that they demonstrated sufficiently proper behavior through self-policing, could serve as moral beacons to errant whites and the vast African majority.

Yet other legislators argued for a consistent restriction across racial lines. Reminding others of the restrictions in place over firearms and the vote, James Hulett argued that exempted Africans were *not* legally equal with Europeans. Rather, the entire event was, in his eyes, a "mistake" that needed rectifying rather than a denial of rights to a class of citizens. Hulett furthered noted that exempted Africans only possessed a portion of "European so-called liberty" and the reinstatement of the ban would be a colonial "blessing" that would protect them from degradation. Liberty became a particularly powerful mobilizing word for the anti-alcohol legislators. Rather than denying exempted Africans liberty by removing their legal right to drink, they were instead providing them with a sense of liberty by freeing them from the degradation and humiliation of alcohol. Dr. Peter Sutherland agreed with Hulett, asserting that "the privilege of obtaining of spirits according to their own free will" was an unthinkable privilege to extend to Africans. Sutherland maintained that such a denial was absolutely necessary as

> the black population of this Colony must remain—no matter how they exempt themselves from the effect of Native law—they must remain for many generations a peculiar people, liable to exceptions on account of their peculiarities. Their peculiarities are such that if we legislate for them, as we legislate for Europeans, we shall be inflicting upon them a very severe evil, an evil they cannot cope with, and an evil which is decimating them all through Africa [for] our Natives who are in a state of tutelage, and who must remain yet a-while minors and children for whom the parents must make due provision.[31]

Men like Sutherland and Hulett ultimately sought to counter the assertions of the pro-alcohol group by challenging the very nature of the concept of liberty. These settlers interpreted liberty through a racialized hierarchy, advocating for European liberty predicated upon self-control in the face of African liberty centered on moral weakness and European paternalism. In this formulation, the right to consume alcohol became not a political right, but rather an expression of moral fitness and ultimately an entitlement for settlers to defend in the face of indigenous encroachment.

The spirited debate over alcohol and the Definition of Natives Bill reveals more than competing settler attitudes toward drink. These debates, indeed, reveal the very construction of race as an ontological category posed in relationship to imagined white settler power. The "native" or "African" is conceptualized in legislative debates as a separate population in competition and contradistinction with the self-imagined settler polity. The specter of alcohol and its consumption render these emergent racial classifications acutely visible in the colonial record, as access overlapped with the ability to properly demonstrate the self-control deemed necessary by settlers for civic life within colony. The very need to define the native in this instance stemmed ultimately from the question of access to alcohol for people within the colony. Thus, the debates over the Definition of Natives Bill offer a crucial understanding of racial formation within a colonial context. Even if the various members of the Legislative Assembly disagreed over whether or not exempted Africans should have access to alcohol, each of the speeches reveal overlapping sets of assumptions about Africans and their relationship to the colonial state. Legislators utilized the larger settler claim that indigenous peoples were the puerile wards of a state that acquired them as well as their lands and therefore must be preserved from the threat of degradation brought upon them by the colonizers themselves.[32] Such a discursive formulation both dodged responsibility for conquest and contained a rationale for policing white settler behavior.

In the midst of the debate over a nativeness framed around exemption and exclusion, legislator Henry Bale took the opportunity to draw upon larger discourses of indigeneity and degradation throughout the larger empire. Disagreeing with a request of African Christians to allow the bill to pass, so that they could share in full privileges with Europeans (including alcohol), Bale argued:

the object of this Bill is merely to deprive them of the opportunities of becoming more degraded than they were in their heathen state. I would much rather that the Natives of the Colony should remain in the gross barbarism which characterized them than they should become as degraded as the Red Indian of North America, or as many of the Natives of the neighbouring [Cape] Colony are. . . . [T]he use of intoxicating liquors by Natives who have been accustomed to civilizing influences for many years is most lamentable.[33]

Such a statement depended upon earlier discourses that rendered Africans as part of a larger schema of global indigeneity, peoples to be rendered distinct from Anglophone settlers around the world. Indeed, Bale's argument matched the *Natal Witness* editorial two decades earlier nearly word for word.

As Natal's settler legislators attempted to grapple with the definition of native peoples in relation to alcohol consumption, they also worked to try to extend the alcohol ban to Indian peoples within the colony. Throughout the 1880s Natal's Legislative Council actively debated whether the alcohol ban should be extended to Indians—making alcohol purely a white privilege and mapping directly onto the discourses of white supremacy that undergirded the colony. Several members of Natal's Legislative Council argued that Indians should also be barred from consuming or acquiring liquor as this would serve to halt the sale of liquor to Africans. Legal debates over Indian drinking complicate a simple white/black divide in Natal's history and reveal the complex, concomitant creation of racial order within the colony. Most arguments either for or against Indian drinking responded to a dichotomized view of the colony as a competition between indigenous Africans and European settlers. Settler arguments for banning liquor either asserted Indians were inherently as degraded as native Africans and disqualified from drinking, or they acted as the conduit by which Africans obtained illicit liquor and therefore must be prevented from betraying the natural racial/moral order of the colony. Likewise, settler (as well as Indian) arguments in favor of continuing to allow Indian consumption of alcohol derived from an estimation of their fitness in the face of native susceptibility, or underlined a shared imperial investment in building a colony amid indigenous lands. Settlers may have relied upon racial tropes to defend their hierarchical society, but they required Indian labor by the late 1870s in order to sustain the sugar industry that dominated the coast, one of Natal's few reliably successful economic ventures. This dependency upon Indian labor led to the defeat of multiple bills aimed at curtailing Indian consumption of alcohol throughout the 1880s. While many of the legislators clearly favored restricting Indian drinking, the idea that such restrictions could limit the continued viability of Indian labor recruitment often undercut votes in favor of restrictive legislation.

Settler politicians mobilized the specter of the degenerate African as a justification for the continued policing of alcohol for nonwhite peoples within the colony. Natal politician James Reynolds made clear his investment in the overall debate, asserting: "I would prohibit the sale of liquor not only to the natives and the Indians, but to all men of colour. If this recommendation is not carried my opinion is we will be hardly able to tell where we are driving."[34] In this speech, Reynolds explicitly advocates creating a white monopoly on liquor consumption within Natal. If settlers could not maintain liquor—and the sociability it provided—as a solely white preserve, then the very distinctions between African and European (and subsequently between whites/nonwhites in general) would break down, obscuring where settlers imagined they were "driving" the colony. Ultimately, Reynolds's speech links white control over alcohol with control over nonwhite populations in general. If the settler state could not restrict nonwhite peoples from drinking, then who, in the estimation of men like Reynolds, was truly controlling the colony?

Yet the opinion was not shared by all of Natal's legislators. Arguing in favor of continuing Indian access to drink, William Darby maintained: "These men have come to this country and have served their five years of service. They are British subjects the same as ourselves. We cannot discover that they are given to the perpetration of greater iniquity in the use of intoxicating liquors than we are. Yet we want to disqualify them, and what is worse than that to disqualify them without notice."[35] Drawing a line between indigenous peoples and all arrivants, of any color, Darby argued that Indians were no more susceptible to intoxication than white settlers—a distinction that implicitly referenced the moral unfitness of natives to drink. Pointing out their shared British subjecthood, Darby argued that as fellow imperial occupiers of the land, Indians should therefore able to consume liquor legally. By furthering the discourse along civilizational lines, Darby argued for Indian rights along a familiar axis of native unfitness.

In 1890 the Legislative Council refined its liquor codes yet again, but this time more thoroughly racializing the statutes. The new law reinforced the denial of alcohol access (save for indigenous beer) to Africans, irrespective of legal or social status, while Indians were subjected to a compromise measure. No longer could Indians purchase alcohol in portable containers; all alcohol had to be consumed on the premises of licensed establishments. White people continued to be under no restrictions regarding consumption, although they did suffer criminal and social penalties for drunkenness.

The partial banning of Indian consumption of liquor elicited a variety of reactions throughout the colony. A significant number of Indians protested the passage of the 1890 law, with over three thousand petitioners specifically joining together in an appeal for the legislature to repeal the act that same year. Led by Anglo-Indian interpreter Frank Ward, the 1890 Repeal Petition offers an illuminating Indian response to the limiting liquor statute. In it, the petitioners make appeals to self-control and proper behavior to claim their own share in alcohol access—and recognition as members of the larger civil polity—within Natal. These claims both echo and challenge settler racial attitudes.

The Repeal Petition began by listing the various origins of the Indian class within Natal—indentured laborers, commercial traders, and freehold farmers in particular make the list—emphasizing that "all of such, on the whole, are recorded to be an industrious and respectable class of people in the Colony of Natal."[36] By asserting that they were respectable and disciplined, the petitioners hoped to make a case for equality with the settler elites who sought to deprive them of access to drink.

Rightfully discerning the relationship between alcohol consumption and recognition as legitimate and disciplined members of colonial society, the Repeal petitioners worked to explain their racial existence within the white/black hierarchy of Natal by claiming to share both imperial affinities and inherent self-discipline with the white settler population. The petitioners deployed a strategy that asserted continuity as British subjects and difference from the indigenous populations in their midst, claiming an exempted status in the hope of legitimizing their claims to full inclusion:

As British-born subjects they were assured of the continuance of all the privileges and indulgences they enjoyed in their Native Land, but . . . to their utter dismay, to be betrayed and vicitimised by the unjust restrictions of said Liquor Law against them, which evidently is inadvertently brought to bear on the Coloured Race, although rightfully intended and justly brought into execution for Kafirs, natives of South Africa.[37]

Noting the white monopoly that settlers wished not only to maintain but also expand over people of color, the Repeal petitioners sought to clarify their liminal position at the expense of indigenous peoples. It is here most clearly that the petitioners occupy the position that theorist Lorenzo Veracini has termed "exogenous others." In Veracini's formation, such populations exist in a settler paradigm ranging from "debased" to "virtuous," where the virtuous are offered limited inclusion provided they assimilate properly, and the debased are to be restricted from acceptance.[38] The moralized divisions settler populations draw between exogenous populations frequently occur along racialized lines of difference.[39] In order to make these claims to inclusion, to "virtue," as an exogenous other group, the petitioners attempted both to establish their credentials as fellow British subjects while simultaneously reinforcing a settler normative standard of division between proper colonists and the indigenes whose lands they occupy.

The petitioners did not attempt to circumvent the racialized hierarchies developing within Natal's settler society; rather, they tried to reaffirm and redirect them. Acknowledging their nonwhiteness, the Repeal petitioners nonetheless insisted that they were hard-working, orderly, and respectable. Furthering this claim, the petitioners marshaled the same gendered tropes of male responsibility that often delineated white claims to respectability with alcohol in Natal:

> Your Excellency's Memorialists beg to state that some of them—as respectable class of men—have for their consumption by the bottle, at their respective homes, with families and friends; but the aforesaid liquor law being against them they are tempted to visit the canteens at unusual hours whenever a dram is required.[40]

The argument within the petition stated that Indian *men*—as householders and providers for their families—must possess alcohol to respectably socialize in their homes. Yet, for the petitioners, the Liquor Law deprived them of the ability to fulfill their position as male providers properly, by tempting them away from home. The case for virtue over debasement led the petitioners to position themselves as respectable male citizens looking to provide for their families, a position undermined by the new law.

Finally, the Repeal petitioners explicitly equated alcohol consumption with full inclusion within Natal's civic polity. The petitioners directly noted that the settlers most invested in depriving Indians of access to drink also worked simultaneously to disfranchise them as voters within Natal. Pointing to their recently successful appeal against disfranchisement, the petitioners linked the right to vote to the right to drink (two privileges expressly forbidden to virtually all Africans). Having won the appeal on a claim to shared rights as British citizens, the petitioners were quick to press their claims based upon imperial affinity:

> The flag that carries the 'Union Jack' will have its just and sympathizing Laws, but not that which is experienced in the Colony of Natal rendered to Her Majesty's Subjects, who are, and may hereafter come into the Colony of Natal . . . but [had] never heard of such indignant and dastardly treatment brought to bear upon them and their unfortunate families by the irreconcilable and irrevocable process of the Liquor Law brought to bear upon a *Civilized Race* in the Colony of Natal.[41]

Ultimately, a sense of both shared imperial affinity and inherent difference from indigenous subjectivity buttressed the Repeal petitioners' claim. Responding to moralizing rhetoric of Natal's settlers, who sought to depict them as inherently unfit for civic (and drinking) equality, the petitioners mobilized raced and gendered modes of behavior to assert superiority over indigenous Africans and a shared investment in the colony with whites. The Repeal Petition of 1890 was immediately disregarded by Natal's colonial establishment who declared it unacceptable to repeal such a law less than a year after it had been put into operation. To the extreme irritation of the governor and legislators, Frank Ward and the petitioners responded exactly one year to the date after the passage of the law, asking yet again for repeal.

Yet not all members of the heterogeneous Indian community agreed with the Repeal petitioners. In response to both the law and the Repeal Petition, a smaller petition was organized in support of the 1890 Law. The 1891 Support Petition underlined ten key points in favor of the new Indian Liquor Law. Chief among them, the petitioners argued that drink was unknown to "proper" Hindus and Muslims and that taking alcohol only served to "degrade" them in the eyes of their countrymen, evoking a similar rationale as the Repeal petitioners, albeit for different immediate ends.[42] The petitioners also reinforced the black/white axis of inclusion, by arguing that the law limited the likelihood of Indians offering alcohol to Africans, resulting in further indigenous degradation through spirituous liquors. The petitioners stressed, "[W]e cannot blind ourselves to the fact that the demoralized amongst our people supply the natives with drink for most pitiable consideration." Such a discursive move sought to distance the bulk of the Indian population from allegations of alcohol smuggling, but it also serves to mark those who did as a degraded minority. In the logic of the Support Petition, Indians were protected by the removal of alcohol's temptations, which served to degrade a minority of the exogenous population and in turn further the moral decline of the far more numerous native peoples.

Natal's governor and Legislative Assembly both resolutely refused to repeal the 1890 law, having taken the better part of a decade to achieve some measure of legal limitation over the alcohol consumption of Indian peoples. Yet the law itself appeared to be rather ineffective in its immediately proposed aims, namely curtailing both Indian and African drunkenness. L. H. Mason, the official protector of Indian immigrants, decried the entire law as a failure. Writing to the governor in 1891, Mason argued that not only were many members of the Indian community feeling roused to political agitation as they felt their rights were being limited, but also that the law perversely increased public intoxication for Indians. Mason complained that after the passage of the law, white canteen owners were serving Indians only full bottles of liquor that had to be consumed entirely on the premises, whereupon, "the Indian after leaving the canteen does not go many yards before the liquor takes effect and he becomes helplessly drunk, half poisoned in fact with Natal rum, some of which is of the vilest description."[43] Referencing the Durban police report for the end of 1891, Mason also insisted that the illicit Indian trade in alcohol to Africans had been lessened—only for white settlers to fill the vacuum in black market activity. The entire stated purpose of the law—the limiting of Indian and African drinking—had not been achieved; indeed, the opposite had occurred, in Mason's view. Why then, did the Natal government consistently refuse to repeal the law?

The Legislature and governor refused to repeal the partial ban on Indian drinking because it fulfilled settlers' racial/political needs rather than their immediate material ones. The enactment of legal restrictions on Indian drinking took place amid an increasingly fierce debate over the very status of Indian people within the colony. An increasing population of both former indentured laborers and urban shopkeepers had become prosperous and established in Natal throughout the 1880s and 1890s. Due to the relative inability of settlers to compel African laborers into providing a reliable labor supply sufficient to their needs, the economy of Natal depended upon a constant flow of Indian migrant labor, particularly in the sugar industry on the coast. Yet they could not legally compel Indian migrants to leave Natal after their terms of indenture were up, nor could they ban the movement of free or "passenger" Indians who arrived primarily to supply the material needs of these laborers. As a result, by the 1880s, a significant number of Indian immigrants and their descendants came to occupy Natal's cities and farms, a development many settlers saw as a direct threat. By the 1890s, Natal white settlers began actively attempting to block Natal's Indian population from exercising the franchise, lest they limit the political and social monopoly settlers desired to enact within the colony. As alcohol stood as a particularly salient marker of inclusion within a settler polity, namely through the discourse of moral fitness, settlers sought to deny Indians the legitimacy of drink as a means of marking them as inherently foreign and ineligible of inclusion.

The continued presence of Indians further troubled the fragile hegemony of the white settlers. Not only did the presence of an additional migrant population challenge the monopoly that whites hoped to maintain in erecting a settler minority state, it also challenged the ostensible claims of moral and inherent superiority that undergirded the entire enterprise in Natal. Sir Frederick Moor, who would later serve as Natal's last prime minister prior to Union, asserted, "It is becoming a colonizing question for Natal. We are importing these Asiatics to settle down, to the detriment, nay, to the expulsion, of the white population."[44] J. F. King, one of the representatives from Durban, put it even more bluntly in 1890, stating, "We are Europeans, and we can only respect Europeans. We can only associate with them, and be happy with them."[45] Yet Natal depended upon both Indian and African populations to support settler ambitions, despite King's cry for separation and distance. Although settlers like King would have ostensibly desired to see a whites-only colony, the reality of Natal's demographics meant that the discursive limits of settlement demanded the establishment of boundaries to civic participation and inclusion. In effect, Natalians attempted to create a whites-only colony psychically and civically if they could not be render one logistically. The establishment of structures of difference and separation were integral to this European-only association, and alcohol, with all of its attendant assumptions of moral fitness and legitimate claims to occupation, served as a critical manifestation of these desired divisions.

It is in this crisis of "comprehending" an exogenous Asian population, one that Jodi Byrd has termed "arrivant settler colonialism," that Natal resembles other contemporary settler colonies.[46] British Columbia, California, and Queensland all found themselves flashpoints in a late nineteenth-century global settler debate over the demographic constitutions threatened by nonwhite immigration. Natal's legislators recognized this as well. In 1888, Cecil Yonge reported before the Legislative Council:

> It is of advantage to know that other colonies have had, and have at the present moment, under consideration this question, and it is gratifying to know that the position some of us take up in this Colony has its support in other parts of the world. It is pleasant to Europeans in this Colony to know that their white brethren in other parts of the world are resisting the introduction of these aliens to supplant them.[47]

In particular, Yonge praised the efforts of Queensland's white settler constituency to resist Indian migrant labor in order to preserve the colony as a preserve of whiteness, even at the expense of economic growth. The presence of a significant Indian population in Natal challenged settler attempts to create a whites-only settler polity that claimed to be the rightful, natural occupants of the colony. Although the Indian population created a unique set of pressures on the settler state, attempts to exclude and marginalize Indians also depended on preexisting settler/native divides. Alcohol consumption served as a particularly visible marker of difference, drawing distinction between disciplined, controlled European colonists and morally unfit Africans. Additionally, Indian men and women worked to avoid the stigma of being seen as degraded exogenous others in Natal society, and strove to make claims of moral respectability. These claims relied specifically on assertions of shared imperial affinities with white settlers as well as histories of civilization in the face of native savagery in order to avoid the same queered fate of Africans in colonial eyes. The passage of the Indian Liquor law of 1890 reveals the struggles over alcohol consumption as a marker of civic inclusion in Natal, and the subsequent battles over drink as the decade came to a close mirrored both the continued challenge Indians offered to white claims to monopoly over citizenship and wider struggles over inclusion waged by arrivant settler populations across the globe.

Race and Gendered Violence under Natal's Alcohol Laws

In October of 1888, as debates over Indian and African drinking took place in the Legislative Assembly, Durban attorney Samuel Rowse sent a lengthy petition to the Arthur Havelock, then governor of Natal. The letter specifically asked for the commutation of a death sentence that had been meted out to two Indian men, Mootosamy and Apparoo, convicted of the rape of Subjan, an Indian woman. The petition, which was signed by several of the jury members on the case, sought to review the evidence in the case and question the culpability of the men involved. The case, and its subsequent petitioning, demonstrate the power of raced and gendered hierarchies within colonial Natal, particularly in relation to alcohol access, offering an essential means of understanding the abstract nature of colonial citizenship and inclusion.

Mootosamy and Apparoo were convicted by a jury in October of 1888 of having sexually assaulted Subjan on a deserted native footpath as they were all returning home from a day at the races near Umzinto village, a coastal community about forty miles south of Durban, known for its sugar production. In her testimony, Subjan asserted that three months earlier she had been walking home alone along the deserted shortcut, where she noticed two men and two boys were following her. Subjan asserted that Mootosamy (whom she recognized) and Apparoo (whom she did not) dragged her into the grass, robbed her of her jewelry, and pinned her down, each man assaulting her multiple times. This assertion was supported by the evidence of the two young Indian boys also on the road, who did not witness the rape itself but could testify to the dragging into the grass and the larger aspects of the assault. As the attorney for Mootosamy and Apparoo, Samuel Rowse worked to undo the damaging impact of such testimony, and sought resolutely to discredit Subjan as a witness primarily by attacking her along raced and gendered lines—all around her use of alcohol.

In order to win reprieve for his clients, Rowse sought to undermine Subjan's authority as a witness—and her legitimacy as a victim—by referencing her purported alcohol consumption. "Upon cross examination, witness admitted that she had taken one glass of rum at the races but denied that she was drunk," Rowse asserted bluntly. He did, however, reluctantly have to admit that "all the witnesses for the crown, although pressed upon this point, persisted in affirming that the woman did not appear to be worse for liquor." Yet Rowse had already begun to contend indirectly that Subjan's alleged rape was actually *her* responsibility, a direct result of her moral permissiveness demonstrated through the consumption of alcohol. In recounting the details of the trial, Rowse worked to posit an alternate reading of the brutal events on that July evening, one that placed the blame squarely upon Subjan's implied immorality:

[T]here was nothing in the Evidence of these witnesses as given at the trial inconsistent with the theory that complainant was drunk and was found lying about on the public Road in a position to her safety if not removed, and that the Prisoners, one of whom (Mootosamy) had been intimately acquainted with her, endeavoured to remove her off the road—that she became restive as inebriated persons usually do, and that they made frequent attempts to get her along the road.[48]

In Rowse's retelling, Mootosamy and Apparoo neither raped nor stole; rather, they offered assistance to a drunken woman by the side of the road, whose own indiscretions had placed her at inordinate personal risk.

Having undermined Subjan's reputation by alleging that she was a drunkard and therefore morally suspect, Rowse then moved to deny the legitimacy her status as a victim of assault. By painting a picture of Subjan not as an innocent victim who had been assailed on her way home after only consuming a legally allowed glass of rum, but rather as a drunken, wanton woman wandering shamelessly without the protection or propriety of her husband, Rowse sought to completely undercut the idea that she had been raped at all. Indeed, by emphasizing her solitary status as well as her public drinking, Rowse could then argue "there is no doubt complainant is a woman of notoriously immoral character."[49] By wandering freely without sanction and in contravention of what proper behavior should be for an Indian woman, Subjan, in Rowse's words, had invited her own assault, if such an assault had even happened. Having demolished her character, Rowse then insisted that it was "physically impossible for the prisoners to have effected their purpose" as Subjan had claimed. Rather, for Rowse, "there was no evidence (beyond the statement of the woman herself) which proved conclusively that, assuming both or either of the prisoners to have had connection with complainant it was *without her consent.*"[50] It is at this point that Rowse's argument finally comes to fruition: Subjan could not have been raped because she was most likely drunk. If she was not drunk, her drinking and her lack of male accompaniment demonstrates her immoral behavior, which means that her body itself was not effectively virtuous to resist male advances. Rowse's gambit was ultimately successful as Havelock was convinced by this gendered reasoning by way of alcohol; he commuted the sentence as requested.

Subjan's story complicates the manner in which alcohol consumption was understood by observers in the nineteenth century as a question of morality. Religious commenters like Mzamo saw African alcohol consumption as a profound form of demoralization, a point shared by the colony's legislators when they attempted to constrain the dangerous specter of indigenous drinking. White men like Swindells and Stransham, who contravened societal expectations around drink, had to maneuver around the idea that they had committed a temporary but undeniably moral failing. Yet the very problem of white drinking relied upon an understanding of African and Indian drinkers as inherently degraded and immoral. Subjan's case moves this even further, offering a sadly familiar tale of morality tied implicitly to raced and gendered expectations. Her assailants received a reduced sentence directly as an understanding of her drunkenness as a marker of her immorality. Raced and gendered understandings of alcohol consumption were often expressed through a lens of morally (in)appropriate behavior, with vastly differing expectations for offenders. Such an outcome recalls Cathy Cohen's assertion that bodies are targeted along a variety of intersections in the midst of white supremacist heteronormativity. In this instance, settler observers interpreted Subjan's aberrant status in relation to alcohol as an altogether larger indication of moral failure. By rendering Subjan queer in relation to gendered and raced norms of behavior, Natal's legal system also made the crime perpetrated against her less serious.

Two years after Subjan's case, the *Natal Advertiser* reported on a "Nasty Case" involving settler men, native women, and presumptions about alcohol, race, and gender. Two European men, a Mr. H. Phillips and R. Williams, were charged in September with supplying liquor to two young native women. One of the women, Nmatu, reported that the men had "enticed" her and her friend Topsy away to a remote beach near Durban "where they gave them drink—the one from a bottle of gin, and the other from a bottle of pontac."[51] However, it appeared that Williams and Phillips did not simply plan for a late-night tipple. Nmatu claimed "the men then caught hold of them and they called out, after which the police came and arrested the four of them." It would appear from this brief incident in the newspaper that the two men assumed that alcohol

consumption for women implied a loose and easy sexuality. Settler discourse asserted that African women drinking publicly, much like Indian
women, demonstrated a particular lack of moral fiber. While generally,
African men were seen as lacking the proper (white) masculine value of
self-control around spirits, African women were rendered promiscuous
and easily accessible for white desires. The news report suggests that the
sexualized interactions between the European men and Zulu women
were distinctly nonconsensual, as the women subsequently cried out
and attracted police attention.

In this instance, alcohol consumption maps directly onto the day-
to-day raced and gendered realities of settler colonialism in Natal. The
Advertiser reported that when Nmatu and Topsy cried out, the first person to respond was a native policeman, who came upon the two men
"holding on by the girls." Immediately Williams and Phillips sought
not to apologize or confess to the officer, but rather to offer him liquor
in hope of winning him over. In this instance the two European men
attempted to use their exclusive privilege to alcohol as a means of purchasing favor with a Zulu man who was legally barred from consumption. In so doing, the men may have hoped to build a masculine alliance
across racial inequalities in order to prevent discipline for their actions
against Nmatu and Topsy. The nameless constable, however, was not
convinced, and soon other policemen joined the group on the beach. The
two women were fined 10s for breaking African curfew laws, but the men
were fined £5 each. While the attendant judge expressed revulsion, claiming "he had never heard a nastier case," the two men were tried not for
attempted rape or for any potential violence toward the native women,
but rather for serving Africans alcohol and thereby breaking laws of racial
distinction. The stories of Subjan, Nmatu, and Topsy illustrate the gendered as well as raced nature of alcohol consumption in the late nineteenth century. In particular, aggressive, invasive displays of masculinity
could be viewed as legitimate in the face of a debased female morality compromised by alcohol consumption. Cases like those of Kumalo,
Subjan, Topsy, and Nmatu provide rare on the ground views of lived
experience under Natal's alcohol laws. Additionally, instances like these,
reported in popular colonial newspapers and sent in reports between

colonial officials, would have informed and helped shape the rhetoric of settler legislators as they passed laws governing alcohol consumption, particularly the major reorganization of liquor law that took place in 1890. Yet at the same time that Indians and Africans found their liquor and *utshwala* rights under attack, white settlers too found themselves increasingly restricted in their alcohol consumption as legislators debated legal restrictions on drink, steeped in the rhetoric of moral fitness yet again.

By the early 1890s, white men who repeatedly fell to the enticements of alcohol had begun to attract pity and sympathy in official circles, instead as being seen as mere moral failures.[52] While debating an Inebriates' Bill in 1894, Henry Bale attempted to humanize white male examples of alcoholic behavior. Standing before the Legislative Assembly, Bale argued that he had known a professional man, who, if he were not incapable of avoiding drink, "would have been an ornament to society and a useful member of the community." This man had asked to be put into prison in order to prevent him from continuing to drink. The request was refused, and the man died impoverished in the streets. Reflecting on the fate of the unnamed colonist and other men like him, Bale continued: "I suppose that this man's will, like the will of so many others under similar circumstances, was enervated, that he was unable to control himself, that he had lost to a large extent one of the attributes of his manhood—the power of self-control."[53] Bale's argument in favor of quarantine over criminalization for alcoholism, however, does *not* signal a change in the raced or gendered assumptions that supported attempts to legally control alcohol consumption in Natal. Rather, Bale *upholds* such formulations through his calls for legal reform. By situating the unfortunate colonist's failing as losing an attribute of his manhood, Bale illustrated the performative and contingent nature of race and masculinity in colonial Natal. If alcohol was a privilege specifically reserved for the enjoyment of whites (and ideally men) who possessed a monopoly over full social inclusion within a settler colony, then alcoholism itself belied the limits of settlement—it was a visceral example of the failing of presumed white male superiority in colonial society. More importantly, this rhetoric privileges self-control, a trait presented as unique to white settlers (indeed, the lack of self-control factored highly into debates over why Africans and Indians should be restricted from drinking).

A year later, Bale continued his drive for leniency, advocating the establishment of settler "retreats" (which naturally, would only be for European men). Speaking specifically about the needs of white settler men, Bale continued:

> [A] drunkard is a curse to his home, a curse to his wife, and a curse to his children, who are influenced not only by his bad example but are brought to beggary and degradation. If, however, that man is confined . . . it is possible that after his restoration he will be able to fulfill his duties as a husband and a father.[54]

Bale's speech underscored the stakes. In his formulation, the destructiveness of antisocial drinking rendered settler men incapable of filling their "duties" as husbands and fathers, which were to produce hierarchies of order and control as well as *reproduce* white settler populations in a colony where indigenous peoples outnumbered them eight to one. White alcoholics ran the risk of degradation, a critical problem in a society that depended upon racial hierarchy. Indeed, the threat of degradation recalled the construction of the African and Indian subject as inherently aberrant and weak-willed in relation to alcohol. White settler masculinity, then, had to be constantly made and remade through the performance of self-control in relation to alcohol, lest the very structure that rendered non-European bodies as queer and degraded in turn define them.[55]

Despite the beginning shifts in views of alcoholism, white self-control over alcohol consumption remained tightly linked to notions of respectability and proper claims to rule in Natal. The racialized component of alcohol as a preserve of white settler enjoyment often served to counter manifestations of the global temperance movement in Natal. While drunkenness was problematic and alcohol a potential vice, the ability to drink served as a racialized marker of distinction that white settlers, particularly moderate drinking men, were reluctant to relinquish. As early as 1881 settlers adamantly protested proposed temperance laws that restricted access to drink and instead offered "wholesome" entertainments aimed at young white men, arguing:

> It does not, of course, matter whether young men play billiards and drink or not, so long as they commit no excesses. There is nothing whatever abstractly vicious in either billiards or wine. All reasonable and reasoning people are agreed upon that point. . . . Nobody disputes the fact that a man who gets drunk makes a beast of himself, albeit often a very ludicrous one. . . . But shall we reclaim them or stop drinking and gambling by establishing teetotal saloons and reading rooms? We think not.[56]

The specific rhetoric deployed throughout the 1880s and 1890s by many settlers marshaled a sense of white masculinity as constituted by moderation and restraint, rendering further restrictions infantilizing, humiliating, and unnecessary.

Likewise, hundreds of petitioners wrote to protest the Natal Legislative Council's temperance-minded attempts to strengthen the Liquor Laws of 1896. The petitioners angrily alleged:

> While the majority of the people of this colony are not what is known as total abstainers, they are temperate and the present Bill is an uncalled for imputation on their character in that its provisions are likely to create an impression in the minds of those who have not the chance of judging for themselves that a very considerable section of the colonists are addicted to excessive drinking and incapable of exercising the self-control which is exercised by the members of all civilized and intelligent communities.[57]

Critically, these petitioners make it known that they are not abstainers, they are self-regulating drinkers. In regards to their drinking, they marshaled a sense of victimization at the wide-ranging proposed changes to Natal's alcohol laws. They interpreted these broad changes as doubt in their inability to maintain sobriety, which served, in effect, to mark their failure to exercise appropriate control over Natal. Bristling at such language, the petitioners insisted that if excessive drinking did prevail among whites it was only in rare cases and did not "in any way justify the branding of the whole community as drunkards."[58]

Although newspapers and legislative debates both indicate that intoxication threatened white settler respectability, ultimately alcohol served as the means of legally defining both nativeness and Indianness. Whiteness was not an a priori condition, but rather was aligned with sobriety through a process that resulted in more detailed racial categories around African and Indian bodies. The rhetoric that linked Africans to wider populations of vulnerable indigenous peoples throughout the Anglophone settler world simultaneously bolstered settler claims to control over both government and spirits. Likewise, the constant debates over alcohol access underscored not only the liminal racial status of Indians within the colony, but also the emergent crises of white settler hegemony that would grip the colony in the first decades of the twentieth century.

Yet, as legal accounts demonstrate, white sobriety (and all that such a condition signified) itself was not automatically or necessarily stabilized even by the law, but had to be perpetually guarded and defended. It is here that the limits of settlement are most apparent in colonial Natal. The inability of settler legislators to deny nonwhite access to intoxicants pointed simultaneously to their own tenuous hold over constructed hierarchies of difference. How powerful were settlers in Natal if their vaunted control was only one careless glass of brandy away from falling away, revealing them humiliated in the dust, like the hapless Martin Swindells?

CHAPTER THREE

The Impossible Handshake

Sociability and the Fault Lines of Friendship

In 1854, John Colenso, the newly appointed bishop of Natal, arrived in the colony and made a preliminary tour. After meeting many of the settler families and colonial administrators in the new colony, Colenso looked forward to meeting with indigenous Africans, with whom he hoped to build productive and close lasting relationships. During one of his first encounters with an African person, however, Colenso remembered that settler administrators (even those ostensibly self-designated as "philo-Kafirs" or liberal-minded on racial divisions) had instructed him on the parameters of friendship with indigenous peoples. He recalled:

> With all my heart [I] would have grasped the great black hand, and given it a good brotherly shake: but my dignity would have been essentially compromised in his own eyes by any such proceeding. I confess it went very much against the grain; but the advice of all true Philo-Kafirs, Mr. Shepstone among the rest, was to the same effect—viz that too ready familiarity, and especially shaking hands with them upon slight acquaintance, was not only not understood by them, but did great mischief in making them pert and presuming. Accordingly, I looked aside with a grand indifference as long as I could, (which was not very long,) and talked to Mr. G., instead of paying attention to the Kafir's presence.[1]

At such an early point in the colony's history, the limits of sociability and friendship had already become clear in the minds of settler administrators. The logics of colonial rule in Natal required an affective division between the African subject and the proper settler; these divisions were to be further entrenched politically and legally through the implementation of customary law for Africans and civil law for European colonists.[2] This moment of unrealized friendship provides a profound and intriguing site of rupture in the colonial record. From Colenso's intimation of the perspective of Mr. Shepstone and the other philo-Kafirs, we can presume that the hierarchized distinctions between African and European were to be understood as a paternalistic form of love. Yet for Colenso, this handshake was not a paternalistic or hierarchal form of love for the African; rather, he imagined his gesture as a more magnanimous, or brotherly act of friendship. If so-called experts like Shepstone and others understood colonial rule as the proper, paternal form of love that characterized settler/indigenous relations, how might friendship or forms of alternate sociability prove dangerous to the desired order? In what ways could friendship and social interaction unsettle hierarchies of race, gender, and colonial power?

As that fraught exchange between bishop and African and settler observers reveals, friendship was both a volatile and capacious term in colonial Natal. As a concept, friendship offered an affective register by which white colonists understood their power relations with Africans. It normalized and domesticated the violence of settlement, putting it in a rhetorical framework that allowed Europeans to understand the power dynamics that existed between them and indigenous Africans in an emergent, hierarchical colonial society. Focusing on the constitutive and constructed nature of raced and gendered hierarchies in colonial Natal, I propose a reading of friendship that underscores its fundamentally protean (and thereby disruptive) nature. Friendship and various forms of sociability across gendered or raced lines could work to either reinforce or unsettle settler power in the nineteenth century, and the legislative record is rife with concerns over improper forms of socialization between Africans and members of settler society. Settlers frequently invoked the idea of interracial friendship to justify their rule in Natal, yet friendship both served to reinforce power relations and simultaneously contained the potential to unravel them.

Settler society in Natal can be viewed as a kaleidoscopic combination of varied actors—Midlands farmers, urban artisans, British and foreign missionaries, and residential officials, for example—who each viewed the province differently yet could and did coalesce around specific interests. The concept of friendship allowed for moments of consensus among differing groups of colonial actors; missionaries and legislators, for example, might find a common rhetorical cause in discussing the potential for friendship with the native peoples of Natal. As a consequence, for settler observers, "friendship" could operate as a signpost, a central point around which many of the broader contradictory and constraining aspects of colonialism in Natal could rally.

At its heart, debates over friendship in Natal demonstrate the aspirations of settler colonialism as well as its limits. The term itself contained considerable rhetorical power that could be marshaled for a variety of purposes; yet it also included inherent instabilities—indigenous peoples had the power to subvert the very gift of friendship offered to them by colonists. Indeed, friendship's very ambivalence contained the potential to not only strengthen but also fatally destabilize the hierarchical power that settlers desired over indigenous peoples and lands. That is not to say that friendship universally described the feelings of Europeans toward African peoples. Some settlers could utilize an idea of interracial friendship as part of larger claims to legitimate rule; other settlers denounced the idea of interracial friendship as an obstacle to the inevitable white dominance over the region. Reading "friendship" as a multivalent process mobilized by settlers as a normative rhetoric yet also fraught with destabilizing potential complicates the contingent nature of settler colonialism. It emphasizes the myriad ways that "bundles of human relationships"[3] could be made and remade in the multisided contradictions of imperial rule. Such an analysis underlies the construction of settler structures in Natal with other contemporary colonies across the globe and foregrounds the considerable contribution of affective discourses (such as that of friendship) to the establishment of colonial power relations.

Friendship carried within it an immense potential for instability and rupture. As Leela Gandhi has argued:

Late Victorian radicalism discursively extended the semantic scope of imperialism to diagnose it as a peculiar habit of mind, discerning within its structure a complex analogical system relentlessly mapping hierarchies of race, culture, and civilization upon relationships between genders, species, classes, etc. In this schema, departure from the self-confirming orderliness of imperial habitation was at once an experience of profound psychic derangement exile to the chaos of a world without taxonomy.[4]

Colenso's desire for a handshake and friendship remained imbricated in larger politics of control, order, and hierarchy typical of nineteenth-century settler societies. Yet, the friendship he wished for cannot merely be reduced to colonial domination and subterfuge. Colenso's privileged pursuit of interracial friendship contained at its heart destabilizing elements; a potential derangement of imperial lines of order lay waiting behind that hand. The bishop's unfulfilled desire offers a view of affective relations that simultaneously attempted to enact a normalized relation across hierarchical power and yet flirted with the possibility of completely upending colonial order.

The friendship envisioned by the thwarted handshake between Colenso and the unnamed African remained unrealized, and would always remain so. The outstretched hands across racial lines always took place in a matrix of unequal power relations, and as much as friendship could destabilize systems of power, it did not completely erase them. Further, the never-bridged distance between Colenso and the African body echoes the work of Frank Wilderson III, whose theorizing on colonialism and antiblackness describes the consummate disavowal of black humanity that white settler colonialism depended upon in Natal.[5] Far from making the African "pert and presuming," the handshake had the potential to bring racialized bodies into close proximity and underline a shared humanity between native and settler that could not be imagined, even by ostensibly liberal members of settler society. As Wilderson has asserted,

"*African*, or more precisely *Blackness*, refers to an individual who is always already void of relationality. Thus modernity marks the emergence of a new ontology because it is an era in which an entire race appears, people who . . . stand as socially dead in relation to the rest of the world."[6] For all of the destabilization of the interracial handshake, for all of the affect enacted in settler imaginations of colonial power, the essential divide between white humanity and African nonhumanity remained unbreached.

For settlers, friendship did not just serve as a distraction from their rapacious violence; rather, it operated as a mode by which they comprehended their interactions with black peoples who were indigenous to the lands they wished to inhabit. Friendship, and the affective register that accompanied it, operated at the core of colonial governance. To be clear, settler claims to colonial domination over indigenous bodies and lands in Natal were not merely justified through this rhetoric. Rather, settlers conceived and understood colonial rule *through* the idea of friendship with indigenous peoples. Nineteenth-century Natal, then, was an affective *state* in both meanings of the term.[7] As a consequence, a queer theoretical read of the centrality of friendship to the settler state allows us to understand how fragile and contingent such a state truly was. Indeed, friendship (and its attendant affective power) functioned similarly to the way Judith Butler has described the creation of gender and heterosexuality in Western societies. A colonial friendship that reinforced the inequities of colonial governance through affective ties was always, per Butler, "in the process of imitating and approximating its own phantasmatic idealization of itself—*and failing*," an action that results in a doomed and endless repetition of self.[8] If both Colenso and the settler observers perceived of their colonial relationship to indigenous lands and bodies as a form of friendship, such affective ties had to be reenacted repeatedly—and were always doomed to fail, belied by the fact that they would always produce hierarchical power dynamics. Settlers, then, continuously engaged in moments of frustrated desire; the never-accepted hand represented simultaneously the failure of friendship to transcend hierarchical domination within a colonial system, and the continued wish to use such kindly feeling to understand the settler project itself.

Consequently, a queer and indigenous read takes the space between the bishop's hand and his intended recipient as a starting point for examining the larger dynamic of the settler state in colonial Natal. Queer theoretical interventions foreground the failed desire and constant repetition of settler friendship in colonial Natal, paying careful attention to how the affective is used as a means to impose normative frameworks of power. When combined with an indigenous theoretical approach that underlines the acquisitive and violent underpinnings of settler colonialism, such a framework foregrounds the power and ultimate limitations of friendship in colonial Natal. However, such a reading cannot, as Jodi Byrd cautions, merely use difference to push back against settler affective claims to create a state that reinforces colonial hierarchies.[9] Rather, such a methodology critically examines the desire of the settlers to render their power relationship as natural and benign through recourse to camaraderie. Such a move keeps the antiblack and anti-indigenous discourses of settler colonialism at the forefront while also privileging the limits of that most ambivalent of gifts, friendship.

Friendship as Gift

While the interracial friendship referenced by settlers could offer either a dangerous sense of instability for colonial regimes aimed at supplanting indigenous peoples or a cover for government officials seeking to naturalize their claim to the colony, this was by no means the only way in which friendship could operate in the context of colonial Natal. To return to the Colenso quote that opened this chapter, it is possible to understand how friendship could paradoxically serve to strengthen colonial hierarchies of power. When standing before an unnamed African man and a host of white settler observers, Colenso despaired over his inability to "have grasped the great black hand, and given it a good brotherly shake," but what would the consequences of such an act of camaraderie have entailed? The scene depicted between the bishop and the African is rife with social inequality, emphasized by Colenso's desire to offer a display of friendship to a native man in a land he had come to occupy. This exchange can be read as one of frustrated desire, as Colenso wishes to offer the gift of friendship to an African subject. It is not a coincidence that Colenso expressed interracial friendship as both a requirement for white settlers and an ideal to be pursued, despite the near-impossibility of its realization. Indeed, the friendship that Colenso wished to offer his unnamed African subject was a loaded one, inextricably linked to larger processes of colonial violence and economic coercion.

Although countless people have written about the positive and destructive aspects of the gift, my reading of the "gift" of colonial friendship in this instance is drawn from two theorists, the French philosopher Jacques Derrida and the American cultural critic Mimi Thi Nguyen. For Derrida, the concept of the gift is in fact a series of actions of homogenization and forgetting. First, the gift must flatten complexities between giver and receiver; the act

> supposes a subject and a verb, a constituted subject, which can also be collective—for example, a group, a community, a nation, a clan, a tribe—in any case, a subject identical to itself and conscious of its identity, indeed seeking through the gesture of the gift to constitute its own unity and, precisely, to get its own identity recognized so that that identity comes back to it, so that it can reappropriate its identity: as its property.[10]

This is quite apparent in the exchange between Colenso and his desired friend. The act of giving friendship entails recognizing Colenso as part of a collective subject group (colonizer, missionary, Briton) while simultaneously attempting to construct a receiving African subject, requiring a bridge across the chasm of hierarchical racial difference.

Secondly, the gift itself by definition creates debt, a sense of obligation or a need for fulfillment between receiver and giver. Yet, for Derrida, this must be ignored, indeed forgotten, in order for a gift to truly exist. "For there to be a gift, there must be no reciprocity, return, exchange, countergift, or debt," Derrida argues. "If the other gives me back or owes me or has to give me back what I give him or her, there will not have been a gift."[11] As a consequence, the gift must *not* be acknowledged as such, or its calculative nature will be revealed, annulling it. As a result, the action of the gift is immediately intertwined with the act of forgetting its very purpose or nature; the fit must be offered but not acknowledged as such, lest it lose its significance or potential power. It is therefore unsurprising that the desire for the gift of friendship remains an abortive one in the mind of Colenso, reduced to a mere wish in an awkward assemblage of dignitaries. Indeed, with this in mind, the warning of the assembled settlers to Colenso that "too ready familiarity, and especially shaking hands with them upon slight acquaintance . . . did great mischief in making them pert and presuming" revealed more than a mere desire to maintain settler distinctions in their refusal of the gift of friendship. Rather, an obvious gesture of friendship on the part of Colenso could have been construed as a very directly offered gift to African observers, and lead to reciprocal demands and obligations as a result.[12]

For Derrida, the power of a genuine gift lies within its unacknowledged nature, a near impossible feat. Otherwise, the gift becomes an instance of calculation, exchange, and indebtedness; it becomes part of an economic calculus of obligation. In such a formulation, a gift has the potential to entrap the recipient unawares: "Unable to anticipate, he is delivered over to the mercy, to the *merci* of the giver; he is taken in, by the trap. . . . Such violence may be considered the very condition of the gift, its constitutive impurity once the gift is engaged in a process of *circulation* once it is promised to recognition, keeping, indebtedness, credit."[13] The friendship that Colenso desired certainly could operate in such a fashion; part of the calculus of such friendship would be to facilitate Africans reoriented as Christian laborers, acculturated to the religious and cultural milieu of colonial society.[14]

Cultural theorist Mimi Thi Nguyen has expanded upon Derrida's work, arguing for a theory of *the gift of freedom*, namely, an ostensibly postcolonial project of gifted liberty in the twentieth century. For Nguyen, *the gift of freedom* is an expansion upon earlier colonial justifications that results "in a cluster of promises" that continuously produces new forms of attachments, events, and obligations that can never be fulfilled or fully realized.[15] This gifted freedom is both the afterlife and continuation of colonial policies of paternalistic care and guidance for "benighted" peoples. Nguyen links the homogenization and forgetting of the gift to larger state operations of power and indebtedness that is impossible for the beneficiary to reciprocate. She has much to offer in theorizing an idea of "friendship" evinced by Colenso as part of a larger project of liberalism and imperial benevolence. "Friendship" was no small part of the British imperial lexicon in southern Africa. Much of Colenso's later political agitation for the rights of Zulu peoples against Natal's settler government would be supported in part by the Aborigines' Protection Society in Britain. The APS informed much of its metropolitan reading public about the work of men and women throughout the empire in their periodical *The Aborigines' Friend*. In this instance, friendship could be used as a means not only to claim a paternalistic interest in indigenous peoples, but also to reserve the right to perpetual protection. Therefore, British friendship to African peoples went hand in hand with a constant support for imperial authority in the region. It was, to draw from both Nguyen and Derrida, a colossal gift that could never be repaid. Instead, African peoples were to be ensnared in an affective relation of constant indebtedness to their enlightened British compatriots, in a repetitive cycle that simultaneously raised and attempted to erase threats to colonial power.

And yet, indigenous peoples could use friendship as a gift to entail affective senses of obligation and reciprocation . Such was the case in 1882, when the exiled Zulu king Cetshwayo kaMpande utilized conceptions of friendship to advance his own interests in southern Africa. Cetshwayo, who had been deposed by the British government following the Anglo-Zulu War of 1879, sought to regain his kingdom with the support of interested parties throughout the empire. Drawing on a motley assemblage of supporters from Bishop Colenso to aristocratic observers from the metropole to social reformers in Natal, Cetshwayo purposefully mobilized the language of friendship to regain power. Cetshwayo's kingdom had been reduced to thirteen smaller chiefdoms, the largest of which was under the rule of a white settler and former confidant of the king's, John Dunn.

While in exile in Cape Town and seeking an audience with imperial officials in London, Cetshwayo frequently stated his "friendship" with and loyalty to Queen Victoria and simultaneously decrying the false friendship of men like Dunn who had replaced him. Cetshwayo had harsh words for Dunn, stating baldly, "When I reigned in that country I treated John Dunn as my friend; his return was to act as a spy between me and the English Government. He told them much that was false; he harmed in all the ways he could; he never could be my friend again; how can I then forgive him and live in peace with a man who treated me so badly after I had treated him so well?"[16] Cetshwayo's invocation of friendship before British observers served as part of his larger strategy to subvert Dunn's control over Zululand and to secure his return to the throne. His declaration of Dunn's false friendship demonstrates one of the ways in which friendship could encapsulate larger questions of imperial stability and colonial order. The rhetorical move was eventually successful, albeit briefly. Cetshwayo subsequently gained an audience with the queen in August of 1882, who restored the monarch to his throne (albeit with a significant loss of territory) while deposing his erstwhile friend Dunn.[17] Indigenous peoples like Cetshwayo kaMpande, who had the resources to bolster their claims to power within the colonial spaces of Natal, had the potential to utilize friendship as a shared language of affect. Yet Cetshwayo's successes were short-lived; he was not restored to his full antebellum territory, and he perished in the midst of a conflict between his supporters and those of Zibhebhu, a competing claimant to Zulu authority.[18]

Affective Attachment:
Colonial Hierarchies and "Kindly Feeling" in Natal

Settlers commonly invoked the idea of interracial friendship while justifying their position within the colony. In an attempt to press for Responsible Government in 1880, Natal's Legislative Council asserted that

The relations which exist between the whites and the blacks in Natal were admitted by Sir Garnet Wolseley himself, during his first visit to the Colony, to be marked by greater harmony and friendliness than he had witnessed between the races in other lands. The Natives and the Colonists have lived in perfect amity together for a period of over thirty years. Nor can better testimony on this point be needed than is born by the well-known fact that the Native Levies called out during the Zulu

War entreated to be led by Colonists, rather than by Imperial Officers and strangers.[19]

The announcement by the Legislative Council is a telling one. The council invoked the idea of interracial friendship as a means of legitimating settler minority rule in the colony; in other words, the "perfect amity" between African and settler demonstrated sufficient domestic harmony in the colony and a sense of profound partnership between Natal's African and settler populations. In the wake of the Anglo-Zulu War of 1879, the claims of Natal's settler government that perfect amity existed between autochthonous and indigenous peoples supported a narrative of settler control over potential African rebellion. By invoking the Native Levies' preference for settler over imperial leaders, the Natal government deployed an interracial affinity (or a form of friendship) in pursuit of settler autonomy.

Likewise, the 1881 Native Commission used the idea of interracial friendship between settlers and Africans in order to justify policies of control over indigenous peoples. At the end of its report, the commission concluded "we have considered the subjects before us impartially and with a kindly feeling towards the Natives. If this does not appear, we shall so far have failed in conveying our sentiments." Not content to simply describe the amity between settlers and Africans, the commission added, patronizingly, "There is, we think, in the Natives, not a little which the Whites generally feel to be attractive, and calculated to win friendliness towards a people with whom they are so closely brought into contact."[20] Both the words of the 1881 Commission and the Natal Legislative Council invoked the idea of friendship with the colony's indigenous African population in order to justify their claims to power and authority.

There is much to behold in the idea of the "kindly feeling," espoused by Europeans toward indigenous peoples in Natal. For Europeans who expressed this kindliness, friendship operated as a collisionary relationship, enmeshed in the extant power relations between settler and indigenous. By positioning themselves as sources of kindness, settlers perpetuated a cycle that claimed to undo the Gordian knots of colonial society through recourse to affect, but neither unwound nor cut the hierarchical ties that bound them.

Settler conceptions of friendship with Africans proved inseparable from larger understandings of power. Even at their most expansive, such views of interracial friendships still arose from disproportionate senses of domination. Harriet Colenso, daughter of the clergyman so vexed by the handshake, was one of the members of Natal's settler community most committed to settler/indigenous cooperation and cohabitation. Yet ultimately her understanding of European/African friendship remained enmeshed in the preexisting hierarchies of power that structured colonial Natal. Responding to a series of questions during the 1904 Native Commission, Harriet Colenso offered a succinct vision for interracial friendship in Natal:

> I think that Natives and we are parts of one community out here. I think we mislead ourselves when we talk about the Native question. It is an odd way of putting it when you come to think of it, because they were here first. It is rather a question of how Europeans are best to live in this country, and we have not only to fit them to our ways, but to accommodate ourselves to a certain extent to their ways and to their country. We have to fall in with one another, to give and take, and the strong have got to bear for the weak. Put it so, that we are the strong. Well, then, we must put up with things; we must make allowances because we are strong and because we know better.[21]

To be certain, Harriet Colenso's conception of Natal in the nineteenth century was a radical one, by settler standards. It fundamentally undermined the idea of the settler exerting unchallenged authority by virtue of conquest and occupation, and demanded Europeans enter into a reciprocal relationship with Africans in order to morally continue their inhabitance within the colony. Yet this visioning still takes as its starting point a position of European superiority and strength. Like her father before her, Harriet Colenso's vision of friendship was still born from a relation of power that sought to justify and reconcile the violence of settler occupation. Friendship, for Harriet Colenso, served as a means of resolving the inherent falseness of the "Native Question," but did not provide an answer outside of a framework of continued colonial rule. Indeed, it instead offered a constant repetition of affective obligation, one that bound Africans and Europeans to a community established through colonial violence and domination. To "fall in with one another," in Harriet Colenso's words, is a revolutionary statement for settler society, yet it still revealed an imaginary bound within the colonial paradigm.

Harriet Colenso's views were largely shared by the American Mission Board in Natal. Celebrating fifty years of missionary presence in the colony, the Reverend Josiah Tyler asserted, "That the heathen, among whom we labour, have been, from the first, and are now, kindly disposed towards us." Indeed, Tyler stated plainly that Africans were "friendly to us, they look upon us as their friends."[22] This friendliness was judged by the pleasantness of their theological exchanges, the mutual reception of missionaries and Africans in each other's homes, and a general sense of civility between minister and potential congregant. Like Colenso, these claims countered more vicious pronouncements of black inferiority, but never truly left a paradigm of hierarchical power.

In his sermon, Tyler considered the kindly and civilizational development of Africans in Natal apparent through their willingness to send their children to work, free of charge, in the homes of missionaries as servants.[23] Here, too, Tyler instantiated a rhetoric of friendship and kindly feeling inextricable from power dynamics within the colony. Despite their best intentions, both Tyler and Harriet Colenso failed to resist the "structural prohibition barring Blackness from the conceptual framework of Human empathy" that Wilderson asserts constitutes the fundamental state of being in settler societies.[24] This prohibition could not be reduced simply to "a lack of goodwill or the practice of rhetorical discrimination," but rather, it encompassed the totality of relations between European settler and indigenous African. It was true, even when these relations constituted a platform of kindly rapport where settlers could attempt to reform the colonial society around them.

Settlers did not universally hold to this ostensibly benign, instrumentalist view of friendship in pursuit of colonial prerogatives. For some settlers, interracial friendship was the antithesis of the social order that they hoped to erect in colonial Natal. For Charles Barter, prominent settler and politician, friendship was inimical to the designs of global settlement. In his 1852 book, *The Dorp and the Veld*, Barter parodied the philanthropic voice of metropolitan British observers and local missionaries like John Colenso, who spoke of friendship and amity, stating, "'We have come to soften, to teach, to civilize, to Christianize them; why should not the two nations dwell together in peace and friendship, on equal terms?'" Yet Barter countered that "this argument is, if possible, still more specious than other[s], but equally hollow and fallacious."[25] For Barter, friendship between the colonist and colonized was impossible, a mere wish of the hopeless do-gooder or prevaricating philanthropist. Barter instead argued that settlement in Natal was part of a larger history of colonialism around the globe, asserting

> the two races, the white and the coloured—be it black, brown, or red— cannot exist in close contact with each other, but on one condition— that of the entire dependence of the weaker upon the will of the stronger. The notion of equality, equality of rights, or equality of treatment, is at best an amiable theory, unsupported by any single evidence drawn from sound reason or experience.[26]

Barter continued, comparing the incompatibility of interracial friendship to the aims of colonialism to other settlement projects across the globe, linking Natal's African population to Native Americans, Aborigines, and Maoris as populations that must be conquered and removed, not befriended. For Barter, the African was destined to either submit or disappear before the approach of white settlement, as had other indigenous peoples around the globe, and thus friendship was a dangerous impossibility. This view of inevitable marginalization and the subsequent rejection of friendship found echoes in the British Parliament. Politician J. A. Roebuck argued in London that colonialism in southern Africa was a natural, if ostensibly regrettable, process of native extermination and settler replacement.[27] In such a formulation interracial friendship between colonizer and African could not exist.

Yet the rhetoric of global settlement and of the denial of interracial friendship was not always used by settlers in favor of colonization. Some observers commented on the *lack* of interracial friendship as a means of critiquing the failings of settler society. Witnessing the movement of Africans from Natal and Cape Town to the diamond fields, Natal settler W. F. Butler harshly critiqued the very system of settler colonialism that debased Africans while holding out a purely hypocritical promise of friendship. Writing to the *Natal Witness*, Butler exclaimed:

> How bitter must be the sense of disappointment with which he learns the real nature of the *role* he has accepted in the new creed and social state; how startling the discovery that this beautiful theory of the white man's love and brotherhood and charity to all men, means in the hard logic of fact the refusal of a night's shelter under the same roof to him; means the actual existence of a barrier between him and the white race, more fatally opposed to fusion, more hostile to reciprocity of thought, mutual friendship, or commonest tie of fellowship, than that which lies between civilized man and the dumb dog that follow him.[28]

For Butler, interracial friendship was a possibility denied by settler selfishness and colonial rapacity. Like Colenso, Butler saw settler society as unwilling to extend the hand of friendship across a racial hierarchy, instead investing in minority control. Unlike governmental institutions that claimed friendship discourse in order to legitimate their claims to authority within the colony, Butler asserted that friendship itself manifestly did not exist. Yet Butler differed from men like Barter and Roebuck, who used the lack of friendship as a means of justifying a theory of inevitable colonization and settler domination. In Butler's instance, this lack of friendship served as a springboard for calls of imperial reform, a challenge *not* to the actuality of settler rule, but to the practice of it as exclusionary. Such a view neither assumed nor denied friendship to advance settler goals, but rather asserted that the lack of friendship perpetuated an unstable inequality between members of the colonial population.

Friendship was ultimately inextricable from the question of how to occupy the lands of indigenous peoples that outnumbered settlers by

nearly eight to one. In his 1885 "Notes on Native Questions," Cecil Ashley admitted as such, bemoaning the fact that Africans, "unlike the Red
Indian of America or the Maori of New Zealand . . . do not fade or diminish before the advance of civilization."[29] Instead, Ashley asserted that
the benefits of European rule had led to an increase in the indigenous
population, offering a constant threat to white hegemony in Natal. To
counter such a threat, Ashley argued for an erstwhile bridge between
friendship and mastery and between settler and African. What Africans
required, Ashley asserted, was a "just, firm, equitable rule" which would
"restore that confidence in our good faith and just intention which many
late events seem, unfortunately, to have sadly shaken in the native mind."[30]
Ashley maintained that Africans were childlike and could only understand the consistent but just power of European colonists and despaired
that settler avarice and weakness had disrupted the natural order of
things. Restoring European rule was essential to avoid spoiling the genuine friendship that Africans exhibited toward settlers, for whom Ashley
believed "there is no enmity of race."[31] Ashley described Africans as desiring European power, wealth, and amity for their own sake, and envisioned
the colonialism as a warm relationship spoiled by undue settler caprice
and harshness. By imagining the colonial project as a reciprocal series of
friendly relationships, Ashley's work simultaneously offered a critique
of settlement while fundamentally leaving its very structure intact.

    Although men like Ashley could imagine and argue for interracial
amity as a means of justifying colonialism, others saw friendship as
ultimately destabilizing of the vision they desired for the colony. Lewis
Hertslet feared that any sort of friendship would fatally undermine the
settler project and the vast hierarchical relations contained therein. In
his 1911 book, *The Native Problem: Some of Its Points and Phases*, Hertslet
echoed the power relations espoused by Harriet Colenso, asserting that
the fundamental relationship between European and African was that
between strong and weak. However, he completely repudiated her other
assertions, arguing, like her father's detractors a half century earlier, that
Europeans should avoid all sentiment in relationships with Africans.
Yet, Hertslet did concede that Europeans should "try to understand [an
African's] point of view, and endeavor—ludicrous though it may sound—

sometimes to put yourself in his place."[32] Here was an affective register that avoided the immediate complications of friendship, and instead offered a kindly form of domination. Rather than be harsh taskmasters, Hertslet imagined European-African relations as a peaceable series of sympathetic hierarchies. Rather than simply "fall in with one another," as Harriet Colenso had suggested, Hertslet advocated that settlers build relationships solely to wield "personal influence" that would push Africans toward "the side of righteousness."[33]

For settlers, friendship served as a signpost, offering a profound orientation device in their attempts to dominate the colonial state they were building in Natal throughout much of the later nineteenth century. As settlers debated the meaning of friendship, they argued whether colonial rule was ultimately based in the power of settler affection for Africans, or if that was a mere delusion that masked the harsher realities of conquest and domination of indigenous lands. Friendship, then, held distinct rhetorical and causal meanings for settlers. At its core, the discussions over friendship with the African touched on the material and structural realities of settler colonialism in Natal. In the midst of the cacophonous, competing voices of colonial Natal, the concept could be used to justify the very presence of Europeans in Natal, or disavowed as a bid to supremacy. Both articulations, however, ultimately cast friendship (and its affective power) as the core structure of colonialism in Natal. Yet as a term, friendship was more frequently utilized to describe social situations *within* racial groups, rather than between them. These same-race friendships, and the moments of sociability that engendered them, were both essential and dangerously destabilizing in the colonial period.

Debating Indian immigration laws in the Natal legislature in 1890, Charles King argued:

> I want our own selves to be occupying this Colony—Englishmen, Irishmen, Scotchmen, Germans and Norwegians very good indeed, but give us our own friends, so that we can associate with them and make our lives comfortable and happy with them. But the very last people that we should try to flood this Colony with are the Coolies.[34]

For King, friendship served as a discursive marker that signified racial similarity as opposed to interracial connection. Friends were fellow European (and ideally English) immigrants. In the context of increased Indian immigration to Natal, King argued that the colony should be set up to preserve and enlarge already existing groups of "friends" at the risk of destabilizing cross-racial connections. Indeed, King later argued expressly for an increase in European immigration to the colony in the face of a potential increase in Indian migrants, saying, "The working men do not object to Europeans of their own kith and kin, their own relations and friends, coming to this Colony. We welcome every shipment of Europeans that comes."[35] The discursive dimension of friendship in King's argument is readily apparent. But this passage also again underscored the affective ties at the heart of the colonial project. White Anglophone settlers were positioned as "our own friends," and the increased association with these people led to comfortable and happy lives. In this formation, Natal existed as an amalgamation of affective ties; the bonds between like-minded and like-tongued people constituting a community of belonging. Friendship, in this context, then, symbolized a sense of collaboration and connection in the face of potential foreign challenges from indigenous Africans and Indian migrants, who could never truly share these bonds of similarity.

As a colonial gift, friendship remained inextricably twined with the larger hierarchies and frameworks of imperialism. Yet friendship also served as a signpost, a rallying point that could collect varied voices within the cacophonous din of colonial Natal. Settlers could either decry friendship as an obstacle to colonial rule, or seek to marshal it as a legitimizing force in their pursuit for white minority rule. Friendship exposed the larger frailties of the settler project, with alcohol serving as both a catalyst for needed moments of same-race sociability and an attendant fear of disruption and disorder. Ultimately, friendship encompassed a variety of competing and contradicting voices within settler society, perhaps most apparent in the desire of Bishop Colenso for that impossible handshake.

This, then, is the true takeaway of friendship in colonial Natal: as an ephemeral signifier, it could paradoxically reinforce desired order at the same time it undermined (but never fully erased) racialized hierarchies. Like the gendered and sexual hierarchies settlers wished to impose in Natal, friendship contained within it an awareness of its own "possibility of becoming undone," a knowledge that resulted in a "compulsion to repeat which is at once a foreclosure of that which threatens its coherence."[36] Indeed, rare moments did occur where the rhetoric of friendship allowed high-status indigenous actors like Cetshwayo kaMpande to make successful demands on imperial power. Generally, however, friendship constituted the panoply of colonial contradictions in Natal. Settlers conceived of their occupation of indigenous lands as a series of kindly exchanges, and yet could never fully escape the very gift that they wished to impose on indigenous Africans. The repetitive, demanding gift of friendship in Natal ultimately reveals fragile contingencies of settlement. The contradictory nature of friendship, its very amorphousness, and the continued desire of colonists for indigenous land (and for indigenous consent to the process of colonization) continued to offer a tantalizing but unrealizable possibility between African and settler, much like that briefly outstretched hand. As the settler colonial state continued to imagine itself the rightful occupant of indigenous African lands, the African person remained "always already void of relationality,"[37] no matter how many affective claims Colenso or others made before the ever-untouched body standing in front of them.

CHAPTER FOUR

The Mission Field

Spiritual Transformation and Civilized Clothing

The mission field offered was a space for Natal's settlers to enact a new normative order for that repositioning of indigenous bodies and places to make them more amenable to colonial exploitation. When Natal's settlers imagined the mission field, they pictured religious institutions hard at work transforming indigenous peoples and lands into productive and exploitable colonial objects. Yet this was hardly an accurate depiction; the mission field remained a site of contestation, negotiation, and reinterpretation for converts, clergy, and colonists throughout the nineteenth century. Missionaries sought to link the internal processes of Christian conversion to visible signs of acculturative change, namely the adoption of Western notions of clothing, domestic arrangements, and family ties. These adoptions overlapped (but not completely) with the order that settlers themselves hoped to enact. Therefore the mission field dictated the heteronormative terms of inclusion yet also provided space for Africans—unequally to be sure—to challenge or redirect the aims of their potential catechists.

By "mission field," I mean the whole bundle of aspirations and actions underpinning Christian conversion efforts in Natal. As such, the mission field denoted both a material process (proselytization primarily within the physical spaces of missionary stations within Natal) as well as a discursive one (the articulation of religious difference to justify settler attempts to occupy African land and reshape indigenous life). It was a key terrain of struggle, in other words, between the ambitions of settler capital and the aspirations of African Christian people. While the mission station itself could function as a "colonial institution *par excellence* [that] communicated many of the essential ingredients of British rule and the capitalist world economy," in the words of historian Clifton Crais, the faith it enshrined simultaneously provided an "integration of cultural symbols and knowledge that could be both hegemonic and potentially revolutionary."[1]

Mission stations in the colony represented a variety of Christian denominations[2] attempting to reorient African men and women toward not only new religious traditions, but also different ways of relating to space, the body, and domestic life. Throughout the latter half of the nineteenth century in Natal, the mission station became a site of intense debate over the progress of the "civilizing mission," particularly manifested by proper displays of dress and inhabitation. These debates were closely intertwined with the aims and goals of the settler state; the colonial government in Natal frequently allotted lands specifically for missionary use in the colony, and also subsidized most educational institutions established by ecclesiastical authorities, particularly those with the express purpose of civilizational uplift for Africans.[3] As with polygyny and intoxicants, the settler state sought to pass legislation that reproduced emerging racial hierarchies, most notably the Clothing of the Natives Bill in 1880. This bill attempted to shore up claims of the superiority of white civilization through appropriate sartorial display within the colony, and built upon previous legislation that had tried to compel Africans to wear suitable clothing, which underlined emergent categories of race and gender.

The intertwined nature of settler legislation and missionary discourses underscores the need to critically appraise the role of the "civilizing mission" as a major organizing force in the establishment of a colonial regime in Natal. It is not simply enough to argue that missionaries offered an ambiguous complicity in the creation of an unequal settler state. The mission field, particularly its role as *both* a physical space and a discursive process, remained integral to the development and implementation of settler colonialism. This chapter relies upon a reading of missionary journals, newspaper reports, and legislative records to identify prevalent discourses about civilization and subsequent attempts to construct legal categories of proper native behavior among the many competing voices that composed the colonial cacophony of nineteenth-century Natal. Such an approach results in a history that critically reads civilizational investments of missionaries against their colonial grain while also privileging the voices of indigenous Africans embedded within these archives. Ultimately, these histories reframe the importance of the mission field and keep its constant and complex relationship to colonial projects firmly foregrounded.

As a site of historiographical investigation, the mission field remains indispensable to understanding the realities of colonial Natal.[4] As in Australia, New Zealand, and parts of Canada, mission activity in Natal aimed to convert indigenous peoples while seeking to maintain the spiritual vitality—and discipline—of new settler arrivals. However, unlike these other colonies, the overwhelming (and increasing) numbers of indigenous peoples in Natal led to a greater emphasis on indigenous transformation as a critical part of the larger settler colonial project. Missionaries desired Africans enter into the spiritual kingdom of Christ at the same time settlers and colonial officials yearned for their absorption into the labor regimes they hoped to institute. While the *amakholwa*, or converted Africans, ambivalently accepted the strictures of missionaries, they frequently utilized missionary access to land and farming techniques in order to advance their material situations in the contested lands of Natal. Natal's position as a struggling white settler society outnumbered greatly by an indigenous population significantly shaped the history and trajectory of Christian mission movements.

Through the rhetoric of the civilizing mission missionaries supported the continued occupation of indigenous land in order to reclaim it and its inhabitants from heathen idleness. Yet, the stations themselves offered conflicting moments of identity formation among settler, indigenous, and imperial actors. For imperial officials, the field justified the colonial project and potentially redirected indigenous Africans toward the economic and social needs of the colony. For settlers, the field offered a sense of contradiction. As a separate space it both alienated labor and land from their grasp, yet still buttressed their claims to moral superiority through religious difference. The mission field presented settlers with a location that both challenged and supported their claims as occupiers of the land particularly through the promise of molding indigenous men and women into appropriately gendered norms within the colony. For African men and women the mission field could denote both a location and a project; it was a site where missionaries, settlers, and a colonial state all sought to fundamentally change them—but it also provided a means of challenging (at least discursively) the supremacy of Europeans in Natal.

Earlier work on Natal's mission history, outside of the near-hagiographies of the mission organizations themselves, offers relatively straightforward interpretations of the role of missions in the colony's political economy. Both Norman Etherington and Jeff Guy place Natal within a larger framework of capitalist settler accumulation and dispossession of indigenous lands, to which missionaries were in many ways explicitly linked.[5] Such readings focus on the economic and social conditions of the African homestead, which allowed Zulu men and women more generally to resist Christian conversion for most of the century. The widespread conversions of Zulus to Christianity in the twentieth century were accomplished principally by the destruction of effective African economic and social independence, leaving a vacuum in their worlds that induced them to choose Christianity. This argument has much to recommend it, although it is too reductionist to be completely explanatory.[6] While a Marxist, economically centered argument rightly focuses on the destructive, material realities that accompanied attempts at religious hegemony, it can obscure, elide, or dismiss indigenous agency in religious affiliation—in part due to the larger narrative aim in explaining the forced absorption of Africans into capitalist systems of labor. Potential converts did not view Christianity as simply one of many commodities on a shelf, making a rational-choice argument for the most practical use of their social and spiritual capital. Indeed, Africans did not accept Christianity within a vacuum. Even as missionaries attempted to mark spiritual transformation through visible acculturation, African Christians pushed back, challenged, and refined discourses on civilization and spiritual change. Nor did missionaries view themselves as cogs in a vast machine of colonial domination—although certainly their work often abetted such efforts in nineteenth-century Natal. In this chapter I critically read missionary- and *amakholwa*-produced texts in order to understand the complexities of discourses surrounding civilizational performance and spiritual transformation. These discourses were produced in relation to and in competition with settler conceptions of civilization and shaped state attempts to reorient Africans toward more recognizably Western, and heteronormative, ways of being.

As with polygyny, the fact that Africans had their own heteronormative concepts mattered little. Settlers and missionaries alike read indigenous practices through a matrix that prized Western practices as the pinnacle of civilization. In such a formation, indigenous modes of domestic inhabitance were viewed as inherently aberrant and in need of correction.[7] This queering of African lifeways undergirded both the settler project more broadly and the mission field in particular. European and American observers positioned Africans along a civilizational spectrum that emphasized their lack of development, an approach that overlapped with mission Christianity's emphasis on material transformation. Indeed, Western Christian observers required the position of the aberrant African in order to bring their own self-identification as civilizers into existence. By identifying indigenous cultural practices as incorrect yet fixable, missionaries simultaneously identified themselves with the true or real set of practices.[8] These practices required perpetual performance, a reenactment and retrenchment in colonial Natal, a process that worked to shore up heteronormativity and settler colonialism more broadly.

More recent writing on mission Christianity has emphasized a variety of factors, firmly grounding the Christian project in its colonial context but also looking beyond conversion as a merely threadbare covering hastily stretched over the true intentions of colonial coercion.[9] Recent work has sought to frame the conversion aspects of mission work as the creation of a "long conversation," a term that allows for agency while at the same time retaining the capacity to analyze the unequal power dynamics of a political economy approach.[10] A conversational approach allows an appreciation for indigenous pushback, recasting, and dialogue, while still acknowledging the unevenness of colonial power. Privileging the agency of indigenous practice and the flexibility of both new adherents and proselytizers situates indigenous practice in the context of colonial capital but does not privilege the latter as the sole, or determining, agent of historical change. Moreover, this approach helps to nuance the particular historical paradox presented by missionaries: "[T]hey were idealists who were deeply and unavoidably involved in the material transformation of the societies where they worked" despite claims to goals wholly independent of the transformative processes of colonialism.[11] At its best, the conversational model offers a critical appraisal of settlement of mission work in Natal that rightfully acknowledges the emotional, social, and spiritual complexities of negotiated relationships between missionaries and potential converts, a needed intervention in mission studies in both colonial and African historiography. Yet I find this approach not to be wholly sufficient for examining the second half of the nineteenth century in Natal, a period where an emergent settler state developed with other contemporary settler regimes across the globe.

Unlike these other locations, Natal increasingly turned after 1880 to the work of maintaining settler power as part of a government of entrenched minority rule, a position increasingly evident in the hardening of racialized laws after the Anglo-Zulu War of 1879.[12] Although the long conversation approach frequently illuminates evangelical power dynamics, the individual autonomy of indigenous adherents, and the complexities of the language of colonialism, it can flatten out the colonial terrain upon which the mission station operated, obscuring the many moving pieces of settler colonial society.[13] To that end, I offer a different take on the history of missions and Christianity in Natal by emphasizing the historically specific and culturally contingent constructions of civilization and settlement in texts produced by missionaries and African Christians. By reading missionary journals, newspaper reports, and legislative reports, I identify prevalent discourses of civilization and subsequent attempts to construct legal categories of proper native behavior among the many competing voices that composed the colonial cacophony of nineteenth-century Natal.

As the settler state in Natal expanded in size and reach in the latter half of the nineteenth century, missionaries, settlers, and Africans each utilized civilizational discourses that connected internal progress to external displays of Westernization. Missionaries advanced a fundamentally normative project that directly linked the spiritual transformation of the Gospel to the adoption of Western norms that upheld notions of what proper gender and sexual orders looked like. For missionaries and many converts, Western notions of clothing, domestic life, and family networks all signaled the true adoption of Christian faith. However, this process was never as unilateral as missionaries intended. While missionaries and the settler state certainly sought to mark indigenous bodies and practices as queer and in need of straightening, African converts often spoke back to catechists and settlers alike, mobilizing religious language to make claims of civilization of their own.

As both concept and undertaking, the mission field worked to link the needs of settlers, missionaries, and colonial officials, granting legitimacy to settlement and sanction to the transformation of indigenous peoples' ways of life. Yet missionaries occupied an ambivalent position in these processes. Christianity could and did exist as a powerful redemptive language that required personal transformation for all believers—while remaining comfortably within preconceived racial and social hierarchies. Missionaries and many settlers alike argued that the Christianization of African men and women would solve Natal's apparent settler "disorder," but they did so believing that the Christianity that they advocated was a system of personal change and sacrifice in which they and all other potential converts were unevenly implicated. White men and women advocated for evangelical transformation that operated squarely in the center of the imperial project: it offered moral legitimacy to their occupation but simultaneously placed restrictions on both them and indigenous peoples as fellow believers—although these limitations were shaped fundamentally by the raced and gendered hierarchies that the project of settlement in Natal was so deeply invested in producing.

Although missionaries were certainly the most vocal advocates, many colonial observers argued for a view of civilization inherently grounded in the redemptive and transformative message of the Christian Gospel.

Missionary George Mason asserted, "[I]f . . . religion can be judiciously coupled with the breaking down of some of their present barbarous usages, then the introduction of universal industry will follow as a matter of course, and will at length bring forth a genuine civilization."[14] Likewise, settler Eliza Feilden groused in her diary that she feared that the colonial government was allowing Africans to "grow more saucy than ever; but if they can be Christianized it may be worth the sacrifice of the present generation of white population."[15] In these formations, the concept of Christianity came laden with its own presuppositions and colonial desires; chief among them the idea of ensuring African conformity to European social and economic imperatives.

This is not to allege that Christianity operated solely as a shrouded superstructure that hid the more vulgar motives of capitalist and colonial exploitation by settlers, colonial officials, and missionaries in a form of grand deceit. Missionaries and some settlers asserted that Christianity must be the primary means of enacting indigenous civilization; any other effort would result in a surface-level transformation that would fail to take root in the obvious pull of regressive indigenous influences. "Those who attempt to Christianize barbarians discarding evangelistic methods, commit a sad mistake," cautioned missionary Josiah Tyler, recalling several instances of "partially" educated Zulus who had reverted to form after a time.[16] Indeed, the very rhetoric of Christianity and civilization suffered an easy slippage in the pronouncements of missionaries and settler observers.

At the same time, many settlers, missionaries, and *amakholwa* genuinely believed in the transformative power of the Gospel, and that spiritual internalization depended upon external change to enact a material sense of the soul transformation they so desired. As Eliza Feilden opined in her journal, indigenous men and women "enjoy their easy taste of barbarism too well to become easily Christianized; Christianity, being a religion of self-denial and moral restraint, strikes at the root of all their sensual enjoyments. Christianity says, 'Up and be doing;' but their feelings say, 'Sit still; what good do we get by exertion?'"[17] There is no doubt about the racism of this statement. Yet, for Feilden, as well as others, Christianity required internal transformation and revolutions in clothing, domestic space, and language that were viewed as the material manifestations of divine transformation. As historian Esme Cleall argues, "Conversion never simply meant a faith-based transfer of allegiance; it had to be embodied in cultural practices. The domestic was an important site where such change was to occur."[18] Thus, the mission field became more than a side theater of the colonial project; rather, it in many ways represented the stakes of settlement—that is, that the bodies and souls both indigenous and settler would be transformed into industrious and moral paragons, albeit unequally and with respect to the hierarchies of power that settlers enacted within colonial Natal.

Clothed in Possibility: Sartorial Claims and Spiritual Transformation

The mission field offered in the eyes of settlers, administrators, and missionaries a particular form of domestic space for Zulu converts: a place where bodies could be redirected toward acceptable norms of behavior that would, in turn, help guarantee social and sexual order. The reproduction of European forms of socialization in the domestic became a marker of "progress" and "civilization" and as a result an indicator of the success of the mission project itself. However, as scholars have been quick to point out, the "domestic" was not a fully formed concept simply imported from Europe to Africa; rather, it was a complicated set of signals and concepts that evolved in relationship to the economic and social structures on the ground in the colony as well as in the individual material and affective relations between missionaries and converts.[19] In order to properly measure the success of conversion (and of their endeavors in general) missionaries relied upon visible markers in African domesticity, particularly in the adoption of proper clothing and home life. Insistence on appropriate apparel reinforced the idea of missionary and mission station as the primary arbiters of spiritual change, casting the mission field as what Nancy Rose Hunt has described as the "spatial center, the pivot that allowed expanding the mission district's borders and domestic knowledge" throughout the colony.[20] Clothing became a primary means of taming the seemingly disordered world of indigenous Africans and a means of denoting hegemonic success for Christ's ambassadors in Natal.

The reliance on externalities like clothing to manifest internal spiritual (and civilizational) change among Zulu peoples is a common theme in nineteenth-century Natal. As early as 1846, missionaries in Natal were providing calico dresses for Zulu women to wear while attending services on the station, only to leave the garments behind for the safeguarded of missionaries until their next visit.[21] While the use of European forms of clothing by Zulu men and women signaled an adoption of social mores and the overall success of the mission field as a discursive project, it also could demonstrate the limits of settlement, as indigenous peoples either resisted sartorial transformations, wore clothing deemed inappropriate, or even worse, reverted back to their indigenous clothing.[22] Writing to *Life and Light*, Natal missionary wife Charlotte Grout despaired over the failed transformation of Nomashinga, a Christian convert in Natal.[23] Despite having been raised from childhood in the Grout's mission school, Nomashinga demonstrated to Mrs. Grout a disturbing "longing for her home and the heathen customs of her people," even though the missionaries offered her a "new dress, slate, and a pencil to draw pictures."[24] The Grouts sought to coerce Nomashinga into enacting the faith she was raised in through sartorial displays, drawing a binary between indigenous practice and Christian transformation. Yet the delights promised by the missionaries appeared to have been insufficient, for Nomashinga chose to leave the Grouts' station and return "home."

That Charlotte Grout phrased Nomashinga's decision to leave the mission school and station as a return *home*, and away from the home the Grouts had endeavored to create for her, is surely significant. Perhaps more clearly than anywhere else does this passage reveal the stakes of the mission field, namely, the creation of a genuine home that supplanted competing indigenous conceptions of the domestic. It is not a coincidence that the mission field sought to articulate material manifestations of transformed homes for converts at the same time that the larger project of settlement sought to domesticate the wild spaces of Natal.

Indeed, in some cases, this reorientation took on an even more personal form, linking the domestic to the familial, as missionaries understood it. As Meghan Healy and Eva Jackson have noted, American Zulu Board missionaries like the Grouts often sought to create new kinship networks among their *amakholwa* charges, a goal most explicitly visible in the missionary practice of renaming converts after baptism either with their own names or those of family members back in the United States. Healy and Jackson assert that for these American missionaries, conversion required a profound ontological shift that demanded that indigenous believers "transform, or break with, kin and ancestors that sustained these homesteads to enter into new and uncertain communities predicated on connection to a new and uncertain god."[25] In the wake of such splintering religious decisions, *amakholwa* were expected to take on the new physical trappings of clothing and household arrangements; it was in this way that their religious conversion could be made legible to mission observers, and the internal spiritual changes made manifest. Missionaries like the Grouts sought to rewrite kinship networks that their Christian formulation had insisted on breaking in the first place, recasting Africans into familial structures that linked new converts into nuclear family structures and away from long-standing polygamous systems.[26] Missionaries worked to enact a heteronormative kinship that explicitly drew Africans into their own European families in an attempt to counter queer kinship formations and produce proper, affective ties to the faith and its attendant physical transformations. Yet Africans did not quietly submit to these mission projects of reorientation and legibility. Healy and Jackson document the ways in which early *amakholwa* like Ira Adams Nembula and Joel Hawes (Mbabela Goba) used alternate names to articulate senses of belonging and space quiet contrary to the simple legibility missionaries may have sought.[27] In this light, Nomashinga's interactions with Mrs. Grout serve as a contestation over family ties and a rejection of missionary attempts to "straighten" her out.

To Mrs. Grout's disappointment, Nomashinga did indeed leave the mission school for her familial home; worse still, she returned to visit the school soon afterward, having discarded the trappings of "civilization" entirely:

> She had taken off the nice garments we had given her, and was ornamented in the native style, with a broad band of bead-work around her waist, strings of beads about her neck and forehead; and her woolly

hair was filled with oil, which was running down over her face and neck. She looked at me very boldly and proudly, as if she would say, 'See! Do I not look better than I did before?' My heart sank within me; and I could not keep the tears back through most of the service.[28]

For Charlotte Grout, Nomashinga's actions manifested a failure to accept the new domestic life—and ultimately, the affective, familial ties—she desired for her to adopt. The act of reverting from "nice garments" to ornamentation "in the native style" represented a material digression that demonstrated a disappointing lack of effective change for the missionary. The emotional reaction that Grout experienced itself reveals the stakes of the mission project in her mind—the work of the Gospel must produce physical transformation that can be observable in the adoption of civilizational norms.

Yet in the end, Charlotte Grout's brief article resolved the "problem" of domestic reorientation envisioned by the mission project. In her final paragraph she revealed that after a few years, she and her husband were "surprised and delighted when we recognized Nomashinga among the well-dressed people. She came to us at once, and introduced her husband, also nicely dressed."[29] In Grout's telling for the missionary magazine, the crisis of mission work has been mercifully averted. Nomashinga, the intrepid Zulu girl and convert has left heathenism and assimilated via proper clothing, and is now paired with a fellow reassuringly Christian husband, also mercifully well dressed. Ultimately, in Grout's account, Nomashinga rejects her preexisting family ties and instead casts herself in a proper Christian family mode—one that is monogamous, nuclear, and marked by ties to a mission station and ostensibly individual rather than communal obligations. Thus the prodigal daughter saga ends happily in Grout's estimation, with the viability of the Christian change reaffirmed and monogamous marriage and proper Western clothing.

Yet to read the document this way misses much of the complexities surrounding dress, domesticity, and authentic faith for indigenous converts. The adoption of appropriate, gendered forms of Western dress served to demonstrate material proof of discursive repositioning of indigenous bodies through mission activity. As Sarah Tyler, the wife of

missionary John Tyler, was quick to note, the transformative power of
Christ could be measured in an assessment of the difference between
heathen antidomesticity and civilized habitation. In an article intended
for metropolitan readership, Tyler emphasized the work of the mission
field in reorienting Africans from naked barbarism to sartorial civilization. Describing a local Zulu convert, the article noted that "when he
became a Christian, he wished to wear civilized clothing; for civilization
and Christianity go hand in hand. Had he not been taught by missionaries . . . we might have seen him to-day, like Umtimuni, wearing his
skins, and brandishing his spears and shield."[30] The article was accompanied by a print of the appropriately clad Christian convert, James Dube,
seated at a writing desk and wearing a European suit.[31] Images like this
reinforced the notion that the mission project existed to recast indigenous peoples in gendered and raced conceptions of civilized attire. Her
comparison of John Dube's civilized status as opposed to that of the
"natural" indigenous state, buttressed by an image of him seated at a
desk and wearing Western clothing, demonstrated in the importance of
a physically observable manifestation of Christian transformation. For
white observers, dress marked the most obvious means of social improvement and the adoption of heteronormative social relations embodied
properly by the "domestic" in Natal. In this iteration, indigenous men and
women left the polygamous world of the *umuzi* and instead embraced
the propertied, individualist, and sartorially appropriate world of Christianity and settlement.

Like Charlotte Grout, Lady Barker experienced a "puzzling" encounter with a *kholwa* servant, Maria, during her stay in Natal in the 1870s.[32]
For Barker, Maria was a perfect servant, primarily for her cleanliness,
dedication, and above all, a Christian faith that she manifested through
frequent recourse to Bible reading, along "with a beaming countenance,
and the sweetest voice and prettiest manners possible."[33] Having been
orphaned at an early age and raised by missionaries, Maria offered Barker
a model of crude piety that she indulgently contrasted with her own,
more rarified variety, and Maria's steadfast attention to the demands of
the Englishwoman earned her a favored place in Barker's household.
Maria was so highly esteemed that when Lady Barker and her family

returned to London, she brought Maria as well, who seemed to reinforce her perceived conversion by acclimating to life in the metropole. After a time, however, a friend of Lady Barker planned to leave for Natal and required a nurse. Barker arranged for Maria to accompany the friend back to Natal, although she claimed to be heartbroken at the loss of a member of the family staff, especially one that signified the success of colonial hegemony and Christian transformation at the heart of the empire. Pointedly, Barker offered Maria multiple articles of clothing to remind her of the material manifestation of her faith and her reorientation in colonial society, among them a "huge Gainsborough hat" and "two large boxes of good clothes."[34]

Yet Barker's ideal of the perfect servant did not survive the return to Natal. Although Maria apparently thrived while they remained in the colonial cities of Durban and Pietermaritzburg, problems arose as soon as Maria's new household moved somewhere further away from concentrations of settler power. Maria met extended relatives that she had not seen since her childhood, and exasperated her new employers by fighting with community members who claimed a share in her newfound possessions. Soon after, she left this new settler family, later presenting "herself before my friend clad in an old sack and with necklaces of wild animals' teeth, and proudly announced she had just been married 'with cows.'"[35] Lady Barker, like many of her contemporaries, interpreted this return by Maria to indigenous social norms over the sartorial markers of Westernized advancement as a direct marker of the failure of the mission field to do its work effectively. Upon hearing the news of the transformation, Barker claimed it demonstrated "how completely her Christianity had fallen away from her, and she had practically returned, on the first opportunity, to the depth of that savagery from which she had been taken."[36] Maria had ostensibly offered Barker an ideal conversion through her orphaned status and her ready adoption of settler norms of behavior; however, her choice to adopt indigenous family connections and clothing demonstrated a rejection of the normative order of the mission field. For women like Barker and Grout, the mission field's transformational work required observable progress that could be ascertained through the adoption of familiar forms of clothing and domestic inhabitance and only maintained through constant surveillance and "improving" contact. And it was always subject to backsliding, making the limits of advancement uncomfortably visible across the mission field.

The writings of Catholic missionaries at the Mariannhill monastery just beyond the city limits of Durban in the 1880s and 1890s indicate that the particular trope of sartorial propriety discussed by Eliza Feilden three decades earlier still held purchase. Commenting on the arrival of their first indigenous teacher to the monastery, a Basuto man named Benjamin Makhaba, the Trappist monks at Mariannhill noted that "though now a good, pious Catholic and real gentleman in taste and manners, may be, had once run naked in the leathern girdle of his race."[37] Late arrivals to the missionary project in Natal, the Trappists at Mariannhill regarded much of the work by their Protestant counterparts as admirable although not very effective, given the significant number of naked, heathen peoples who surrounded their station. Writing some years after the establishment of the monastery and mission, the Trappists at Mariannhill maintained that the "Native's wardrobe is wonderfully empty. All that the man requires is a girdle of skin or short tails, and he is quite *a la mode*. . . . Children swarm about in the kraals like little swine with no patch of dress other than that with which nature has provided them."[38] This description is particularly significant in its use of "empty" to describe the clothing of the local population; contemporary settlers would have used the same word to describe the land they inhabited prior to European occupation.

However, by the 1880s, Europeans groused that *empty* was an ironic word to use, as men and women they viewed to be nonindigenous natives had moved into lands settlers regarded as formerly vacant lands and were crowding out ostensibly rightful white occupants. These pseudonatives, in the eyes of settlers, threatened the legitimacy of their occupation and challenged the emptiness settlers imagined for the landscape of Natal with a sartorial emptiness they viewed as dangerously different. Indeed, the designation of the numerous naked children as "swine," a wandering animal population that despoiled the landscape but were useful if properly used, uncomfortably echoed settler presumptions about both their place as well as the place of indigenous peoples within the colonial project. Everywhere the newly arrived Catholic missionaries looked, the nudity of indigenous peoples demonstrated their spiritual and material destitution and need of reorientation.

Mariannhill served two purposes: to educate both poor white European children and local native children on the principle that both came from places of abjection and need of the charity and uplift that the Church could provide. Of course, Mariannhill's clergy did not conceive the mission field as an equal, multiracial space of spiritual transformation; like their contemporary mission workers at other stations, the Trappists argued that the transformative message of the Gospel was required by all, although it operated within a profound social and political hierarchy in Natal. Thus, missionaries at Mariannhill could claim that all needed to be changed by the sacrifice of Christ while maintaining that the demands placed by the faith were different based on the social circumstances of the colony. The primary marker of this hierarchy was, of course, clothing, which symbolized the larger stakes of civilization and the project of the mission field (and colonialism at large).

But in the rude and dirty state in which the children came from the kraals, it was natural enough they could not and never would be set aside the more decent and refined European boys. That was by the Trappists never intended. They never meant, never once thought of placing the nauseous 'green' Kafir, whose only covering is one of the 'dirt of ages,' at the same table as their poor but clean and respectable orphans and destitutes. That was to be a matter of time. The Native boy must first put away all that is loathsome and disgusting.[39]

The decency and refinement of the European boys, despite their destitution, comes from their apparent relationship to the trappings of civilization, namely Westernized clothing and habits of cleanliness, approved by the Trappists. The "green" African, newly arrived from indigenous lifeways outside of settler and Christian norms, was more than a mere other in missionary eyes. They offered a destabilizing danger to the cleanliness and respectability of European boys, and had to be quarantined. In effect, the Trappists viewed the "uncivilized" African as a queer threat to the proper growth and reproduction of civilizational norms in the colony. The very nudity of the African body presented a danger, a contagion that could be caught by white settlers and therefore had to be ameliorated in careful degrees. African nakedness, then, was not just a disgusting spectacle; it was also a destabilizing challenge to the heteronormativity of civilizational Christianity the Trappists sought to enact. In this way, the pathologization of the African body is more than mere hegemonic racism or cultural chauvinism; it is a form of queering that sees the African body as a threat to the continued existence of white civilization in Natal.[40] Although the Trappists claimed that both groups of children were deserving of the transformative work of Christianity, the actual implementation of that work—and its visible markers thereof—remained significantly different, and bundled firmly with racialized notions of appropriateness.

While clothing served as a marker of proper Christianization, its mere presence did not indicate authentic spiritual transformation; the destabilizing threat of the non-normative body still loomed. Such a threat occurred in 1856, when Eliza Feilden noted that her male servant, Friday, had acquired an inappropriate garment from a Zulu woman: "Once a 'sister' came to see him in a pink frock; next day I went into the kitchen and asked for Friday. The pink frock looked up and grinned; the girl had given it to him."[41] It is noteworthy that Feilden described Friday literally *as* a pink frock. His civilizational growth, measured in clothing, was not merely wrong; the garment moreover became a metaphor for his failure at normativity. Feilden noted that Friday wore the frock for a few days until he demonstrated a "growth in understanding" that such a garment was "not a man's attire."[42] For Feilden, Friday's attire showed both his inability to perform his gender correctly as well a lack of intellectual sophistication. Indeed, African attempts to adopt Western clothing styles did not always result in white approval or agreement that the mission field was producing suitable fruit. When the Mariannhill missionaries observed African men and women in Western dress in the early 1880s, they were not convinced that the civilizational trappings had brought about either social change or spiritual transformation, and said so in damning terms:

Zulu 'gorillas' that had previously run wild and naked over the land now promenade[ed] in Indian file quite *comme il faut*, real Kafir ladies and gentlemen got up in all the latest Paris costumes. And yet the whole thing was the greatest deception on earth. Our reader will often have read with delight in his youth of the silly lion that stalked with majestic gait in the skin of an ass, or the equally stupid daw that strutted proud in borrowed feathers. History once more repeated itself. The Kafir brunette flirting barefoot along—for to boots they had not as yet aspired—attired in Belgravian robes of glaring hues was neither more nor less than a whited sepulcher full of rottenness within; and the *vertgalant* dressed in a second-rate soldiers' abandoned garment forcibly reminded one of Mephistopheles in the habit of a son of St. Francis. The Christian's uniform each bore; but they were servants of Satan still.[43]

For the Trappist observers, this scene evidenced a monstrous failure of the mission project itself. In this tableau, unconverted Zulus wore the vestments of the European; they draped themselves in the coverings of civilization, of advancement, of material and religious progress, but without having made the necessary changes to justify them. They were, to the Trappists, committing a brazen sartorial lie by claiming garments that they had not properly earned. They were, ultimately, ersatz Christians, maliciously covering their aberrant bodies with the clothing of the civilized.

As missionaries asserted that the adoption of Western clothing signified the true transformation of the Gospel, then the presumption of indigenous peoples to wear such clothing without proving their conversion had to be rejected as an atrocious falsehood. The Trappists' denunciation underlines that clothing commonly served as a visible marker of internal spiritual transformation. Further, that clothing's successful adoption required the adoption of particular gendered and sexual expectations. The Trappists had reasoned that African nudity indicated the very unfitness and aberrance of Africans without Christianity.

The modesty afforded by proper garments served notions of heteronormative respectability—but they were being worn *queerly* in violation of their proper normative function. The ferocity of the Trappists' denunciation invokes Judith Butler's analysis of heterosexuality as "performatively constituted through an imitation that sets itself up as the origin and the ground of all imitations. In other words, heterosexuality is always in the process of imitating and approximating its own phantasmatic idealization of itself—*and failing.*"[44] The Trappists, like other missionaries, set themselves up at the sole purveyor of authentic transformation; this display of African men and women constituted a despicable copy in their eyes. The civilized image that the Trappists had hoped to see in the Africans parading before them was merely "as an incessant and *panicked* imitation of its own naturalized idealization" to again borrow from Butler.[45] Although the idea of transforming Africans into civilized Christians was the ostensible goal, proper transformation was never truly or even permanently possible. As Emma Tarlo has observed in colonial India, British observers were adamant that Europeanization was necessary for indigenous subjects, but then balked at mimicry that was too close to the authentic subject, as it blurred the distinctions between the civilizers and their ostensible charges.[46] Indeed, observations like those of the Trappist missionaries reveal moments of African agency in the midst of an ostensibly unidirectional granting of the clothing of civilization—and the attendant anxiety that these indigenous disruptions caused.

The anxiety over indigenous dress evident in writings from the mission field illustrates the ongoing contestations over meaning that operated within the dynamic spaces of Natal's evangelizing project. For as much as missionaries hoped to effect a material transformation in the clothing of Zulu men and women in order to mirror the interior changes they yearned to see, their erstwhile indigenous charges frequently disputed this connection between cultural assimilation and religious change. Indeed, in many instances Africans successfully challenged attempts by settlers and missionaries to reorient them, often by making direct recourse to the same spiritual claims that their European counterparts made. In her diary, Eliza Feilden once again recounted an amazing instance of missional redirection by her servant, Louisa:

> She came to me on Saturday, 'You know me want?' 'What do you want, Louisa?' 'Me want go church, all man love God; go church, not work

Sunday.' 'Quite right, Louisa, you shall go to church. I cannot walk
so far, so we have church here to worship God. You must come soon
back at night.' 'No! me stay all night, me go church, me not work, God
rest.' So I suppose we must help ourselves on a Sunday in future.[47]

In this exchange Louisa cleverly and firmly asserts her own autonomy
from Feilden's work demands by turning Christian rhetoric against her.
Settlers assumed that proper Christian action would require indigenous
peoples to submit to hierarchies of order and command, in order to demonstrate genuine religious commitment. Yet in this instance, Louisa
successfully countered Feilden's reasoning by using a shared Christian
language. In so doing, she demonstrated spiritual commitment through
physical action, yet also did so independent of Feilden's desired work
goals.

Likewise, the shared language of Christianity in this instance constrained Feilden from being able to further compel Louisa to work, as
she had appealed to a religious sense of duty that superseded duty to her
mistress. Although Feilden did use this occasion to grumble in her journal that "She talks of love to God, but does not strive to please her mistress, and, so far as I can judge, she does not know that she is a sinner,
and yet I suppose she is as good a specimen of a convert to Christianity as most of these."[48] This exchange shows Feilden's attempt to use
religious language to compel Louisa, as a convert, into correct patterns
of obedience that acknowledge her hierarchical power as a mistress over
Louisa's work and ability to rest. However, according to Feilden's diary,
it appears that Louisa continued successfully to resist further attempts
at compulsion through continued recourse to Christianity. According to
Feilden, Louisa "went to church as usual in the afternoon, but I told her
she must be back before six in the morning to make breakfast. She
arrived when I was washing the breakfast things and putting them away,
and expressed no regret."[49] As a result, Louisa claimed a form of piety
that rejected attempts to redirect her as a native servant into "appropriate"
forms of action. Rather, she utilized rhetoric of spiritual transformation
to engage in worship practices that freed her from Feilden's oversight.
The exchange between Louisa and Feilden offers an instance of visible

indigenous resistance through recourse to Christianity, and for evidence of conversion as a pathway to new forms of agency, if not freedom, for African women as well.

In her imagining of Nomashinga's personal thoughts, Grout hinted at her charge's internal motivations. Reading the article against the grain, it becomes possible to see how Nomashinga herself might have articulated Christianity, the mission field, familial ties, and domestic spaces very differently than Charlotte Grout did. Although she may have chosen to leave the mission station, Nomashinga did not leave it permanently, having made her significant visit in new clothing soon after leaving. Rather, it seems that Nomashinga contested and reframed the domestication project that Mrs. Grout envisioned as central to the mission field. By returning to the mission school dressed in her very best traditional clothing, Nomashinga could have been making a profound statement about home and family belonging. Such a reading echoes Elizabeth Elbourne's assertion about the stakes of writing about the complexities of mission Christianity and indigenous agency: "[I]t is easier on the pen to celebrate resistance to westernization than to understand the partial incorporation of western myths and technologies, but this natural tendency cannot do justice to the ambiguity, pain, and partial accommodation that are the stuff of everyday life."[50] Quite possibly, the transformational work of Christianity did not necessarily require sartorial assimilation; rather, Nomashinga chose to return to present both her spiritual affiliation as well as her own articulations of internal change by retaining indigenous clothing. The resultant bricolage produced by blending indigenous clothing and foreign worship service could offer a profound witness to transformation and a claim by Nomashinga to belong in multiple spheres, a claim that Mrs. Grout's binarized worldview would not enable her to comprehend.[51] When Mrs. Grout observed Nomashinga, she described her as looking "boldly and proudly," which might show a desire to assert her place in both worlds—or perhaps, her rejection of the need to choose between them.

As with Charlotte Grout's, Barker's reports on Maria reveal multifaceted indigenous responses in this exchange. As European observers sought to open the conditions of possibility by dramatically foreclosing others, such as the return to ostensibly savage vestments, women like Maria and Nomashinga did not simply accept this redirecting along colonial lines of order. Rather, by rejecting Western clothing it is not readily apparent that Maria was rejecting Christianity—but perhaps that she was refusing to enforce the hedge that missionaries, settlers, and administrators sought to erect between unclothed heathenism and civilized *amakholwa*. Maria's adoption of indigenous clothing as well as her acceptance of marriage into a rural Zulu community articulates the existence of family and continuity outside of the mission stations that sought to take the place of her parents, who had died at an early age. Thus, Maria's story of traveling from Natal to London and back does not necessarily, as Lady Barker would have it, represent "an amazing instance of the strength of race-instinct."[52] Instead, Maria subverted the claims of settlers, missionaries, and officials to dictate unidirectional terms of civilizational attainment.

Possibility in Print: *Ikwezi* and the Domestic Rhetoric of the Mission Field

By making observable progress toward the ultimate goal of Christianity, missionaries offered a vision that imagined the mission station, settler establishment, and imperial power as interlocking, interconnecting aspects of evangelical life in the colony. Nowhere was this more obvious than the pages of *Ikwezi* (Morning Star, which ran from 1861 to 1868), the first Zulu-language newspaper published in Natal, produced under the auspices of the Esidumbini Mission Station under the direction of American missionary Josiah Tyler.[53] *Ikwezi* is a curious source, for it is difficult to determine exactly who has written which piece, and the archaic Zulu is exceedingly difficult to comprehend in some passages.[54] The brief-lived newspaper offers a critical vantage point for viewing the attempts of missionaries to enact a form of African transformation centered on the domestic.

The very first issue of *Ikwezi* established its role as a conduit between settlers, missionaries, and Zulus. The ostensible goal of the paper—to facilitate the creation of a literate class of educated, native Christians by providing them a forum for education, exchange, and self-improvement—

fit well within the rhetoric of the mission field. In the first article, "Izindaba ngokuqala kwa le ncwadi" (The first news from the paper), an unknown contributor celebrated the long-desired arrival of a Zulu-language newspaper, explaining the significance for Christian Africans in obtaining access to such a means of expression:

> All the white people, they have newspapers. Some are printed every day in the morning and in the evening. If a white person is not receiving a newspaper, we say he's poor; if he's not poor, we say he should be pitied greatly, because he sits not knowing anything about what's happening to people like him in other nations. So then, why can't *we* have books? There are so many of us who read at all of these mission schools![55]

From the very beginning *Ikwezi* demonstrated the mimetic strategy employed by many Christian Africans in order to make claims to belonging within colonial Natal. For the author, *Ikwezi* allows the imagined Zulu reader to claim knowledge and access to power in a manner similar to Europeans. By possessing a newspaper, Zulus could become *like* white people by gaining knowledge of other peoples around the world, knowledge that can potentially be used to their advantage. This knowledge was contained in a portable fashion, a newspaper, which allowed for the further reproduction of European social conventions; namely, the creation of a domestic space where printed material provided a form of familial socialization, discussion, and uplift.

The article's reference to the role of domestic space became more explicit as it continued, illustrating a familiar turn toward rendering the home as a site for demonstrating physically meaningful civilizational and spiritual transformation: "We greatly love that we are constantly seeing books in the homes of black people and it is such love that leads us to produce this newspaper."[56] The founders intend *Ikwezi* to facilitate the creation of European-style domestic inhabitance as a means of demonstrating Christian conversion and civilizational readiness. Finally, the close of the article made clear the idea of the mission project serving as a bridge that linked settlers, missionaries, and indigenous people through vehicles like *Ikwezi*. The author exhorted indigenous readers to "write of your customs as well as those of the whites—do not fear, for you are addressing each other."[57] By encouraging *amakholwa* to write to the paper and describe their customs in print, the author provided a vision of *Ikwezi* as a conduit for conversations between African and European Christians. Such an exchange would encourage Africans to set up domiciles that resembled those of their Christian catechists, places where they could read and learn more about the world around them.

In some issues, *Ikwezi* articulated the overlap between the missional and the colonial projects at large. In January 1863, a prominent article announced:

> The nation of Natal is now progressing. By the construction of bridges across rivers—and roads under repair—good homes are increasing— the land is being farmed—sugar cane and cotton and coffee and some food grow. . . . Black people are being taught in schools, this is going well, they are accepting the truth of God's Word.[58]

The author linked Natal's material progress—roads, bridges, farms, homes—with the Christianization of indigenous peoples; although both may have been more aspirational than real (Natal remained one of the least successful sites of proselytization throughout the century).[59] Nonetheless, the linking between the two concepts is quite explicit.

While *Ikwezi* ostensibly provided a place for a newly literate, educated Christian Zulu class to discuss issues of importance to them, the American missionaries that produced the paper also insisted upon providing updates of news and information about the wider world in order to better inform their charges.[60] As a result, articles in *Ikwezi* described geopolitical events around the world, with particular emphasis on settler society within the United States.[61] American missionaries writing in *Ikwezi* occasionally articulated images of other indigenous peoples and settler rhetoric—in Zulu. The most apt example of this in *Ikwezi* occurred in the August 1863 issue. The article offered a line drawing of an indigenous North American man standing in a wild forest, observed by a child securely tied to a swaddling board placed in a tree. The accompanying text read as follows:

> This picture shows a North American Indian! Here is a child. Some children are hung up in trees. Indians in the country of America are Red people. There are many tribes. Some are believers. Some are in darkness, they are constantly fighting. Among the Sioux peoples, it is said that a girl will reject a man who does not bring her the scalp of an enemy.[62]

By presenting the information about the Sioux in such a manner, the editors opened multiple conditions of possibility. First, such reporting sought to reproduce the European (and American) idea of newspaper reading as a properly domestic activity of exchanging and discussing information. In addition, however, it was an outgrowth of the civilization/religious transformation discourse in Natal; indigenous peoples in Natal were to become "native settlers" in the colony. They could own land, build dwellings recognizable to Western observers as proper, and more importantly, could view other indigenous peoples through a mental rubric of settlement.

In the depiction of the Sioux that the Esidumbini missionaries offered in *Ikwezi*, a stark division was made between a "wild" and undomesticated people and the potentially transformed, civilized subject reading about such a tribe in the newspaper itself. Such a move by an American mission paper reproduced imperial logics not "through a detachable and remappable 'frontier' or 'wilderness' . . . [but] through the reproduction of Indianness that exists alongside racializing discourses that slip through the thresholds of whiteness and blackness . . . that are necessary conditions of settler colonial sovereignty."[63] Christian Africans were invited to observe the "exotic" peoples of the world from the vantage point of civilizational occupation, commenting on the wildness of men who remove scalps in order to perform savage rituals of love. By denoting these people as warlike and in darkness, the article worked discursively to underline who is and who is *not* civilized; instead of creating a sense of global indigeneity, the article worked to foster an idea of a global settlerdom, producing a vision of a wild North American people from the vantage of settler to other would-be settlers (that happen to be native) in Natal.

Ikwezi did not survive the departure of Josiah Tyler from the Esidumbini station in 1868. However, the periodical remains an invaluable part of Natal history, not simply because it is the first extant newspaper printed in Zulu, but also because it offers a unique look at the challenges of the imagined contours of the mission field in early colonial Natal. In such a formulation, the mission attempted to bridge the perceived divisions between settlers, missionaries, and indigenous peoples, while continuing to invest in notions of successful domestic mimicry as an a priori condition for demonstrating successful Christian transformation. Simultaneously, *Ikwezi* seriously viewed indigenous peoples as contributing members of the paper, albeit still in line with missional goals of creating Christ-centered fellow settlers. It is in this tension between desired reorientation and conditions of possibility that the discourses of civilization opened up by the mission field are most keenly visible. *Ikwezi* offered a mixed space of transformation, where missionaries imagined creating physically changed native peoples who emulated settler views, while *amakholwa* responded to and challenged these assertions.

Reproducing the Domestic:
Edendale as Mimetic Space and Civilizational Challenge

As with clothing, adherence to the contours of a proper domestic space might be evidence of a physical manifestation of Christian change. The act of colonial domestication, of rendering landscapes hospitable to proper occupation, of redirecting rivers and streams and veldt to suitable and sustaining settlement overlapped here with the process of the mission field. Men and women were expected, upon conversion, to render their bodies—and the houses and clothing that covered them—as visible markers of that internal soul change. Settlers and missionaries alike viewed the viability of Christian conversion primarily in terms of dress and domestic habits. They regarded the successful acculturation physically demonstrated by indigenous peoples as material manifestations of the true adherence to the new faith. The experiment at Edendale offers an example of how that aspiration unfolded inside the parameters of a built environment expressly designed for such purposes.

Founded by missionary James Allison on land purchased from departing Boer leader Andries Pretorius in 1851, Edendale became both a model mission settlement and a profound curiosity in Natal.[64] Of particular interest to settlers, missionaries, and colonial officials alike was Allison's plan to extend land tenure to his African convert community. Edendale's community members consisted of a diverse group of Africans (Basotho, Zulu, and other ethnic groups among them) who purchased the lands upon which their homes were built, and most endeavored to construct European-style homes in stark contrast to indigenous houses. As a result, through the course of the nineteenth century Edendale offered observers a model of African land tenure as well as reproductions of European cultural norms.[65]

Visitors repeatedly made mention of Edendale's central distinguishing feature, its sizeable chapel, erected at a cost of over £1,000. Upon visiting in 1875, Lady Barker remarked upon the grandeur of the building and how "nearly every penny of which has been contributed by Kafirs, who twenty-five years ago had probably never seen a brick or a bench, and were in every respect as utter savages as you could find anywhere."[66] For Barker, the establishment of a chapel marked the high point of the mission project at Edendale, having successfully inculcated Africans with a sense of Christian duty. Yet it also demonstrated a commitment to notions of proper domesticity—the bricks and benches that she declared to be lacking previously in Zulu homesteads. The following year, a letter to the *Natal Witness* praised Edendale, paying particular attention to the costly chapel as well as informing readers that "the natives of the village have neat little cottages, of green-brick, well finished and kept as tidy as those of the most scrupulous white people; and around these houses may be seen young orchards and prolific gardens of ample extent."[67] Reports like these linked the religiosity of the community at Edendale, expressed by the visible outpouring of money and effort in building the main chapel, with an additional form of industriousness, the building of proper domestic space. Reports throughout the 1870s, described Edendale largely as an orderly model village, an example for other Africans (and indeed for straggling Europeans) to follow. These positive descriptions rested primarily on indigenous peoples' creation of spaces that Europeans recognized as proper homes. Such domestic spaces functioned as orientation devices, reinforcing settler claims to a civilizing project in Natal at large while simultaneously allowing Africans to claim their own form of belonging. The domestic and home operated as a shared set of signals within the mission field that both supported settler hegemony and bolstered indigenous autonomy.

The project of creating a recognizably domestic space in Edendale attracted considerable settler attention as a successful project in mission acculturation. In 1879, the *Natal Witness* reported on an interracial event held at Edendale during the Anglo-Zulu War and took time to lavish praise upon the development of the mission station:

> [T]he civilization of the Edendale settlement is no mere artificial growth, which accident may sweep away in a few years' time. It is no house built upon the sand of a merely personal influence which may be withdrawn. It is rather a house built upon the rock of natural adaptiveness, of sterling moral and intellectual qualities, of a capability for the assimilation of the complex conditions of civilized life.[68]

It is no coincidence that the analogy of the "house" is used to describe the civilizational status of Edendale. The term functions both as a Christian allegory, reflecting Christ's exhortation to build faith upon a solid foundation, and as a mirror of the domestic spaces that had earned Edendale such attention from settlers—the European-style homes and the emulous furnishings within. Continuing to praise the advancement of Edendale's native citizenry through their adoption of settler norms, the *Natal Witness* correspondent looked ahead to the potential resolution of the mission project, opining that, "The future of an institution which requires continued supervision and direction from those who have been instrumental in starting it may very reasonably be doubted. Leading strings and apron-strings are all very well in infancy, but they are a sign of want of *manly existence*, even of imbecility, when their presence is visible in later life."[69] The *Witness* article argues that the mission field

has successfully achieved its goals in places like Edendale. For some readers, Edendale's accomplishment might have been to link the removal of
"apron strings" with a true and proper course of masculine action. It
may also have shown that maintaining Africans like those at Edendale
in a state of tutelage would be infantilizing and ultimately degrading to
"manly existence" for both colonial society and Africans themselves.
And yet Edendale's establishment as a mimetic space of domestic reproduction could visibly unsettle the underpinnings of the colonial project
in Natal.

The tension between proper reproduction of domestic space and
clothing—so critical to demonstrating both civilizational and Christian
conversion—were in full force when Lady Barker paid her visit to an
Edendale household: "I was specially invited to look at the contents of
the good wife's wardrobe hung out to air in the garden. . . . I did not possess anything half so fine. Sundry silk dresses of hues like the rainbow
waved from the pomegranate bushes; and there were mantles and jack-
ets enough to have started a secondhand clothes shop on the spot."[70]
The description here is an intriguing one; Barker seems at turns cele-
bratory, envious, and dismissive of the sartorial possessions of an Edendale housewife. Echoing her earlier description of the poorly reproduced
"English bedroom," Barker's observation of the clothing hanging out
to dry seems to signal both approval and yet a desire to distance herself
from this attempt at reproduction. The idea that a Zulu woman might
have so fully absorbed the civilizational lessons of church and closet cannot be openly countenanced in such a description—as a result, Barker
praises the unnamed woman for her collection of fashionable gowns
while also faintly mocking the wardrobe as excessive, comparing it to
a "secondhand clothes shop." Implicit in this description is the fundamental tension between the civilizational pretensions of the mission project, as well as the potential disorder that might result if such goals actually
came to fruition. As a consequence, women like this Edendale *kholwa*
must be celebrated but also despised for their excessive decoration and
their failure to *truly* become like their settler models through proper gendered behavior. White observer praise was tellingly limited to a future
present in part because the actual present was much less safe ground

when it came to evidence of civilizational success.[71] While some settlers (like Feilden), colonial leaders, and missionaries were agreed in
advancing the mission field as a raced and gendered project of reorientation, the fears of its *actual success* in granting Africans the civilizational
trappings to claim a shared Christian and settler status along with an
equal right to occupy the land would lead these coalescences to splinter
throughout the final decades of the nineteenth century.

The positive reports offered by myriad colonial observers at Edendale cast Africans as proper inhabitants reproducing settler norms by
building square houses, planting orchards, and filling these spaces with
the latest furnishings. The voices of different members of the colony—
settlers, administrators, and missionaries, each with differing aims and
objectives—coalesced around the mission field in this model village, linking Christian transformation to the idea of becoming a proper occupier
of the land. Such rhetoric, paradoxically, reinforced and justified European settler claims to the land while simultaneously sowing seeds of
a profound indigenous challenge to settlement. Settlers, missionaries,
and colonial officials used the production of appropriate domestic spaces
by Africans in order to praise Edendale as a model of Christian faith and
civilizational development. In so doing, they also recognized and produced their own claims to legitimacy. These praises were more than
condescending acknowledgment of African mimicry of Western social
norms, and certainly more than the arrogant delight at ostensibly seeing
their own values reflected back at them. Rather, these observations demonstrate an investment in shared modes of settlement and occupation
of the land. By articulating home and the domestic as an orientation
device, settler observers discursively attempted to justify their own raced
and gendered claims to occupation and yet offered others the ability to
do so as well.

For all of its exceptionality, Edendale would not remain untouched
by the shift in colonial attitudes in the years following the Anglo-Zulu
War in 1879. As Europeans slowly grasped that a white settler majority
was not to materialize, the loose coalitions that supported the project
of assimilation engendered by the mission field crumbled. Imperial officials, particularly following political reversals and military overextension

across the globe, decreased investment in the transformation of indigenous peoples, content to devolve authority increasingly to a settler
minority regime, culminating in the granting of Responsible Government in 1893. Settlers, for their part, worked to secure their control in a
racialized hierarchy in Natal, limiting perceived threats to their authority. In 1879 the *Natal Witness* had argued that Edendale's progress meant
that the time was ripe for native Christians to assume equality within
the structures of Natal. A few short years later, as settlers intuited that
they would never possess the logistic majority they craved, public opinion had largely turned against the notions of civilizational progress,
Christian development, and potential political equity across racial lines.
As Norman Etherington has documented, concerted government efforts
to limit African attempts to buy land only began to occur in force after
1880 and particularly to limit African economic survival in order to
protect settler farming interests in the last decades of the nineteenth
century.[72]

The extent of the changes in colonial coalitions regarding the mission
field is abundantly clear in an 1880 *Natal Witness* report on a war monument erected at Edendale. Far from the immense praise heaped upon
the converts previously, the correspondent claimed:

In vain in the whole of Edendale we looked for any very striking evidence of Christianity. There were missionaries and a Bible; to these
we are accustomed. We have seen them where the missionaries had as
yet made no converts—clothed pagans, aye, even clothed cannibals,
we have seen—a pair of trousers is not an evidence of faith. . . . We
saw the European inhabitants of the City of Maritzburg treated with
marked contempt, kept standing in the sun as inferiors, in the presence of the preachers of a gospel of humility, and of the pampered
'Makolwas' of the station.[73]

In the hardening racial attitudes of a post–Zulu War settlement, African
Christians found that their attempts at reproducing settler society through
mimetic domestic displays were interpreted very differently. Despite the
positive statements evinced prior to 1880, indigenous people frequently

came to learn that "flourishing Christian communities (at least those with which missionaries were happy) were always located in the future."[74] Settlers now saw these attempts as threats on their minority rule status, ands sought to degrade, discount, and dismiss such sartorial and domestic claims on civilization and inclusion. The mission field as a space that buttressed colonial occupation eventually lost coalitional support in colonial Natal not because of the failure of the mission project at creating *amakholwa* who could reproduce effectively civilizational trappings, demonstrating internal conversion; rather, support faded in the latter decades of the century precisely because the project had become such a threatening success.

Discourse to Practice: The 1880 Clothing of the Natives Bill and Civilizational Rhetoric

As settler legislators sought to shore up minority rule following the Anglo-Zulu War they attempted to delimit native peoples increasingly through racialized and restrictive legislation. In 1880, the Natal Legislative Council debated the strengthening of a preexisting Clothing of the Natives Bill in order to combat the moral and spiritual challenge of Africans continuing to appear "naked" within the colony. Mr. Garland, a member of the legislature, insisted that the government must "demand that every Kafir should be clothed to stop the spread of immorality," arguing that he had "been asked by men in high places in England—'What has your Government done for the Natives of Natal?' and I was compelled to answer—'Nothing for their elevation or Christianisation.'"[75] In the rhetoric of legislators like Garland, the continued adherence of Zulu men and women to indigenous norms of clothing demonstrated a lack of civilizational (and ultimately Christian) assimilation within Natal. Settlers and missionaries both asserted that Christian transformation, which had so routinely been directly linked to acculturation via modes of dress, had failed to make the inroads they had as yet hoped for, given that larger numbers of Africans continued to resist Western clothing norms.

The discussion of the bill was influenced strongly by the opinion of imperial administrators and the metropolitan public. Prominent legislator and future prime minister John Robinson reflected upon the indecency of native nakedness and its implications for Natal's reputation back in metropolitan Britain:

> It has long been a matter of remark, and especially by new comers to the Colony, that our Natives should be made to clothe themselves, and I need only remind the House of an instance at Home—as a powerful incentive to us to take some measures to remedy the present state of affairs—in which the chaste mind of the Lord Mayor of London was inexpressibly shocked, not by seeing the stern, naked reality (*laughter*) that confronts us daily, but a photograph of that spectacle.[76]

For Robinson, the nakedness of Africans in the colony had created a different kind of problematic exposure for the colony. The idea of British observers in the metropole disparaging African nudity ran the risk of demonstrating settler failure to bring about civilizational uplift among their native charges, and potentially revealed that the "stern, naked reality" of colonial life in Natal was not as morally upright as its settlers desired.

These concerns were echoed by J. C. Boshoff, who framed the question of nakedness in terms of harming potential British emigration to the colony:

> I should like to know why a respectable family man coming from London here should see a lot of the niggers coming before him in this condition. (*Laughter*). He and his family of boys and girls will all run away. Surely it is the duty of the Council to take these disgraceful scenes away. I think it would be one of the best things that could happen to pass this law.[77]

In Boshoff's argument, African nudity and lack of civilization threatened both the order of the colony and the likelihood of attracting other settlers to further improve the region. Boshoff's rhetoric underscores the fears of white settlers "running away" at precisely the moment of panic over the lack of a European majority. African nakedness, then, became shorthand for larger questions of an uncivilized native majority that undermined the continued security of white arrivals.

It is not a coincidence that as the 1880s dawned, colonial documents recorded continued settler frustration with indigenous failure to transform at the same moment that the state sought to increase the strength of its minority rule over the colony. "Barbarism and nakedness are almost synonymous terms," bellowed Robinson during the debate. "As long as we conserve nakedness we conserve Barbarism."[78] Legislator John Walton concurred that clothing of some sort was needed for Africans and added a financial incentive in the process, arguing, "anything that will tend to civilize the natives will assist us in governing them. . . . [I]t will not only tend to civilize the natives but will tend to increase the revenues of this Colony."[79] Alexander Walker agreed that African nakedness represented a lack of civilization, and also argued that nakedness threatened degeneracy and improper sexuality for settlers, stating, "I should not like to see any Kafir come into my House in a naked state. If the Law will not help me, then, I say, I am justified in taking a stick or a bludgeon to enforce decency being observed. It is not the decent but the indecent Kafirs I want protection from."[80] Such an argument again uses the domestic, but this time as a preserve of civilization threatened by the naked indigenous body.

Debates over African nakedness and civilization differed along gendered lines for the settler legislators. Thomas Garland argued at length with multiple legislators over differences in the way that African male and female nakedness were viewed by Europeans:

[T]he indecency and immorality is so revolting that it is a common remark amongst ladies.

[Mr. Millar (*interposing*): I do not think that they object much]. It is a common remark amongst ladies that it is most abominable the sight that is present, especially by the female portion of the community, in their nakedness.

[the Colonial Engineer, Albert Hime (*interposing*): is it the men or only the ladies that the ladies object to?] (*laughter*).

I am speaking especially of the immodest dress of the females.

[Mr. Walton (*interposing*): the want of dress of the females.]
Yes it is a well-known fact that the men are better clothed than the women.
It is a well-known fact that a woman of 16 has only got a couple of inches of fringe round the loins (*laughter*).[81]

Garland initially shaped his disagreement with African nakedness in terms of the displeasure of white women observers. Yet legislators deemed female nakedness specifically problematic and debasing.

This distinction between male and female nudity was not a lone occurrence in the debate. Indeed, the Charles Mitchell, the colonial secretary, asserted in 1880:

[W]hen one sees the fine noble form of a naked Kafir and then sees in this city the same being clothed with a few rags such as an Italian *lazzarone* at Home would almost disdain to wear, that is sufficient to make those who have not indecent ideas and lewd thoughts own that the naked man was the far preferable spectacle of the two. As regards the women, I say nothing.[82]

Mitchell offers a description of indigenous manhood that is invested in an idea of the native existing in his "natural state" rather than being corrupted by the bricolage that resulted from the contact zones of the mission field (and of colonial Natal at large). While potentially lionizing the attractiveness of indigenous clothing and bodies, it nonetheless reinforced an idea of African men and women as both inappropriately sensual and in need of consignment to a space apart from European society. Mitchell's statement is a curious form of heteronormative discourse as well. His preferential praise for the noble form of the naked African man is underscored by a denial of "indecent ideas and lewd thoughts." Mitchell viewed the nude male African body with respect and admiration, but not that of the African woman. Mitchell's almost voyeuristic enjoyment of the nude African male form not only opens up queer erotic possibility, but also serves to further denigrate African women's bodies as degraded and an incitement to lust in the eyes of settler men. Settler discourses over African clothing refer to more than civilization; they also reinforce heteronormative hierarchies of gender order.

At the same time that debates over the Clothing of the Natives Bill demonstrated gendered divisions in the policing of indigenous civilization, the legislators also argued over the nature of defining racial categories through dress. Michael Henry Gallwey, the attorney general of Natal, cautioned that the law should be made applicable to all peoples regardless of race; Indians, Europeans, and Africans should all be compelled through the law to wear clothing. In response, legislators complained that Indian workers were also violating civilizational demands for clothing. Mitchell disagreed that the law was applicable at all, stating that, "the great empire of India has gone on for something like a century with Englishmen and Englishwomen submitting to the fact of Natives being very little more clothed than our Kafirs are here." Fellow legislator Mr. Mellersh concurred, arguing

> Here, last week, or a little before, the whole of the Coolies were going stark naked, except for a little bandage round the loins, and nothing has been said about it. We never hear of any attempt to clothe the Coolies, and that is because they are afraid if any attempt of that kind were made it would stop their immigration here. So much for our morality. As to the Kafirs, I do not think they are a bit more indecent than the Indians.[83]

Both Mitchell and Mellersh were challenged by other legislators who maintained that Indians as well as Africans should be clothed. In this moment of debate, the problem of the naked, brown body presented a concrete challenge to the idea of settler hegemony. In this instance, both Indians and Africans were discursively coproduced as impediments to the triumph of European settlement, and particularly as threats to the moral structures necessary to secure a white colonial future.

The larger hardening of racial attitudes in Natal after 1880 significantly undermined the consensus that conceived of the mission field as a space of possibility that could accommodate the aspirations of missionaries, the potential coercive power craved by settlers, the legitimacy claimed by colonial officials, and potential for some indigenous converts. "They are here as immigrants on sufferance, and are not citizens," thundered the editor of the *Natal Witness* in 1880, noting that precious few Africans had completed the arduous process of acquiring exemption from Native Law as well as negotiating the byzantine laws that prevented black suffrage, proving themselves unfit "for the privilege of a citizenship they do not enjoy, have never demanded, and, perhaps, value but little?"[84] Although the transition itself did not occur immediately, as we have seen in the previous chapters, the 1880s demonstrate a particular shift in Natal politics, where settler claims were on the rise, imperial intervention on the decline, and missionaries and indigenous peoples both found themselves affected by an increasing move to restrict African access to land, power, and a share of genuine belonging in the colony.

Scholars have noted that southern Africa, and the larger British imperial world, underwent a significant hardening in racial attitudes as the century wore on. Evangelical humanitarianism and the generosity of spirit demonstrated by British imperial officials and colonists around the globe appeared to be substantially on the wane by the end of the century, replaced by a dim pessimism regarding the closing of an ostensible gap between the civilized capacity of Europeans and indigenous people.[85] Numerous factors have been posited to explain this hardening, as coined by a variety of historians, ranging from substantial indigenous resistance in India (1857), Jamaica (1864), Afghanistan (1877), and southern Africa (1879) to the rise in evolutionary thinking and the scientific recasting of racial difference to immutable characteristics. As part of a global discursive network, Natal was undoubtedly affected by these larger shifts. However, in addition to these global hardenings, Natal had its own local catalysts that facilitated a change in social attitudes, primarily on the part of white colonists.

Natal had been annexed by the British in 1843, and championed from mid-century as a new territory for white settler occupation. It was imagined by multitudes of Europeans as a space that, like contemporary colonies in North America and Australasia, would become a white-majority location, ready to be filled by settlers, who would soon become the majority of the population. While this came to pass in most other settler colonies, this did *not* happen in Natal in particular. Indeed, the population of indigenous peoples, through cross-border immigration and reproduction, skyrocketed, while the white population grew at a far slower pace. Throughout the 1850s, 1860s, and 1870s, settlers still believed that they would somehow become the proper majority of the society they hoped to build; in the years immediately following the Anglo-Zulu War in 1879, this became far less certain. Indigenous people had not only rather rudely refused to vanish,[86] they continued to resist settler desires to compel them into amenable labor relationships and continuously flouted social conventions through the survival of practices like polygamy and *ilobolo*. As a result, settlers began to accept their failure at reproducing contemporary patterns of settlement, and instead began to seek to shore up their status as a minority regime, a process crystalized by the granting of Responsible Government to Natal's Legislative Council in 1893.

Missionaries—as well as the mission field—were not immune to these shifting tides. As Esme Cleall maintains, "there is no doubt that changing registers of race altered the discursive web within which missionaries operated."[87] Theological innovators like Colenso, who demonstrated excessive proximity, were shunned by larger settler society, and the rhetoric of later missionaries like the Catholic Trappists in the 1890s showed a profound sense of white superiority over inherent, genetic black inferiority. More importantly, the mission field itself could no longer work as a larger coalition that encompassed the very different goals of settlers, missionaries, colonial officials, and the *amakholwa*. At the heart of the field's failure lay the conception of indigenous converts as becoming "native settlers" who could, through mimetic claims, be full citizens of a British imperial colony. The recognition of white minority rule by settler government, combined with a decrease in direct action by the imperial administration, rendered the idea advanced by Lady Barker as late as 1876, that of a transformed, Christianized black population filling Natal, impossible. Instead, stations like Edendale were denigrated as failed reproductions, and settler legislators worked in concert to block African purchase of land and ability to develop economic or political power in the colony.

And yet, while the mission field ceased to operate productively as a concept that could contain a variety of colonial actors, it does not mean that indigenous peoples failed to articulate their own demands and desires in light of the changing conditions in a hardening Natal and global context at large. In 1899, Solomon Kumalo wrote to *Inkanyiso yaseNatal*, the newly constituted Zulu-language newspaper run by missionaries, insisting:

> We hear enough Good News in religious books and in the churches. In a newspaper, we desire news that both tells us of the government and official ministers as well as offers assistance for people here on earth.[88]

Kumalo's letter offers an indigenous challenge to the narrative of restricting rights and declining mission possibilities. In the pages of a mission newspaper, Kumalo asserted his status as an educated *kholwa* and demanded access to knowledge available readily to white readers. The potential goals of the mission project—of education and transformation—paradoxically would allow an early generation of elite Africans to articulate identities and counter-colonial claims in print as the twentieth century dawned.

CHAPTER FIVE

"To Become Useful and Patriotic Citizens"

Education and Belonging

In an 1894 parliamentary debate over education in Natal, Prime Minister Sir John Robinson declared, "We hope that the future Natalians will not only be full men, but will be . . . strong men as regards their own capacity to do their work in life, and strong men as regards their ability to become useful and patriotic citizens."[1] For Robinson, formal education in Natal offered an essential part of creating a "useful and patriotic" citizenship among the colony's white population, enabling settlers to claim legitimacy as the rightful occupiers of the land both within the colony and in the wider imperial world. Yet Africans and Indians also pushed for education in order to access social mobility, increased wealth, and a measure of autonomy within an increasingly stratified racial system in the late nineteenth and early twentieth centuries. Missionaries and the colonial state both sought to provide education, to reach various groups with the colony, and to secure funding for these intellectual enterprises. As indigenous Africans, Indian migrants, and British settlers all clamored for access to education, Natal's settler legislature attempted to foster institutions that forced various peoples into roles most amenable to an emerging colonial hierarchy. The piecemeal creation of educational institutions in late nineteenth-century Natal offered opportunities for social advancement but also operated as a disciplining space that produced raced and gendered identities through the collisions of competing peoples.

Education did more than fill children with measured, quantifiable knowledge. It also provided social capital within colonial Natal. Access to education allowed one to claim sophistication, intelligence, and a sense of distinction within the colony. Education (or the ability to be educated) offered a critical means of asserting one's claim to citizenship. It is for this reason that Natal's settler government secured vastly unequal sums of public funds to support education for the children of settlers, while spending markedly less for Indian and African peoples. In 1891, the state allocated £3,200 for Indian education, £2,500 for Africans, and £37,000 for Europeans.[2] In 1896, the Legislative Assembly reported educational spending for Europeans at £38,574, Africans at £5,599, and Indians at £1,825.[3] By 1907, European funding had ballooned to £112,000, while Indian funding had increased to £5,700.[4] The amount of government funds spent on average for individual students remained particularly lavish in European education compared to African or Indian counterparts at the time of Natal's absorption into the Union of South Africa in 1910.[5]

Nonwhite peoples were allotted less funding for two critical reasons. First, because settlers tended to view Africans and Indians as intellectually and socially inferior to them as a general class, Natal's legislators expressed considerable ambivalence regarding any attempt to expand their educational access. Second, despite this assumed inferiority, Natal's settler government also feared that access to formal education would undermine its attempt to hold a monopoly over power in the colony. The records of Natal's legislative debates are full of anxious discussions over the destabilizing potential of Indian or African claims to equality and full citizenship due to their educational status. Africans, Indians, and settlers alike viewed education as a means of claiming a share within the future of the colony. As a consequence, the settler government attempted to control access to this social resource, and direct it in ways that most clearly secured the political and social future of Europeans within the colony.

Conversely, Africans and Indians used education to contest settler claims to hierarchical power in Natal. They did this in a variety of ways. First and foremost, they attempted to increase educational access for their own communities to engage settlers on their own terms, to increase their social mobility, and to advance their claim to inclusion within the colony. However, in other instances, Africans and Indians challenged the presumptions of settlers to control or shape their allotted education. African students recruited to attend the first government-sponsored training school at Zwaartkop responded to state coercion by voting with their feet—one class of students elected to run away from the establishment, and the Africans' continued refusal to attend classes forced the school's closure within a few short years.[6] Similarly, the Natal Indian Congress published a lengthy petition protesting the government's decision to limit Indian education to less affluent schools, and to deny students access to an equal education. Both actions showed resistance to settler attempts to shape nonwhite lives along a racial hierarchy and on terms more amenable to the colonists.[7] Education became another battlefield in Natal where ideas of citizenship, inclusion, and civilization were all fiercely debated.

Education was not simply a system overlaid atop preexisting raced and gendered divisions, however. Indeed, debates over education, both in the creation of legislation and in the responses of people impacted by that legislation, created, maintained, and reified gendered and raced distinctions. Furious legal debate in the halls of Natal's legislature at the turn of the century refined and reinforced racial distinctions as people marked as "Indian" increasingly found themselves squeezed out of publicly funded schools, and shut out of opportunities for industrial training and formal education for people understood as "native" or "African." Natal's legislators increasingly used access to educational institutions as a benchmark for measuring the distinct and privileged status of European settlers, and jealously guarded social and imperial prerogatives as a means of consolidating the power of a white minority. These raced distinctions were not self-evident; they were reasoned, articulated, and wholly invented through often tortuous logic and constant strained analogies with other locations like Canada, the United States, Australia, and the Caribbean, as illustrated in this chapter.

Ultimately, settler debates over education in Natal and the resultant legal statutes developed demonstrate neither the confidence of legislators nor the clarifying objectivity of the law, but rather the very opposite. The myriad contradictions and challenges of colonial rule confronted

Natal's residents daily; the legal scaffolding that supported colonial education indicates that settler power was never fully realized and had to be recalibrated constantly. The question of education in Natal was, at its heart, a process through which racial distinctions were made and remade, and classifications established with an aim to securing competing claims to a future in the colony. Consequently, we cannot simply view education in Natal through a racialized lens. Nineteenth-century legislators argued about the education of white children in the same breath that they voiced concerns at Indian ambition or their imperial duty to use education to uplift indigenous Africans. These concerns, motivations, and legal remedies were developed completely in process with each other, and as such, demonstrate that hierarchies of power and and racial classifications were profoundly intertwined in colonial Natal.

Likewise, the act of providing for the education of the colony's children raised many questions about futurity and social reproduction in Natal. These questions crystallized around developing conceptions of gender. Discussions concerning the particularities of training boys versus girls in Natal's schools provide an intimate look at gender discourse's manifestation in the materiality of law and school institutions. These institutions in turn were tasked with the maintenance and reproduction of the gendered norms they were creating. European boys' schools in Natal disciplined children into the raced and gendered norms expected for the ruling settler minority. Likewise, schools for settler girls and African girls alike served as spaces to train for domestic management and create properly heteronormative, family-directed women within the colony. Studying the development of educational institutions in Natal uncovers the gendered and raced expectations imagined by those who sought to create productive citizens (or noncitizens) in the colony.

Education, then, reveals the fears, anxieties, and aspirations that undergirded settler society in Natal. The constant missteps and piecemeal development of policy reveal the state's weaknesses at crafting a future that ensured the dominance of a settler minority in the face of other peoples' determination to be part of that future. Simultaneously, educational policy planning showed the potential power of state-created apparatuses to mark those inside and outside a marked circle of power.

Education, and the myriad debates surrounding its practice, implementation, and reform, provides an essential platform from which to view the complex interplay between local and transnational, material and discursive, which characterized settler colonial logics and their limits in Natal.

Creating Colonial Education

The development of educational institutions in Natal predated the British annexation of the colony in 1843. The first Western missionaries arriving in the 1830s offered forms of educational instruction fit for the propagation of Christianity among the indigenous population, particularly after the ascension of Mpande kaSenzangakhona in 1840. By 1850 a considerable number of American and European mission stations dotted the colony of Natal, and religious instruction took place independent of government support.[8] The formal incorporation of the colony of Natal as a separate polity from the Cape in 1856 altered colonial funding and the status of African education in particular. Part of the royal charter incorporating Natal stipulated that £5,000 of tax money must be set aside for "Native purposes." This clause, which rankled settlers in the colony, was an imperial rather than a local colonial condition, and could not easily be removed.[9] This mandated fund soon helped offset some of the expenses of missionary educators in the province, and bolstered some of the rhetoric of the civilizing mission.

Prior to the Anglo-Zulu War, the government approach to African education could best be described as piecemeal. European and American missionaries had begun to receive grants-in-aid from the colonial state beginning in the late 1850s, creating an education-on-the-cheap system where the government partially subsidized the efforts of clergy in both educating Africans and creating a class of Christians, known as the *amakholwa* (believers). Institutions like the printing press and school center established by John Colenso, the bishop of Natal, as well as the American-missionary-directed schools of Amanzimtoti (later Adams College) and Inanda Seminary began to receive modest government stipends in 1870, and while their funding remained steady, there were no increases in the allotments for nearly two decades.[10] This piecemeal approach avoided completely alienating white settlers that disapproved of educated Africans, while slowly allowing for the creation of a very small minority of Africans with formal Western educations who could serve in the expanding colonial bureaucracy by the 1860s and 1870s. African education remained primarily implemented by missionaries, a move probably appreciated by the mission educators who had submitted a formal petition to the Natal government in 1879, requesting additional funding for their endeavors.[11] For the colonial government, funding missionary education allowed them to help shape what was taught, helping to fit African education into a mold more in line with European interests.

Following the official granting of independent colony status to Natal in 1856, work commenced toward establishing formal educational institutions for European children in the colony. Most education prior to 1856 in the new colony was on a private basis or assisted by local religious institutions. The arrival of John Colenso as the bishop of Natal in 1855 provided some standardized training for European children as well as African children in the environs in and around Pietermaritzburg. The creation of the position of inspector of education by the Natal government in 1859 was an attempt to encourage and standardize education for the children of settlers. Due to the large size of the colony and the relatively limited size of the settler population, the position involved continuous travel and observation. Under the direction of Robert Mann, the first inspector, Natal's government established high schools in Pietermaritzburg and Durban in 1863 and 1866, respectively. Both schools were begun rather informally as spaces where the male youth of the colony could obtain formal education in preparation for either further study beyond the colony or to fill the ranks of Natal's expanding bureaucracy. Both institutions' successes were intertwined with the relative stability and success of the colony more generally; during financial difficulties or warfare, attending populations often shrunk precipitously.

The further growth and establishment of European schooling in Natal reflected changes within the colony. Schools increasingly became more than just places to obtain intellectual qualification and career advancement. They also created a sense of imperial nationalism, linking the far-flung colony to the metropole though powerful self-imaginings of English cultural identity. As H. G. Mackeurtan, a second-generation settler and

lawyer in Durban, recollected fondly: "One of the characteristics of public school education is that feeling, which we English, for lack of a fit-
ting term in our own language, term *esprit de corps*, a feeling that runs
deep and strong in the heart of every Briton, whether he be of the homeland or of the dominions beyond the seas."[12] This esprit de corps, a sense
of English feeling nonetheless inexpressible in the English language,
undergirded much of formal education for settler children in Natal at
the close of the century. Government-assisted schools worked to reflect
a confidence that Natalians hoped to embody. In the years following the
granting of Responsible Government in 1893, a newly triumphant settler minority sought to underline its own authority and continuity through
its schools. These institutions were self-consciously English in that they
reproduced metropolitan mores as a way of claiming civilization, authority, and order in the face of mounting African and Indian challenges.[13]

Following in the wake of the government-established high schools
in Durban and Pietermaritzburg, settlers created other boys' schools
throughout the colony, with elite schools concentrated within the midlands region. Hilton College was founded in 1872, and education expanded
significantly in the years after the Anglo-Zulu War, with the addition
of Weenen County College and Michaelhouse College by the end of
the century. These schools became elite boarding institutions within the
region that allowed a rising rural farming gentry among Natal's white
male population to access social capital and assume places of importance within the colony.[14] The intensely hierarchical nature of these elite
schools, in which junior students experienced harsh discipline and legitimated violence at the hands of their elder compatriots, reinforced notions
of power among the students. In addition, these schools became centers
where masculinity operated as significant form of social capital; young
male Natalians learned how to dispense justice and endure punishment,
ideals that were viewed as particularly necessary for young men training for positions of leadership within the colony. While these institutions were undoubtedly shaped by their location within the midlands,
urban government schools in Durban and Pietermaritzburg also struggled with questions of discipline, order, and training future leaders of
the colony.

In the years following the Anglo-Zulu War, the colonial government sought to formalize and systematize state control over education. This centralizing tendency applied to African education as well as European and Indian counterparts, although it was done far more cheaply, a particularly unfair move given that African taxes contributed a substantial percentage of the colony's annual budget. Rather than build government schools for Africans, the colonial state at first worked to increase grants-in-aid to extant missionary schools. The government funding supplemented (and in many instances sustained) these educational enterprises, without committing the government to the overall responsibility for implementing a new system. In 1884, the Natal Legislative Assembly passed a sweeping series of changes for African education into law. Law No. 1 of 1884 stipulated that all institutions wishing to continue receiving government funding for African education had to incorporate some form of industrial education as part of the curriculum. The law also created the position of inspector of native education, an individual who served as a liaison between the government-assisted schools and the settler government in order to coordinate larger educational aims that were amenable to the desires of the Legislative Assembly. The law also implemented the brief-lived Zwaartkop Native Industrial School for Boys. These three changes initiated by the 1884 law—the implementation of industrial education, the oversight of a government inspector, and the establishment of a government school for African boys—represented a profound move by the Natal settler government toward centralizing colonial educational institutions for Africans, with decidedly mixed results.

The passing of industrial education requirements within the 1884 law reflected settler interests in shaping the nature of African education. As the settler state sought to standardize education, more generally, providing manual labor skills offered a means of challenging the idea of native laziness, inculcating industrious habits among people, and making them more readily available as parts of a colonial workforce. As Keletso Atkins has noted, settler attitudes toward ostensible African laziness were rooted in racialized conceptions of African labor as undeveloped insomuch as it failed to reproduce observable European standards. As such, appeals for industrial training for Africans reproduced predominant colonial

and capitalist rhetoric.[15] As early as 1869, calls had appeared in the settler press urging for the training of Africans in industrial education in
order to pull them more firmly into the orbit of colonial control.[16] The
increased move toward centralization in post-1879 Natal meant a push
toward shaping not only African education, but also African lifestyles to
pull them further into the orbit of settlers.

Nor was the interest in African industrial education limited to settlers
alone. As part of the 1881 Native Affairs Commission, mission-trained
authors and *amakholwa* William Ngidi and Magema Fuze answered a
series of questions regarding the state of African education. Both men
argued that education should be made available to all Africans, with a
particular interest in industrial education. "It would be a good thing
throughout the whole land if the people were educated," asserted Ngidi
and Fuze in the colonial record. "I do not mean the preaching of the law
as coming with cannon to blow up the world. I do not like teaching by
fear. What we want is to learn how to make chairs, tables, and similar
things—in fact, industrial teaching."[17] Yet both Fuze and Ngidi argued
that industrial education should follow classroom instruction, adding that
"the child should be first taught to read, and then following upon this he
should have a useful implement put into his hand, and be told 'Learn
that business.'"[18]

In the midst of this move toward industrial education, Natal appointed
a new inspector of native education. The first inspector, Mr. Fynney, died
while on sick leave in 1888, merely three years into his appointment.[19]
He was replaced that year by Robert Plant, whose views on African education would prove formative in the last decades of the colony and beyond.
Plant, a veteran of the Anglo-Zulu War, actively sought to further governmental control over the direction and scope of African education,
although he frequently encountered effective resistance from missionaries and Africans themselves.[20] For Plant, educating African peoples
stemmed from the obligations of the state to provide for all of its inhabitants, but this provision required government intervention to produce
an indigenous population that benefitted settler interests. In his 1889
annual education report, Plant produced a separate note titled "Minute
on Native Education." In this piece, Plant set forth his larger aims for

African education. For Plant, African education existed "to qualify the native youth for the effective discharge of their probable duties in life. These, for the present generation of school children, are those connected with the stable, kitchen, nursery, wagon, or farm."[21] While he acknowledged a "few will rise higher than these things, will become teachers, mechanics, clerks, &c.," he also asserted that existing educational facilities already more than sufficiently educated these limited numbers of Africans, particularly Adams Training College and Inanda Seminary, the American-missionary-run institutions near Durban.[22] Plant envisioned the larger mechanisms of state-sponsored African education to provide lightly educated laborers without attempting to create an elite educated class to challenge settler dominance. These assertions were couched in paternalistic phrasing of racial and evolutionary dominance, one that viewed Africans as charges to be simultaneously protected and uplifted, in spite of their lesser civilizational state.

As such, Plant echoed exhortations from the settler government that Africans be compelled to develop skills that would render them materially sufficient and useful to Europeans. Yet he also embodied the contradictory impulses of encouraging the development of manual skills while actively seeking to limit labor competition with settlers. Arguing that European education existed to give children an advantage in a market already crowded with unskilled laborers, Plant insisted that African education should produce "intelligent manual labourers, who are willing to perform the duties of the different departments of labour already referred to in an intelligent manner." Ultimately, Plant argued that pushing industrial training was not necessarily the best tactic for Natal's government strategists. First of all, it was both costly and unsustainable to force nongovernmental institutions to equip themselves with formal industrial education centers in order to receive limited government grants. Second, such training could prove injurious to settler economics, and thus, classroom education should probably be separated from the idea of industrial education. These meditations were undoubtedly influenced by Plant's own experience with the final condition of the 1884 law: the construction of the Zwaartkop Native Industrial School for Boys. On paper, the institution seemed particularly suited to the grand plans the

Natal government imagined for Africans. Yet, the question of industrial education and its utility for both settlers and Africans brought the experiment to a crashing halt as African students made very clear what they wanted from education, regardless of what settlers had envisioned.

The Zwaartkop Native Industrial School for Boys was an ambitious program, born of a larger aim of centralizing government control over education and circumventing the previous practice of educating African students cheaply through subsidizing nongovernmental institutions. The school took in both day students and boarders, and while it was headed by a European, it had African instructors for both classroom and industrial education, which included carpentry and wagon building.[23] Yet the school, which opened in 1886, was a costly failure, and closed six short years later, to considerable embarrassment. Zwaartkop's lack of success arose primarily from a resolute lack of interest in it from the African communities who resided near the institution. Although Zwaartkop had been implemented before Plant's hiring, he nonetheless presided over most of its tenure and eventual demise, and his recommendations that industrial education be rendered separate from classroom education must be seen in light of this contested school. Plant noted ruefully in 1889 that the local community had insisted at the opening of the school in 1886 that "they did not wish for a school and would not send their children, and from the very first they have kept their word."[24] Indeed, the school lurched from crisis to crisis in its brief existence. African students made their displeasure with the institution abundantly clear on multiple occasions; in 1888 all of the boarding students ran away, returning only briefly afterward.[25] Later, Percy Barnett, the superintendent for education, surmised that colonial officials, who were "amateurs" in the field of education, had not bothered to account for issues like intertribal conflict between the different indigenous peoples in the region as well as the lack of any missionary support and poor domestic management.[26] By 1892, Plant and the government admitted defeat in the face of continued indigenous intransigence, and shuttered the school.[27]

Yet the closure of Zwaartkop did not mean an end to attempts at expanded government centralized control over African education. Indeed, the idea of African education served as a larger moving target that contained contradictory and competing settler plans for indigenous peoples. First, many settlers viewed African education as a duty required of Europeans that justified their continued presence in and domination over the colony. Yet African education also contained within it a potential threat of disorder. By encouraging the education of Africans, even if it furthered settler economic and social aims, Europeans ran the risk of undermining the developing racial hierarchy that existed within Natal. Moreover, by insisting on industrial education, Natal's white population ran the risk of setting up potential competitors in a colony structured around protecting the settler minority. As a result, Natal's politicians worked to limit the scope of industrial education. In 1895, the government began to refuse grants to any schools that might encourage Africans to compete with white laborers or any that operated newspapers or printing presses, which had the potential to create a dissident educated readership aware of the machinations of Natal's settler politicians.[28]

While Natal's government or local mission agencies had attempted to provide educational assistance for European and African children since at least the 1850s, it was not until the 1870s that the beginnings of formal educational assistance began to appear for Indian children in the colony.[29] The 1872 Coolie Commission strongly recommended the establishment of educational systems for Indian children; the Reverend Ralph Stott urged the establishment of schools as soon as possible, for there was "nothing more likely to tend to keep the Coolies on estates and satisfied, than the establishment of schools on estates."[30] The commission noted that Indian men and women were themselves already organizing schools to meet their needs, but specifically requested more assistance with regard to funding and staff. A schoolteacher, Chinnah Villay, noted with pride that his small schoolhouse was growing as more students attended with each passing week.[31] Another Indian interviewee, Rangasammy, complained that Indian children were "spoiled for want of teachers" and begged for more schools to be built.[32] In 1878, Natal's legislature passed a law to establish the Indian Immigrant School Board in an attempt to create a systemized structure for the education of Indian children.[33] Establishing the board took considerable time and effort; an inspector was hired only in 1881, and early attempts to establish systemic education at the expense of the settler sugar farmers who employed Indian labor ran into hostility.[34] This hostility arose, in part, both from planter suspicions that Indian education would cut into the regular supply of labor for sugar production, and from anti-Indian sentiment among the wider settler community, a sentiment readily visible in the legislative debates.

Despite the existence of the Immigrant School Board, actual plans for educating Indian children remained somewhat nebulous. In 1881, Natal's Legislative Assembly debated what exactly should be done to establish regular education services. Charles Mitchell, the colonial secretary, offered a plan in which planters, Indian workers, and the colonial government would each contribute to cover expenses—planters would supply land and housing, families would provide school fees, and the government would offer teaching salaries and books. In discussing the extent of Indian interest in education, future prime minister Harry Escombe noted that 37 of the 123 children attending government schools were of Indian ancestry, and showed a strong disposition toward continuing education. Escombe further argued that Indian children "should be encouraged in education, in which I believe they will be as successful as any children in the world."[35] Indeed, the early 1880s showed an ambivalent feeling by settler legislators on the question of interracial education; as the school system was still small and somewhat rudimentary, it was less of a problem that Indians and Europeans attended the same schools, but Mitchell argued that though Indian children were equally intelligent as Europeans, there was "no objection whatever to their mixing with English children, *except on the ground of race.*"[36] The increasing appearance of Indian children in government schools throughout the 1880s would make the "the ground of race" more salient as colonial institutions grew in size and complexity.

The 1881 debates about the growth of Indian education were also steeped in rhetoric about native Africans in the colony. In the midst of discussion of increasing educational opportunities, politicians debated over what official government structures should be established in favor of African education. Charles Mitchell in particular stated that while he believed it lamentable that no official government support for African education had been established at present, it was due primarily to the fact that "one race wants to be educated while the other does not."[37] In response, the attorney general, M. H. Gallwey, placed blame for the failure of government-based education for Africans squarely on the shoulders of the Legislative Assembly. Gallwey noted that Henry Bulwer, the lieutenant-governor of the colony, had made provisions for European, African, and Indian education separately, but plans for African education had been scuttled by the Legislative Council, which could not agree on whether to encourage formal schooling or labor apprenticeship for Africans.[38]

It is not a coincidence that questions about Indian education were caught up in simultaneous debates over the education of Africans. Rather than thinking of the two as fundamentally distinct and discrete units, the debates of legislators reveal that questions of racial distinction, colonial hierarchy, and formal education were profoundly intertwined. Discussions of educating Indians could not occur without remarking on the progress made at civilizational uplift for indigenous peoples, or for the fears of racial amalgamation in European schools.

This intertwined understanding of race and education among settler leaders was readily apparent as early as 1875, when then-Associate Inspector of Schools Robert Russell wrote as part of a Special Report on Government-Aided Education that Africans and Indians had indisputable (albeit abstract) rights to belonging within the colony—either through prior inhabitance or through imperial claims—yet, the real conflict arose with the idea of their intermixing with European children.

> The question is not whether they shall be educated, but whether they shall be allowed to sit side by side in the same schools with our children. . . . Their social position, however, is not high; and the characters of some of them would hardly bear scrutiny. Their ways of thought, and their habits and customs, are often widely different from our own. These considerations, and not the fact of mere difference in colour, are the causes of wide-spread feeling against them.[39]

Russell saw racial distinction not as simply inherent, but as part of a matrix of differing cultural and social norms that became most salient in the quotidian interactions of the classroom between differing groups. This, in his estimation, was the biggest problem with interracial education, beyond that of the "mere difference in colour." Yet he also acknowledged that the desire for education by nonwhite peoples within the colony served as a beneficial endorsement of English colonial hegemony, and should be "encouraged rather than checked," as it spread a shared linguistic and cultural framework that benefitted settlers in Natal.

And yet, Russell viewed the largest problem of interracial education as one that impinged upon and threatened the inherent "rights" of European settlers:

At the same time, it must be clearly understood that white people have 'rights' which they cannot afford to part with; and that not the least cherished by them is that the sense of honour, decency, and manliness inculcated in our children shall be fenced from injury by ever possible security. Let us hope that with the adoption of needful safeguards all ill-feeling on this subject will gradually disappear, and that in time we shall see white and coloured children vying with each other in the attainment of the mental and moral qualities necessary for discharging successfully the domestic, civil, political, and religious duties of their common home.[40]

For Russell, solving the question of interracial education ultimately lay with the establishment of settler hegemony. If African and Indian children could acculturate to the shared demands of their settler counterparts, then the reasons for ill-feeling among colonists would vanish and all could compete within educational institutions, developing the necessary skills for expanding their shared inhabitance of the colony. It was a utopic and necessarily vague conclusion to a settler crisis of competition.

As settlers debated over how to construct educational institutions, African and Indian peoples made their own claims, and pushed for a greater share in access to government education. Settler legislators were forced to note that despite their belief in African disinclination toward learning, "there is a great desire amongst them in some of the large districts to obtain education."[41] The growth of *amakholwa* communities like those in Edendale undoubtedly reflected some of the formal pushes for education among Africans. Likewise, the increase of Indian children in government schools throughout the 1880s can be read as a way of making claims to belong in the larger structures and spaces of the colony. Yet the tensions envisioned by Russell did not abate over time, even with the increase of students partaking in government education. Rather, the increased presence of Indian students led to a stronger sense of racial threat and differentiation by Natal's settler politicians, and they sought to arrest these changes after obtaining Responsible Government in 1893.

The contents and tenor of legislative debates after the granting of Responsible Government reveal a settler legislature attempting to defend its own prerogatives as the sole legitimate leaders within civic life and to delineate what shape education would take in the growing colony. The potential legitimacy and access offered by education lent urgency to these debates, which resulted in the repealing of previous legislation and abolishing both the Indian Immigrant School Board and the Council of Education. In their places, Natal's Legislative Council created a centralized Department of Education, responsible for the education of all racial groups in Natal—European, African, and Indian.[42]

Education and the Logics of Settler Rule

In 1894, Frederick Tatham, representative to the Legislative Council for the city of Pietermaritzburg, entered the wider discussion with the publication of his book, *The Race Conflict in South Africa: An Enquiry into the General Question of Native Education*. A staunch opponent of African education under any circumstances, Tatham wrote and published the essay in the hopes of convincing a significant number of Natal's white settler population of his views. Tatham ultimately opposed African education on the grounds of intrinsic evolutionary character, civilization, and the continuance of settler governance. For Tatham, education created Africans who were artificially advanced but utterly unable to rise above their essential barbarism. Such peoples became challenges to the proper racial and civilizational order of the colony. Tatham argued that these were not simply the feverish conjectures of a man obsessed with white supremacy in a land dominated by indigenous peoples; rather, he claimed his analysis stemmed from a thoughtful consideration of other settler societies. To do this, Tatham turned to the history of the United States after the Civil War, arguing that chattel slavery had kept Africans safe and protected.[43] It was this "safety" that had protected African Americans from the inevitable degradation and destruction that native North Americans had experienced.[44] Thus, for Tatham, the history of Reconstruction in the contemporary United States served as a cautionary tale for unthinking do-gooders in Natal who wished to educate their black peoples. Africans were incapable of civilization; they would inevitably return to violence, sloth, and degradation, and drag down principles of proper settler government with them. The implementation of white supremacist rule in the southern states of the United States was thus a return to proper order and a check on the destructive tendencies of African savagery, and should be well noted as an object lesson by Natal's white citizens.

Tatham's jeremiad against African education operated from more than sheer racial animus. It revealed the larger questions of domination, of government, of identity in colonial Natal, and demonstrated how debates over education revealed the deeply contested claims of legitimate belonging within the colony. Through a veil of disingenuous concern, Tatham warned that the probable result of African education would be "a black Parliament in Natal," a fate that would lead to black degradation and European destruction.[45] His analysis reveals the heart of the settler project not just in South Africa, but also in other settler societies. Tatham's paranoid prose clearly signals the making of racial categories through the collisions of bodies in this nineteenth-century context—such a cross-cultural encounter created shock waves that crystallized into formations of race. Secondly, Tatham's text exposes the central weakness of settler societies, masked as inherent strength. The project *must* be preserved; the violence of occupation *must* be legitimated, or it will all fall apart, all will be demoralization, all the futurity will have been for naught, and all will *still* result in native genocide. Such a rhetorical approach posits a process of inevitable indigenous annihilation as a result of settlement, arguing that Natal's settlers should outright oppress Africans throughout a racialized order (and thereby preserve their native charges) rather than allow an *unavoidable* African genocide that would result from the failure of white domination. Such a view was not unique to Tatham; it has previously been espoused in print by Charles Barter, an active member of Natal's legislature in the 1860s and 1870s.[46]

Although Tatham's bid to ban nonwhite education outright was ultimately unsuccessful in colonial Natal, his settler rhetoric was shared by observers both in the colony and beyond. In 1885, Cecil Ashley, youngest son of the social reformer Anthony Ashley Cooper, the 7th Earl of Shaftesbury, published his opinions on indigenous education in South Africa in the *National Review*. Ashley, who had traveled extensively in southern Africa, agreed with Tatham's initial remarks, noting that "unlike the Red Indian of America or the Maori of New Zealand, the Kafirs do not fade or diminish before the advance of civilization."[47] Yet for Ashley, this was not indicative of a larger genetic, predetermined inferiority. Rather, he felt education did not facilitate the wasting away of indigenous Africans but instead transformed them into positive, directed workers that maintained the power and productivity of the colony. It is this view that Natal's settler politicians more widely chose to embrace rather than that of their colleague in the Legislative Council. In 1895, following the passing of more restrictive government legislation regarding industrial education, Frederick Tucker, a former member of the Council of Education, penned a letter to the *Natal Witness* and subsequently published a pamphlet on the topic. Turner's argument differed substantially from Tatham's, although it did accept as a starting point African intellectual inferiority and lack of civilization.[48] Tucker argued that the colonial state had an obligation to fund the education of indigenous Africans, and that the fear that industrial education would compete with settler labor was vastly overblown.[49] For Tucker, colonists not only had an obligation to African education by virtue of the revenues Natal gained through taxation, but they also owed the native population out of a sense of fairness and good faith. Depriving Africans of education was certainly a calculated move by colonists to shore up political and racial hierarchies, yet Tucker found this to be both shortsighted and unfair to the indigenous population.

These larger settler debates surrounding the education of Natal's population demonstrate both the co-creation of racial categories and the fears of settler legislators at losing the monopoly over power they possessed in the colony. On its surface, at least, education carried with it the potential for social advancement; this had been behind many of the drives for centralizing and formalizing white educational systems within the colony, and in turn had also led to increased demand from Indians and Africans for a share of the educational bounty. In the years immediately following Responsible Government, the debates took a profoundly sharper turn, as legislators began to evince more openly fear at the potential claims to civic equality that education might offer Indians and Africans in Natal. During the 1894 session, John Bainbridge warned of the problem of continued African and Indian education. He spelled out the destabilizing potential of education bluntly:

> I see grave consequences that may ensue. If you educate the Native and the Coolie, and he competes with the children of the white people and passes them, you cannot keep those higher offices closed against him. And what is the consequence? He is brought up beyond labour, he is in a sphere in which he has no occupation; he is an educated man. What is the consequence? You are breeding up at the public expense a lot of public agitators who want their rights—we will have the case of Gordon in Jamaica over again. Is it desirable that we should spend our money in this way?[50]

Bainbridge offered a straightforward imperial calculus. Education provided a sense of investment in a colonial system, and a sense of entitlement to critique that system. The educating of nonwhite peoples in Natal was not only ill advised, it was inherently dangerous. Bainbridge and others in Parliament believed the chief aim of government was to maintain disproportionate power and control for the educated, "civilized" European minority. Education not only gave Africans and Indians the words to articulate their disaffection but also the social capital to make claims to belong in a society that settlers wished to reserve solely to themselves. In addition, Bainbridge invoked the specter of George Gordon, the mixed-race parliamentarian in Jamaica executed on flimsy evidence as a consequence of the Morant Bay Rebellion in 1865. Bainbridge's rhetoric explicitly cast educated Africans and Indians as potential threats, dragon's teeth sown among the fertile lands of the colony, only to spring into treacherous actions against the legitimacy of the settler state.[51]

It is not a coincidence that Bainbridge's arguments against an expanded educational access in Natal immediately followed the laudatory comments of John Robinson that opened this chapter. Robinson's speech praised the potential of education to assist in making Natalians "useful and patriotic citizens." The subsequent discussion in the chamber revealed this core issue behind education in Natal—who can become a citizen. As Bainbridge's speech makes clear, education offered the destabilizing potential of inclusion within the body politic to nonwhite peoples.

Perhaps made oversensitive to the bluntly articulated nature of white supremacy in colonial governance, legislators worked to soften the overall tone of the argument over education. Following Bainbridge's remarks, Frederick Tatham formally withdrew his measure that baldly stated governmental opposition to educating Africans, a document that included the words, "this House desires to place on record the fact that it will not approve any action on the part of the Government having for its effect the raising of the Native into competition with the European." Echoing this rhetorical shift, politician Cecil Yonge moved the terms of the discussion to that of morality, couching his opposition to interracial education more broadly:

I will satisfy myself with simply referring to the question of Native and Indian education. I trust that the day is near at hand in our little Colony when no longer will such a thing be possible as to see the Indian child, the Kafir *umfaan*, and the white cherub walking hand-in-hand down our streets to partake of instruction at the same school. By all means educate these coloured children if you think necessary, but educate them according to their level, according to their morals, but do not educate them with the child whose greatest tribute, whose most precious earthly value, is its morality. Do not educate our children with those children who, however young, however deserving of support they may be, have no idea of, and have not the opportunity of learning, the value to them of the morals and the morality which we desire and expect to see inherent in our own children.[52]

Certainly morality in this instance is a coded phrase for fear of inter-racial intimacy, but it is telling that the move to debate the morality of interracial education casts the matter of education less in terms of maintaining settler prerogatives and more in terms of the safety of the community. Yet Yonge's speech still utilizes civilizational rhetoric (as seen in chapter 4); the rationale for separate African and Indian pupils from European ones comes down to questions of uplift or degradation in morality. This is not far afield from the larger attendant fears over non-white suffrage, which frequently justified a white monopoly on the privilege through discourses of civilizational fitness and civic advancement.

Indeed, in 1896, the Legislative Assembly attempted to ban the franchise outright for Indian voters, only to have the move negated by Britain as a piece of class legislation, targeted specifically at one racial group. Natal's settler politicians saw these questions of education, labor, and political supremacy as interlinked. That same year, future prime minister John Robinson maintained that "Indians should come into this Colony for labour purposes and for fixed periods, but we do not want the population of this Colony to be predominated by a majority of Asiatic voters." He further maintained that though Indians had many qualities that had benefitted Natal, "when they aim at acquiring political dominancy, it is our duty, as representing the European electors of this Colony, not merely to protest, but to interfere."[53] While fellow legislator Harry Escombe thought some higher educated Indians should possibly be allowed the franchise, he nonetheless agreed that "the electoral rolls throughout South Africa as regards English Colonies must be kept absolutely confined to persons of European race."[54] Two years previously, John Bainbridge had explicitly linked the education of Indians to the fear of settlers losing political dominance. Specifically arguing against continuing bursaries or other state funding for Indians, Bainbridge related a conversation he had had with an Indian youth:

The little fellow came to me one morning, after I had got my breakfast, and he said: 'I was in the House last night.' 'Oh,' I said, 'were you?' 'Yes,' he said, 'and I was very much pleased, very much pleased; it is a fine institution.' 'Well,' he said, 'I have a great ambition to be there, and I hope to be there one day.' 'Indeed,' I said, 'I do not think so.' 'Yes,' he said, 'Don't you think that the Coolies are the coming race?' I looked at him, and said it was absurd. . . . I do not say, keep these men back if they like to educate themselves, but do not do it at the country's expense.[55]

As Bainbridge's story makes clear, settler politicians linked Indian education explicitly to fears of losing political control by the 1890s, and this fear governed political legislation throughout the next decade. Subsequent settler legislation sought to limit interracial education between Indians and Europeans, and to further minimize the potential political and social mobility for Indians within the colony.

For settler legislators, the questions of Indian education were inextricable from the threat of Indian political competition within the colony. In 1888, John Philip Symons, member for Umvoti County, argued explicitly against continued allowing of Indian immigration into the colony, framing it directly in line with larger questions of settler rule. Using the very space of the Legislative Council to prognosticate the precarious future of white settler rule in the face of the Indian "threat," Symons argued:

Are we to have an Indian population growing up in our midst side by side with ourselves? Are we someday—all those who remain of us or those who come on—to see that gallery, instead of being filled up with the bright faces we see there now, filled with a lot of blacks, and your chair, Sir, occupied by a man with a turban? I do not want to see that. I want to see this country a country filled with white people. I want this country to be the home of Englishmen, the home of Europeans, and I want to see the blacks put in their proper place. It was only yesterday a gentleman said to me, 'What is to be the future of this country?'[56]

For Symons, the questions of futurity, stability, and orderly settler rule were bound up in the maintenance of racialized power. The advancement or further inclusion of Indians within the colony risked transforming the political gallery into something monstrous—the bright faces of European politicians replaced with that of uncivilized turbans and black visages. Symons expressly referred to settler order requiring "blacks put in their proper place," a categoric linking that placed both Africans and Indians as properly below the rule of white leaders. Education, and the social value that accompanied it, had the potential to disrupt these carefully organized hierarchical structures.

These racialized fears linking education to citizenship are readily visible in the pages of the 1904 Native Affairs Commission. The commission interviewed a significant number of settler leaders and missionary representatives, while addressing multiple African respondents as well. Multiple European observers spoke disparagingly of African education as a form of undermining racial hierarchies within the colony; education, it seemed, allowed Africans to make claims to citizenship and potentially suffrage—something that settlers were unwilling to acknowledge. Frederick Moor, former secretary of native affairs, put it most explicitly when he asserted before the commission:

At this stage in our history we can tolerate no terms whatever of political or social equality, and it is something deeper than any doctrines and dogmas or laws that implants that feeling in every white man's brain. It is a racial instinct which, in its tendency, is wiser than any laws which we might make to bring about terms of equality between the races. It is more honest for us to say to these people: 'You are not our equals, and we cannot accept any such position,' than to preach to them any condition of equality, which in our practice towards them would be immediately broken.[57]

For Moor, education and other paths of advancement opened the question of social equality, thereby dooming the racial hierarchy that underpinned Natal society. Indeed, African observers who sought to use education as a path to social advancement supported these assertions. Standing before

the commission, African storekeeper Mark Radebe asserted that education provided a means of social improvement, stating, "[W]e have tried
at various times to raise our people, and the only method of raising our
people will be education, and trying to make up schools, and trying to
teach the people."[58] For Radebe and others, education itself offered a significant means of claiming belonging in a colonial society. These claims
furthered settler anxieties as they sought to find ways to control African
mobility, both physical and social.

Many of these larger anxieties surrounding settler minority rule and
education were on display in the 1903 Natal Teachers' Convention, held
in Durban. The conference brought together a wide variety of (white)
teachers throughout the colony, and held informative panels and work-
shops over several days. In the opening remarks, Ernest Belcher, assistant
master at Durban High School, stressed that education played an integral role in reinforcing hierarchies of power within the colony. "Teachers
are aware that intimate contact with a race of inferior social and intellectual capacity, engaged in 'menial' labour, and bearing on their shoulders the whole substructure of the common industries, is debilitating and
demoralizing to the white children," Belcher announced.[59] For Belcher,
teachers offered the first line of defense against the corrosive effects
of an African majority within the colony. Education served primarily to
inculcate and reinforce structures of power; white boys and girls needed
to learn their particular roles in the colony. Further, education could serve
to inoculate the settler population against the negative effects of excessive acquaintance with the Africans they were destined to rule. Rather,
colonial education had the express purpose of creating a sense of duty that
reinforced the role of the settler at the top of the social order. This social
education, in turn, was explained as a creating a form of charity or self-
lessness that colonists then extended to their indigenous charges. Indeed,
Belcher stated baldly that "education [could not] permit white children to
grow up ignorant that their very first duty is to care kindly for their inferiors and dependents."[60]

The minutes of the convention are an illuminating source, for they
provide considerable insight into the operation of power, education,
and settler futurity in Natal. In particular, speeches governing classroom

discipline reveal much about the expectations for students training to take their role as future colonists, but also much about the views of Africans in the colony, who were regularly depicted as grown children in need of firm instruction. As James Forbes, former head of Durban High School and subsequent founder of the Berea Academy, admonished in a paper on discipline:

[C]hildren must be governed, to a great extent, in the same way as men are, viz., by the adaptation of plans to be fixed and uniform tendencies of human nature. At the same time, absolute and unquestioned authority must be maintained by a judicious mixture of force and influence. It was a great mistake to consider instruction the first thing. Discipline came first, and was the only basis on which systematic study could be successfully pursued.[61]

Forbes's instructions are significant in that they reveal more than classroom management techniques. They are, at their core, a means of understanding the psychology of control and domination that characterized settler society. Settler children were to learn that proper colonists did not revel in the wanton extension of pure force. Such actions were brutal, and ultimately regarded as profoundly unmanly. Yet as Robert Morrell has demonstrated in his study of Natal's elite boys' schools, corporal punishment was respected in general as a means of maintaining order among European children.[62] Although patriarchal authority had to be measured and restrained, it was still deemed quite necessary. Students were to learn the correct exertion of authority, a sense of implied and assumed strength that could be exerted without risk to the colonist. Indeed, Forbes cautioned teachers to "never give a command which they had not the ability and intention to enforce, for a rule successfully broken was an inducement to further disobedience."[63] Such admonitions were clearly repeated in the halls of government in Natal, as settler legislators feared to make unenforceable laws, particularly over the African population.

Maintaining and furthering settler racial hegemony were central subjects discussed at the convention. As H. V. Ellis, headmaster of Hilton College, wondered in his presentation, "How shall we train our Natal boys and girls to take up the noble burden of the white man?"[64] Continuing with the themes in the convention, Ellis maintained that the largest threat to the security of the colony lay primarily with excessive contact between Europeans and Africans, leading to a breakdown in civilizational order. To offset this, Ellis maintained that efforts should be redoubled in maintaining cultural purity for white colonists. This included only allowing African attendants who were fluent in English (eliminating the damaging association of isiZulu on proper English speech) and practicing Christians. For Ellis, African contact had to be isolated and controlled in order to create culturally appropriate European rulers in the colony.[65] Secondarily, European children had to remember that they were daily examples of civilized behavior to Africans. With this in mind, settler children had to behave in ways appropriate for civilized men and women at all times, lest Africans gain the wrong idea. This was roundly echoed by Robert Clark of Durban High School, as well as Robert Plant, inspector of native schools, who despaired at European laziness and unwillingness to do simple chores that were performed by their African servants.[66]

Likewise, Belcher argued that "teachers are aware that intimate contact with a race of inferior social and intellectual capacity, engaged in 'menial' labour, and bearing on their shoulders the whole substructure of the common industries, is debilitating and demoralizing to the white children."[67] In this instance, the rhetoric of morality took a different turn, however. As nonwhite peoples were designated to do manual labor, their association with white children will lead to "demoralization," or a distraction of European students from their more lofty callings. Belcher was joined by the convention's chief speaker, Dr. George Parkin, a Canadian education expert. Parkin echoed Belcher's fears about nonwhite education, and added that he had seen similar examples in his tours of the United States, arguing that "white people living in touch with the black people had been dragged down to the level of the blacks. There was nothing of the cheerful about the homes of the poorer whites in the black States."[68] Drawing upon a global settler colonial framework much like Tatham had, Parkin encouraged both the separation of white students from their darker counterparts, and for the limiting of the nonwhite vote to a small minority that could evince civilizational fitness.

Making Men and Women in Natal's Schools

Colonial education was not simply a rhetorical space where racial hierarchies were crystallized, reified, and reproduced. Education, and the
institutions created to facilitate it, also served to create and reinforce
gendered distinctions. Indeed, discourse and debate surrounding African education in the late nineteenth century reveal much about the operation and deployment of gender in the colony. From the very beginning
of missionary involvement in education for Africans, the figure of the
African woman raised particular concern. The "kraal girl" figured prom-
inently in missionary reports, offering the image of an African woman
rejecting oppressive heathen institutions for the comparable liberality
of Western missionaries and their offers of education.[69] As part of their
attempts to reorder and reshape African lives and souls, missionaries
tried to change the social structures that had made the *imizi* a viable
institution. Educational institutions, then, could provide the space for re-
training Africans into gendered forms of labor that missionaries deemed
more appropriate for the *amakholwa*. Rather than perform the ostensible
drudgery of agricultural labor, African women were to be retrained in
domestic arts, which involved profound transformations in relation to
dress, household work, and child rearing.

Debates over African education and its larger role in achieving the
aims imagined by settler elites in Natal frequently invoked and reproduced gender distinctions within the colony. The move to provide industrial education for African students took on a profoundly gendered
element in the context of late nineteenth-century Natal. Missionary institutions often found it far easier to accommodate the governmental
demands for industrial education for their female students, as students
were required to learn needlework and other domestic activities.[70] These
activities required considerably less financial investment than industrial
education for male students, which required significant capital to provide
instruction in woodworking, blacksmithing, printmaking, or other tasks.
Schools were assessed for a variety of factors, from quality of education
to the effort "taken to encourage conformity with European habits."[71]
Schools that excelled in particular areas earned comments in the annual

report, and particularly commendable schools were praised for their ability to enforce the adoption of European clothing and Western standards
of hygiene, and they generally emulated the lifestyles of their instructors. In his 1891 annual report, Inspector Robert Plant offered particular
praise for the acculturating practices at Inanda Seminary, which combined Protestant Christian instruction with industrial training for women.
For Plant, Inanda was a model institution in its training African women
either to work for European mistresses or to create *amakholwa* homes
that reproduced Western cultural models of domesticity. "I am convinced
that such education given to Native girls will go very far to solve the
problem how to create 'wants' in the Native life," Plant asserted. "With a
wife who has had such a training a man will have to work to obtain the
many things which his wife regards as absolute necessaries."[72]

In creating educational institutions that served African women as well
men, settler administrators and missionaries entered a complex and
shifting working relationship. Both groups wished to transform African
women along European cultural lines that made them more accommo-
dating to the demands of settler capitalism in Natal. They also sought to
weaken the hold of the *imizi*, which functioned as a successful social
bulwark against both colonial social transformation and Christian conversion. Missionaries and administrators recognized that the existence
of *ukulobola* and polygamous marriages sustained both the economic and
social unity of the *umuzi* and thus sought to undermine Natal's Native
Code of 1891, which had enshrined these practices as distinct components of customary law, in effect giving government sanction to these
dissident practices. The crystallization of polygamy and *ukulobola* within
the larger customary law code served to bolster colonial authority and
harden the traditional and gendered authority of African elder men, an
act that historian Jeff Guy has described as "an accommodation of patriarchs."[73] This legal maneuver attempted to foster a sense of legitimacy for
settler government over indigenous peoples, and draw them into an alliance that sacrificed the autonomy and agency of African women. Yet this
action distinctly contradicted the transformations envisaged by missionaries and colonial education administrators. The last decades of the nineteenth century in Natal, then, offered a contrast between transformative

aspirations and a symbiotic colonial state that drew legitimacy from existing traditional African customs.[74] It is in the heart of these contrasting,
contradicting moments that gender becomes most acutely visible in the
colonial record.

While a variety of institutions offered education and training for African women, the two most prominent centers for women's education in
colonial Natal were Inanda Seminary and Mariannhill. Inanda, which had
been founded by American missionaries in 1869, provided a standardized education that combined industrial education with a classic great
books curriculum, constructed in consultation with the colonial administration. Inanda graduates were trained extensively in a variety of texts
and were encouraged to develop their academic and intellectual potential in order to serve as productive members of *amakholwa* society. Inanda
frequently earned the praise of Robert Plant in his annual reports, as
its educational objectives often matched with those of colonial administrators. This was not the case for Mariannhill, the Catholic mission and
school founded by Trappist monks in the 1880s outside of Durban. Franz
Pfanner, the abbot of the monastery and head of the institution, sharply
disagreed with Plant's theories, particularly those concerning the education of African women.

Pfanner's vision for Mariannhill involved strict racial segregation
between African and European students, and a particularly minimal
education for African women. For Pfanner, the first generation of African Christian women had no need of formal education aside from the
barest necessities to make them proper wives for African men, who should
in turn serve as dutiful manual laborers. Pfanner believed that African
women should have "as little education as possible," arguing that for
these women, catechism, prayer, and very little written indigenous language sufficed; any other learning (including the English language) would
serve simply to make women servants for white masters and not properly
humble wives.[75] Pfanner's restrictive views for African women not only
stood in strict contrast to the goals of other institutions like Inanda, but
they also operated at loggerheads with the colonial administration, which
sought to pull African women into Natal's economy on terms amenable
to settlers. Pfanner's proclamations earned ire from both African and

settler women; one 1889 letter from the Mapumelo mission asserted that Pfanner was "two centuries behind the present times . . . an echo from the dark ages," who denied the coming "day when the now evident Zulu shall become enlightened men and women alike."[76] While Pfanner and other Mariannhill teachers actively discouraged bringing Africans into European service on the grounds that it increased interracial contact and led to corruption, they nonetheless deployed the rhetoric of labor, progress, and work to justify gendered distinctions in education.

Debates over domestic versus academic education also characterized discussions of settler women's education. E. J. Moore-Smith, the head-mistress of Ladies' College in Durban, summarized the main goals for women's education among settlers in Natal, arguing for training that made women more than "capable housewives and housekeepers," but women who could serve on committees and prove "fit wives for men who may at any time become leaders in the political and social life of Natal and South Africa."[77] At its heart, women's education sought to train new leaders among Natal's colonial elite. Moore-Smith's speech makes clear that this training served to make women intellectual partners for their presumed white male husbands, and to take on the duties of assisting in government, either through running committees, offering tactical advice, or efficiently offering general spousal support.

In general, settler government in Natal saw education as a necessary part of training and maintaining social power in the colony. Educational facilities became social as well as governmental institutions that facili-tated the creation and reproduction of raced and gendered hierarchies essential to the maintenance of hierarchical control in Natal. Education became a commodity highly prized by settler administrators and settler families alike; it allowed men and women to claim positions of signifi-cance within the colony, and it reinforced senses of moral and cultural superiority. The social capital offered by educational institutions allowed men and women to claim a share in the colony and a sense of responsi-bility that justified their minority claims to citizenship and suffrage in the colony. The social capital and civilizational distinction offered by educa-tion was a commodity that settler legislators attempted to jealously guard as the colony expanded. By the turn of the century Indian and African students had begun to make sustained claims to their own share of education, and risked upsetting the carefully created and reinforced raced and gendered hierarchies that bolstered settler rule. Consequently, discussions of education in nineteenth-century Natal offer a unique window into understanding larger fears over citizenship, suffrage, and inclusion in a deeply contested colonial society.

Refracting Futures in Natal and Beyond

In the years following the Anglo-Zulu War, Natal's settler government attempted to maintain control as the grand demographic equalizing they desired steadfastly refused to arrive. Throughout the 1890s, Natal's legislature passed increasingly restrictive legislation that put Indians and Africans under the permanent control of the white minority. Simultaneously, political and economic changes bound Natal ever more tightly to the other settler polities in southern Africa. The Boer War and eventual defeat of the Transvaal and Orange Free State resulted in a more tightly connected labor market, one that could more effectively lure African men from Natal to the gold and diamond fields. In addition, the granting of Responsible Government to Natal in 1893 led to increased settler control over indigenous and Indian affairs, limiting the potential for imperial intervention. By 1910, when Natal joined the Union of South Africa, the united settler governments had begun a systematic stripping of nonwhite suffrage and access to land, moves that would culminate in the hardening of legal means of exclusion under apartheid. The twentieth century saw the entrenchment of raced and gendered hierarchies of power in Natal and South Africa more generally. These hierarchies of power, however, have their origin in the second half of the nineteenth century in Natal.

Queering Colonial Natal is significantly influenced by much of the historiographical work developed as part of the so-called "imperial turn" in the last two decades of British history. These approaches emphasize the interconnectivity of the domestic and colonial realms, privileging social formations that challenge such an easy binary between at home and away.[1] When read alongside constant and creative indigenous attempts to respond to and reinterpret the terms of British claims of sovereignty, official metropolitan fears that settlers would be unable to maintain a discretely bounded area of control allow us to see how empire rarely functioned as core–periphery models have suggested, with power emanating from metropole outward. The disjuncture between the aspirations of officials and the actual experiences of colonists provides meaningful challenges to dominant rhetorics of empire. Studying how bodies move through colonial and frontier landscapes—and importantly, how multiple observers *interpreted* these movements—allows for an understanding of how power operated within an imperial context, an understanding that acknowledges *both* empire's incredible capacity for violence and the continuously incomplete attempts at enacting hegemony. Natal in the latter half of the nineteenth century provides an ideal site for such study, particularly as the settler population tended to identify themselves with Britain and the empire, even after the Boer War and on the eve of incorporation into the Union in 1910.[2]

Queering Colonial Natal has challenged historical interpretations that privilege either the idea of a domestic/imperial divide (where empire happened over there and was completely unknown to and non-influential in the domestic lives of metropolitan observers), or the idea that empire was an accidental development largely controlled by top-down action through Whitehall.[3] Rather, nineteenth-century British imperialism can be best understood as a kaleidoscopic array of overlapping connections.[4] Ties of print, affection, commerce, resistance, and migration linked men and women in Natal to varied and constantly changing points across the imperial landscape. To describe these points of connection as kaleidoscopic requires a moment of explanation; such a device provides symmetrical arrangements through mirrors, which refract only to the extent that exact repetition creates new arrangements.[5] Of course, the mimetic effects created between Natal and other points in the empire were far more aspirational than properly replicative. When settlers agitated for Responsible Government, they specifically drew upon precedents in other settler colonies and sought to define their political situation against a variety of nonsettler colonies throughout the empire, although they did not immediately reproduce conditions that occurred anywhere else. Likewise, Indian arrivants articulated a sense of common British subjecthood stretching from India to Natal to London when attempting to resist the settler state's racialized legislation, particularly in relation to alcohol in the 1890s. These purposeful invocations of other places within the empire demonstrate a profound, overlapping, and ever-changing assemblage of locations in pursuit of a variety of aims. Exchange between metropole and colony certainly did happen, and it undoubtedly operated with a power imbalance in favor of the metropole. But average citizens were aware of the empire, and did debate the meaning and significance of imperial reach and (inter)national politics. The interactions between Natal and the wider empire were myriad, mutable, and multidirectional as bodies and goods traveled within and without the colony.

The kaleidoscopic connections that linked Natal to the empire, particularly as a contemporary settler state, become salient in the discussions of race and masculinity that surround debates, laws, and resistance in the colony. As British settlers, Indian laborers, and African inhabitants sought to claim a sense of belonging in the colony, they interacted with, threatened, and directly confronted each other in Natal. The race and gendered identities that they co-created in relation to each other worked to structure the hierarchical formulations that undergirded settler society in Natal. The very nature of colonial occupation as well as land and labor appropriation required forms of discursive rationale. Settler notions of racial superiority and of patriarchal access to land were not fully formed on arrival but arose in daily collisions with varied actors in the colony. While discursively created through quotidian interactions, these ideas had material import: their creation helped to shape material realities of dispossession, legal restriction, and government actions against indigenous peoples and Indian laborers. The piecemeal legal solutions to separate Africans, Indians, and Europeans occurred through a lengthy process of trial, error, and innovation on the ground. When John Robinson declared in 1894 that "I think we may lay down as an axiom that the franchise right is a race privilege," he first referenced the history of interactions between Africans, Indians, and Europeans in the colony and made comparison to other settler societies to justify an idea of a whites-only vote.[6] Likewise, the 1880 debates over the Clothing of the Natives Bill revealed the histories of racial creation and hierarchy in the colony. Arguments for legally mandating Africans to be clothed relied primarily on the dangers that could arise from African male servants in proximity to young European children, an aspect of colonial service that had occurred in the previous decades in Natal. Various legislators then asked if clothing laws applied to Indians as well, and jokingly asked if they as white men were to be compelled to be clothed through legislation.[7] The constitutive creation of racial categories then became calcified through legal action in Natal.

This is not simply to argue that the colonial period in Natal, particularly after 1879, was some form of undifferentiated negotiation between settlers, indigenous peoples, and Indian migrants. Far from it; the settler state possessed considerable coercive power, supported by military might. Yet the attempts of settler elites to use state power to secure full advantage often shifted, faltered, or even failed in the face of resistance from Africans and Indians. Historians of early colonial Natal have frequently stressed the limited power of the state, and settler society in particular.[8] The queer indigenous theoretical approach in *Queering Colonial Natal* has privileged the power of rhetoric in the making of legal and political exclusions within the colony, rather than simple negotiation. This involves a serious reckoning with the economic coercion that fundamentally underpinned colonial policy in the British Empire of the late nineteenth century. Undoubtedly, British colonies—Crown as well as settler—were established in pursuit of resources and the securing of particular modes of production that benefitted the imperial state. Indeed, anxieties about proper forms of race and gender played fundamental roles in the pursuit of these economic objectives. While my methodology is deeply influenced by the work of critical theorists and cultural historians working primarily within the fields of indigenous studies and queer theory, this is not to presume that such observations are inattentive to the root economic structures that supported settler colonialism in Natal and elsewhere.

Consequently, this book takes seriously the contention that race and gender did not exist simply in the realm of the identitarian or "merely

cultural," divorced from the larger economic, legal, and political structures of colonial Natal.[9] As a colony of British settlement, Natal's racialized hierarchy privileged settlers and their descendants explicitly over the
indigenous inhabitants and subsequent Indian migrants both socially
and economically. The establishment of Native Law and orthodox forms
of marriage—for settlers as well as for indigenous peoples—pivoted
upon questions of state recognition of "proper families." These families
were undoubtedly connected to the political economy of the settler state.
Although opprobrium surrounding the believed impropriety of polygamy
and *ilobolo* filled both newspapers and speeches in the Legislative Council
in the 1850s and 1860s, white settlers relied upon indigenous demands
for cattle in marriage negotiations in order to compel them into working
on their farms for a wage. Indeed, many settlers viewed indigenous social
customs merely as obstacles to be removed to the achieving of European
prosperity—a prosperity ironically curtailed by the endemic racism of
the settler class.[10] This racist hierarchizing was not just stubbornness on
the part of Europeans that rendered them immune to economic opportunities; rather, it was the very discursive *and* economic mechanism that
undergirded the entire settler project in Natal, even if it worked against
their immediate material interests. The dilemma surrounding African
polygamy and other marriage practices existed expressly within the conflict of settler economic coercion and the effective resistance that indigenous social formations offered in the face of such pressure. As Judith
Butler has argued, "[T]he regulation of sexuality was systematically tied
to *the mode of production* proper to the functioning of political economy,"[11]
and in no place was this truer than in nineteenth-century Natal, where
settler legislatures argued over the proper forms of marital formation for
whites, Indians, and Africans with an eye specifically to the viability of
the colonial project.

　　Likewise, laws restricting alcohol access in nineteenth-century Natal
along racial lines demonstrated more than a cultural reading of settler
colonialism. Intoxicants represented commodities grown and created
within the confines of the colony, but more importantly, the consumption of intoxicants by nonwhite peoples in Natal served as a drag on settler economic productivity that demanded the compulsion of people of

color. The multiple attempts of settlers to render drinking a white (and relatively male) monopoly throughout the nineteenth century bespoke specifically raced forms of citizenship within Natal, but it also demonstrated the socioeconomic conditions of the colony itself. Indeed, race has operated not as a fig leaf covering the larger, lurking economic substructures of imperialism; racialization instead frequently conditions the very modalities of economic domination.[12]

Nineteenth-century Natal was more than a small British settler colony on the southeastern coast of Africa. It was a space of recurrent collision between a variety of peoples—British merchant, indigenous African, Indian migrant among them—where the logics of settlement and the politics of belonging refracted and cast multiple shadows across the landscape. While British settlers arriving in Natal imagined themselves as part of a larger contemporaneous movement of emigration and occupation that stretched across the globe, the specificities of Natal's demographic developments and the constant negotiation of indigenous peoples challenged this aspirational development. To live in Natal in the second half of the nineteenth century meant responding to a settler state that increasingly attempted to control the economic, social, and political dimensions of the colony, but never managed to fully subordinate its occupants. Natal's emergent settler state sought to monopolize claims to legitimacy and rightful occupation through appeals to stabilizing notions of race and gender. Yet missionaries, indigenous Africans, and Indian peoples all used these notions to stymy and challenge the state at every turn.

The post-apartheid South African state has inherited many of the colonial legacies of its predecessors. Larger questions of civilization, order, and control live on in an ostensibly postsettler colonial nation. While South Africa has transformed considerably (as the now-named province of KwaZulu-Natal can attest), it still retains many of the mechanisms of a state that secured power for a select few at the expense of a majority of its citizens. In addition, the ascendance of President Jacob Zuma in 2009 has revealed a complicated series of responses to the centuries of queering undertaken by a settler regime.

As with indigenous negotiations in the face of settler biopolitics a century before, contemporary Zulu attempts to use a discourse of tradition to reject the queering of their social formations can result in a blatant appeal to heteropatriarchy. These discursive attempts mirror earlier settler formulations of defining a sexual other outside of conceived normativity. While addressing a crowd in isiZulu in KwaZulu-Natal on Heritage Day in 2006, then Deputy President Jacob Zuma stunned observers by announcing bluntly that "as a man," he was personally against the idea of same-sex marriage, calling it "a disgrace to the nation and to God." Zuma further asserted that homosexuality was a repulsive and wholly foreign concept to Zulu culture, stating, "When I was growing up an *ungqingili* [a gay man] would not have stood in front of me. I would knock him out."[13] Roundly criticized by local and international organizations, Zuma tendered a half-apology for his statements.

This pattern seemed to be repeated when King Goodwill Zwelithini, the ceremonial head of the Zulu nation and direct descendant of Shaka's younger brother Mpande, made his own culturally articulated claims to Zulu heterosexuality. On January 22, 2012, standing before a crowd of observers marking the anniversary of the Battle of Isandlwana between Zulus and the British, Zwelithini allegedly claimed, "Traditionally, there were no people who engaged in same-sex relationships. There was nothing like that and if you do it, you must know that you are rotten."[14] In response to the media furor, the Zulu Royal House and other political figures claimed that the speech had been mistranslated. However, the language was ambiguous enough for Zulu speakers and linguists to conclude that it was more than likely that the king intended to demarcate homosexuality as nontraditional and "un-Zulu."[15] Despite national and international criticism, no apology was forthcoming from the Zulu Royal House.

These traditionalist recourses to antigay rhetoric are unsurprising given the context of British colonialism and the heteronormative logics of settlement. When indigenous sexuality was rendered *queer* in the eyes of British observers seeking to establish heteropatriarchal and biopolitical forms of control over the colonial spaces of Natal, Africans did not passively receive this designation. Although Zuma raged against British reporters' reinscriptions of colonial sexual stereotypes of his dehumanizingly excessive heterosexual appetites, he in other moments fell back upon a patriarchal assumption of power relationships and sexuality that echoed colonial assessments. When challenged in court during his well-publicized rape trial, Zuma asserted that he had no *need* to rape, for he was an *isoka*, a masculine man with enough prowess and activity to justify his desirability to women.[16] Such a response is laden with assumptions of masculine power and attraction as well as a "traditional" understanding of (hetero)sexual power dynamics. Zuma's defense, therefore, hinged upon deploying a rhetoric of powerful heteronormative masculinity, a move that underlined gender dynamics as normative rather than queerly excessive, as British observers had claimed in the previous century.

Public rejections of homosexuality as "un-Zulu" also reveal larger issues of race, colonialism, and modern sexuality. As Neville Hoad has demonstrated, African denunciations of homosexuality can also put pressure on the idea of gay or queer as a universal signifier.[17] First, such refutations discursively recognize the Western roots of gay (as well as LGBT) as an identitarian marker. Locating these universal categories as impositions over indigenous bodies underlines the ways that "settler definitions of modern sexuality became hegemonic for all non-Natives, as well as for Native people who sought ties to sexual modernity."[18] The individually realized sexual subject under the category of "gay" or "LGBT" resembles the normative sexual figure imagined as a product of European colonial violence against indigenous peoples. African scholars have noted for years that there may have been nothing inherently queer in their own societal terms about same-sex relationships or other forms of sexuality marked as aberrant by the settler state and closely allied Christian institutions.[19] To them, a postcolonial badge of solidarity with "queerness" may in itself serve to perpetuate new universals stamped upon African bodies by Westerners, this time by the evangelists of queer theory and sexual modernity. African rejections of homosexuality, particularly in a Zulu context, while undoubtedly perpetuating reprehensible justifications for violence against people who engage in nonheteronormative sexual activity, also potentially challenge the underlying assumptions of universal sexual subjects produced through colonial violence.

The entanglements of race, gender, class, and sexuality in contemporary South Africa flow in part from the contradictions of the settler colonial state. Studying discrete yet interlocking aspects of the colonial project in Natal—questions of state control over marriage and social reproduction for settlers as well as indigenous peoples, the legal managing of alcohol, the civilizational claims of the mission field over African and settler bodies, and finally, the politics of access to education in the colony—reveals the ways in which colonial inhabitants instrumentalized race and gender to claim legitimacy and belonging in a highly contested space. A queer indigenous reading of race and gender in Natal does more than simply illuminate the inner workings of a multiracial, complex colony in southern Africa. Rather, such a view allows us to see how questions of occupation, belonging, indigeneity, and settlement played out both in Natal, and across the wider expanse of the British Empire, challenging easy claims to power and authority, or at the very least, hoping to "unsettle" them.

Acknowledgments

This weird, weighty collection of words in front of you was only possible through the support and love of many people.

My book has multiple origin points, but two of them start at the University of Illinois, Urbana-Champaign, where I began a PhD under the enthusiastic direction of Antoinette Burton. Antoinette has remained a steadfast friend and ally over the past decade, and so much of my work has been produced in conversation with her whether while drinking a chai latte, sharing snarky asides, or pushing to develop a rage-based historic practice. While at Illinois, I also began taking isiZulu classes under the direction of Tholani Hlongwa and later Bheki Madela. Language classes culminated in a transformative summer with the Zulu Group Project Abroad (GPA) program sponsored by Fulbright-Hays in 2009. Learning with Audrey Mbeje, Thabile Mbatha, and Nelson Ntshangase and living with the Mkhize family in Manqongqo made me a better scholar and radically transformed the way I thought about living and working in Mzansi.

My time in South Africa has transformed me in so many ways. I have called Durban and Pietermaritzburg home often over the past decade, and I'm particularly grateful for the local community I've enjoyed in KwaZulu-Natal. I was extraordinarily fortunate to find an intellectual home in the final years of the History and African Studies seminar at

194   *Acknowledgments*

the University of KwaZulu-Natal, and I lament the breakup of such an intellectually rigorous and thoughtful group. Jeff Guy pushed me to be a better scholar in every way, and is profoundly missed. My heartfelt gratitude goes to Keith Breckenridge, Catherine Burns, Marijke Du Toit, Liezl Gevers, Karthigasen Gopalan, Eva Jackson, Vukile Khumalo, Baduduzile Luthuli, Ashley Morris, Simphiwe Ngwane, Kyla O'Neill, Julie Parle, Nafisa Essop Sheik, Stephen Sparks, Jo-Anne Tiedt, Goolam Vahed, Suhail Vawda, and Thembisa Waetjen for their wonderful conversations and good cheer. Mwelela Cele, at the Killie Campbell Africana Library, offered invaluable advice and needed friendship. Zama Gumede, Bongiwe Mbhele, Senzo Mkhize, and Mbali Zulu made navigating the difficulties of nineteenth-century archives easier, and I'm so very grateful. My subsequent trips back to South Africa to refine the manuscript were sustained by close friendships with dear friends across the country. Thank you so much to Liz Ampofo, the Basckin siblings (Daniel, Rachel, and Sophia), Lauren Beukes, Charl Blignaut, Kelly-Jo Bluen, Danielle Bowler, Scot Brimson, Dan and Stuart Buchanan, Louise Ferreira, Erin Fourie, Lauren Fox, Inger Harber, Dean Hutton, Vashna Jagarnath, Karen Jeynes, Marc and Liz Kalina, Mlungisi Khambule, Charl Landsberg, Shéla McCullough (and the entire clan), Gugulethu Mhlungu, T. O. Molefe, Samesh Naidoo, Zama Ndlovu, Jabu Ngema, Jen Norins, Amy Nortje, Mbali Ntuli, Mvelase Peppetta, Bob Perfect, Sekoetlane Phamodi, Richard Pithouse, Jonathan Ramayia, Dexter Sagar, Saadiq Soeker (Shiraz), Michelle Solomon, Melita Steele, Sita Suzanne, Liz Tilley, Damien Williams, and Melanie Winter.

This book could not have been contemplated or written without the support I received at Washington and Lee University in Lexington, Virginia. I loved serving in the history department, and I remain indebted to Molly Michelmore, Kameliya Atanasova, David Bello, Mikki Brock, Ted DeLaney, Sarah Horowitz, David Peterson, Nicolaas Rupke, and Stephanie Stillo. Molly deserves specific praise as a friend, department chair, manuscript reader, and absolute rock during my four years in Lexington. Multiple research trips to South Africa between 2015 and 2017 were sponsored by the university's Lenfest summer research fund, and a pretenure leave in the fall of 2017 allowed me the needed time and energy to finish the final manuscript. This essential funding of my work would have been impossible without the support of Jennifer Ashworth, Jinky Garrett, Kara Hemphill, Meredith McCoy, Taylor Anne Moffat, and Michelle Rothenberger. I have been fortunate indeed to work with an amazing intellectual community in the heart of the Shenandoah Valley and wish to thank Aaron Abrams, Kevin Beanland, Melina Bell, Rebecca Benefiel, Sarah Blythe, Christa Bowden, Alex Brown, Julie Phillips Brown, Elicia Cowins, Elizabeth Denne, Tamara Futrell, Deirdre Evans Garriott, Genelle Gertz, Leah Green, Paul Gregory, Adrienne Hagen, Maggie Shapiro Haskett, Mohamed Kamara, Wan-Chuan Kao, Suzanne Keen, Elliott King, Michael Laughy, Robin Le Blanc, Andrea Lepage, Jemma Levy, Ellen Mayock, Turk McCleskey, Rose Mary Sheldon, Elizabeth Teaff, Ricardo Wilson, and Paul Youngman.

Much of *Queering Colonial Natal* was inspired by conversations with the amazing students I worked with at Washington and Lee. Arlette Hernandez's brilliant analysis and critical observations made me a better thinker and scholar over our shared tenure at the university, and advising her capstone paper on the gaze of the colonial camera was one of the best moments of my career. I am also deeply indebted to the students of my Queering Colonialism seminar taught in fall 2015 and winter 2018 and wish to thank Trichia Braavi, Stephanie Chung, Dana DeSousa, Kelly Douma, Mililani Ganivet, Olivia Hunter, Brittany Lloyd, Mark Martin, Jack McGee, Edward Miller, Elizabeth Mugo, Matthew Rickert, Ben Schaeffer, Jake Sirota, and Muskaan Soni. Thanks also to students Adit Ahmed, Tyra Barrett, Teddy Corcoran, Samuel Gibson, Ayub Herman, Catherine Hoy, Truth Iyiewuare, Makayla Lorick, JoAnn Michel, Cloy Onyango, Alejandro Paniagua, Joelle Simeu, and Shaun Soman.

Living and working in Confederatelandia was, to put it mildly, a challenge. But the constant care of people around me made life possible. I could not have learned to find my way or appreciate so much of the world around with me without the endless kindness and inspired insights of Deborah Miranda. My community of friends and colleagues in Staunton has sustained me over many a dreary day. Endless thanks to Shandra Aber, Chris Beery, Raven Beverage, Sydney Bufkin, Bree Carr, Claire Casto, Matt Casto, Joseph Clemmer, Jason Fitchko, Austin Hatter, Coye Heard, Jims Hinkle, Thomas Hurt, Meg Johnson, Steve McCormick, Rocky Parker, Bobby Perkins, Will Rinaldo, Scott Roberts, James Larrick Rule, Abby Shirkey, Pete Stallings, Tina Stelling, Scott Toombs, Lily van Diepen, Dee Williams, and Megan Williams. Caleb Dance has been my closest friend in this strange valley, and I treasure the conversations, absurdities, and general survival strategies we shared in a never-ending confederacy. Charmi Neeley has pulled me back from more ledges than I can recall, and Cassie Knick always helped me fight another day. Being adopted informally into the family of Lyndon Sayers and Florentien Verhage kept me sane on many a hectic afternoon; spending time with Sam and Owen Sayers also kept me grounded when anxiety or rage seemed to pop up unbidden.

I'm generally terrible at sequestering myself away to write (although I did a decent amount of final revisions at home); this is very much a book written and theorized in coffee shops. To that end, I must mention Blue Mountain Coffee, Pronto Gelateria, The By and By, The Bean Green, and Coffee Cartel—thank you for putting up with a bleary-eyed professor with a laptop and a half-smile who squinted at an electronic box for hours on end at one of your tables. Many thanks to the veritable army of people who have offered to read through chapters, stumble through drafts, and help untangle the Gordian knots of my tortured prose. Sincerest thanks to Anne-Marie Angelo, Jason Bruner, Emily Burrill, Meghan Healy-Clancy, Karen Kelsky, Jessica Levy, Dan Magaziner, Victor Roman Mendoza, Joseph Pierce, Liz Thornberry, Coll Thrush, Wendy Urban-Mead, Sarah Watkins, and Michael Yarbrough. Jill Kelly and Lauren Jarvis saw me through every step of the writing process, and I'm indebted to their kind hectoring and brilliant feedback.

I want to thank my new community at the University of San Diego who have welcomed me kindly as I finished the final pages of this book. I'm glad to be part of the history department and to work with scholars and friends including Ryan Abrecht, Tom Barton, Jason Crum, Josen Diaz, Colin Fisher, Michael Gonzalez, Jim Gump, Persephone Lewis,

Molly McClain, Channon Miller, Clara Oberle, Mychal Odom, Kenneth Serbin, Kathryn Statler, and Yi Sun.

Portions of this book have been workshopped, partially published, and transmuted under the careful eyes of friends and editors. Chapter 2 was workshopped at the Symposium for Global Cultural Encounters between the Material and the Immaterial, 1750–1950, held at the University of Michigan in 2017. I'm particularly grateful to Stefan Hübner, Simon Layton, Harry Liebersohn, Elizabeth Matsushita, Ted Sammons, J. Barton Scott, Teresa Segura-Gaura, Fenneke Sysling, Emma Thomas, Kira Thurman, Moritz von Brescius, Shuang Wen, Albert Wu, meLe Yamomo, and Yurou Zhong for their feedback. Specific thanks must go to the great people at the University of Minnesota Press, especially my incredibly supportive editor Jason Wiedemann. Thanks also to Neville Hoad and Alan Lester for their generous reading of the manuscript in various stages.

Writing a book is an exercise in terror and narcissism, and I am so grateful for the people who put up with me at my weirdest and most ridiculous, who showed me new paths and who made it all seem less terrifying. How lucky am I to thank all y'all—R. Shawn Abrahams, Wendy Belcher, Annie Bethancourt, Sarah Bond, Crystal and Finn Boson, Alex and Tim Briggs, Andrew Brown, Brandi Brown, Kevin Butt, Amber Butts, Jodi Byrd, Nancy Caciola, Joshua Cerretti, Marisa Charley, Lauren Cole, Terri Coleman, Tequlia Cooper, Margaret Dickerson, Kim Yi Dionne, Rachel Dobric, Suz Fisher, Mick Gieskes, Jim and Kelsey Goodwin, Daniel Gonzales, Brian Henry, Amenie Hopkins, Sue Haglund, Kim Icreverzi, Cáel M. Keegan, Mark Kurai, Danielle Lorenz, Anastasia McGee, Munier Ahmad Nazeer and Mitsuko Clemmons-Nazeer, Cassie Osei, Yumi Pak, Shaista Patel, CJ Penso, Stella Won Phelps, Archana Prakash, Melissa Rhoades-Rudder, Ginny Robinson, Zach Sell, Brett Shadle, Mel Shaw, Leah Smith-Enciso, David Tong, Katie Walkiewicz, Theresa Warburton, Rob Wildeman, and Barb Yau. Mark Daku has been an incredible travel companion and a participant in havoc from Maputo to Fort Worth. Joanna Davis-McElligatt has listened to every one of my fears, pushed me to be a better scholar, and reminded me to be accountable to multiple sets of ancestors.

My family, especially Bill, Violet, Daniel, Kristen, Michelle, Mike, Cathy, Sherry, Denise, Theresia, Pam, Shamika, and Shauntay—thank you for holding me all these years. Dorothy Dresser, I miss your quotidian love every day. Above all, thank you Diana Tallie, the best mother in the universe. All the good things I am in this life are due to her; the bad parts are entirely my fault.

I still can't believe I wrote a book, y'all.

Notes

Archival Sources

Killie Campbell Africana Library, Durban, South Africa
  Debates from the Natal Legislature
  Natal Evangelical Alliance
National Archives, Kew, London, United Kingdom
  Colonial Secretary Office files (CSO)
Pietermaritzburg Archives Repository (PAR), Pietermaritzburg, South Africa
  Attorney General's Office files (AGO)
  Colonial Secretary Office files (CSO)
  Secretary for Native Affairs Office files (SNA)
Rhodes House, Bodleian Library, Oxford University, Oxford, United Kingdom
  Natal Missionary Files
  Cecil Yonge Scrapbook

Introduction

1. The term Nguni language speakers is somewhat unwieldy to describe the African peoples who lived in Natal prior to British annexation, but it underscores the lack of a unifying descriptor for these groups in the 1830s and 1840s. Historians have discussed at length the process by which these peoples came to be known as Zulu, and their disparate dialects systematized as isiZulu. Much of this process took place throughout the colonial period, in response to settler attempts to achieve hegemonic control in the colony. In general, I will use the terms "indigenous" and "African" interchangeably to describe these Nguni language speakers throughout the book, and occasionally "Zulu" where such designation seems most appropriate. For more on the complexities of these terms see Jeff Guy, *The Destruction of the Zulu Kingdom: Civil War in Zululand 1879–84*, 3rd ed. (Pietermaritzburg: University of

KwaZulu-Natal Press, 1994); Benedict Carton, John Laband, and Jabulani Sithole, *Zulu Identities: Being Zulu, Past and Present* (New York: Columbia University Press, 2009); Michael R. Mahoney, *The Other Zulus: The Spread of Zulu Ethnicity in Colonial South Africa* (Durham, N.C.: Duke University Press, 2012); Robert J. Houle, *Making African Christianity: Africans Reimagining Their Faith in Colonial South Africa* (Bethlehem, Pa.: Lehigh University Press, 2011); Norman Etherington, *Preachers, Peasants, and Politics in South East Africa, 1835–1880: African Communities in Natal, Pondoland, and Zululand* (London: Royal Historical Society, 1978); Peter Limb, Norman A. Etherington, and Peter Midgley, eds., *Grappling with the Beast: Indigenous Southern African Responses to Colonialism, 1840–1930* (Boston: Brill, 2010).

2. By this I mean largely the Anglophone settler colonies/societies of Canada, Australia, New Zealand, and the United States. The demographic was similar in Natal's contemporary colonial neighbor, the Cape Colony, and there was even more demographic disparity in British settler colonies in the twentieth century, namely British East Africa (Kenya) and Rhodesia (Zimbabwe). Natal joined the Union of South Africa in 1910.

3. As Michael Mahoney has convincingly argued, the "Natal Africans" of the mid-nineteenth century were not a homogenous "Zulu group," as they would later become under more centralized colonial intervention and indigenous resistance in the later colonial and early Union period. Mahoney, *The Other Zulus.*

4. Mary Anne Barker, *A Year's Housekeeping in South Africa*, 2nd ed. (London: Macmillan, 1879), 207.

5. Henry Rider Haggard, *Cetywayo and His White Neighbours; or, Remarks on Recent Events in Zululand, Natal, and the Transvaal*, 2nd ed. (London: Trubner & Co., 1888), 68.

6. A considerable amount of scholarship exists on indigenous forms of resistance, accommodation, and reinterpretation to nineteenth-century British imperialism; of these, some of the more relevant examples are Keletso E. Atkins, *The Moon Is Dead! Give Us Our Money! The Cultural Origins of an African Work Ethic, Natal, South Africa, 1843–1900* (Portsmouth, UK: Heinemann, 1993); Elizabeth Elbourne, *Blood Ground: Colonialism, Missions, and the Contest for Christianity in the Cape Colony and Britain, 1799–1853* (Toronto: McGill-Queen's University Press, 2008); Jean Comaroff and John L. Comaroff, *Of Revelation and Revolution*, Vol. 1: *Christianity, Colonialism, and Consciousness in South Africa*, 1st ed. (Chicago: University of Chicago Press, 1991); Clifton C. Crais, *White Supremacy and Black Resistance in Pre-Industrial South Africa: The Making of the Colonial Order in the Eastern Cape, 1770–1865* (Cambridge: Cambridge University Press, 1992).

7. Tony Ballantyne, *Orientalism and Race: Aryanism in the British Empire*, Cambridge Imperial and Post-Colonial Studies Series (Houndmills, UK: Palgrave, 2002).

8. Judith Butler, "Imitation and Gender Subordination," in *Inside/Out: Lesbian Theories, Gay Theories*, ed. Diana Fuss, illustrated ed. (New York: Routledge, 1991), 307–20.

9. Robert Morrell, *From Boys to Gentlemen: Settler Masculinity in Colonial Natal, 1880–1920* (Pretoria: UNISA, 2001).

10. Benedict Carton, *Blood from Your Children: The Colonial Origins of Generational Conflict in South Africa* (Charlottesville: University of Virginia Press, 2000); Jeff Guy, "An Accommodation of Patriarchs: Theophilus Shepstone and the Foundations of the System of Native Administration in Natal" (Paper presented to the Conference on Masculinities in Southern Africa, University of Natal, Durban, 1997); Mark Hunter, *Love in the Time of AIDS: Inequality, Gender, and Rights in South Africa* (Bloomington: Indiana University Press, 2010).

11. Michel Foucault, *The History of Sexuality*, Vol. 1: *An Introduction*, trans. Robert Hurley (New York: Vintage, 1990); Ann Laura Stoler, *Race and the Education of Desire: Foucault's History of Sexuality and the Colonial Order of Things* (Durham, N.C.: Duke University Press, 1995); Ann Laura Stoler, *Carnal Knowledge and Imperial Power: Race and the Intimate in Colonial Rule* (Berkeley: University of California Press, 2002).

12. Anne McClintock, *Imperial Leather: Race, Gender, and Sexuality in the Colonial Contest* (New York: Routledge, 1995).

13. Qwo-Li Driskill, Chris Finley, Brian Joseph Gilley, and Scott Lauria Morgensen, eds., *Queer Indigenous Studies: Critical Interventions in Theory, Politics, and Literature* (Tucson: University of Arizona Press, 2011); Lorenzo Veracini, *Settler Colonialism: A Theoretical Overview* (New York: Palgrave Macmillan, 2010); Jodi A. Byrd, *The Transit of Empire: Indigenous Critiques of Colonialism* (Minneapolis: University of Minnesota Press, 2011); Caroline Elkins and Susan Pedersen, *Settler Colonialism in the Twentieth Century: Projects, Practices, Legacies*, 1st ed. (New York: Routledge, 2005); Annie Coombes, ed., *Rethinking Settler Colonialism: History and Memory in Australia, Canada, New Zealand, and South Africa* (Manchester: Manchester University Press, 2006); Scott Lauria Morgensen, *Spaces between Us: Queer Settler Colonialism and Indigenous Decolonization* (Minneapolis: University of Minnesota Press, 2011); Andrea Smith, "Queer Theory and Native Studies: The Heteronormativity of Settler Colonialism.," *GLQ: A Journal of Lesbian & Gay Studies* 16, no. 1–2 (2010): 1–2, https://doi.org/Abstract.

14. Some of the limited examples of settler colonial theorizing in Natal can be found in Morrell, *From Boys to Gentlemen*; Jeff Guy, *Theophilus Shepstone and the Forging of Natal: African Autonomy and Settler Colonialism in the Making of Traditional Authority* (Pietermaritzburg: University of KwaZulu-Natal Press, 2013); Nafisa Essop Sheik, "Customs in Common: Marriage, Law, and the Making of Difference in Colonial Natal," *Gender & History* 29, no. 3 (November 2017): 1–16.

15. When referring to settlers I prefer to use the terms "autochthony" and "autochthonous" to differentiate from indigeneity and indigenous and to seek to avoid using the term "native" where possible, given its particularly vexing history in southern Africa. Autochthony is different in this context as it seeks to be a replacement form of indigeneity, one that is claimed and understood through previous claims of indigenous peoples.

16. Patrick Wolfe, "Settler Colonialism and the Elimination of the Native," *Journal of Genocide Research* 8, no. 4 (2006): 388.

17. Great Britain Parliament and Thomas Curson Hansard, *Hansard's Parliamentary Debates*, vol. 116 (London: Hansard, 1851), 272–76.

18. Charles Barter, *The Dorp and the Veld; or, Six Months in Natal* (London: William S. Orr and Co., 1852), 171–72.

19. Aileen Moreton-Robinson, "Whiteness, Epistemology, and Indigenous Representation," in *Whitening Race: Essays in Social and Cultural Criticism* (Canberra: Aboriginal Studies Press, 2004), 75–88.

20. Sara Ahmed, *Queer Phenomenology: Orientations, Objects, Others* (Durham, N.C.: Duke University Press, 2006).

21. Mark Rifkin, *When Did Indians Become Straight? Kinship, the History of Sexuality, and Native Sovereignty* (New York: Oxford University Press, 2011); Cathy J. Cohen, "Punks, Bulldaggers, and Welfare Queens: The Radical Potential of Queer Politics?," *GLQ: A Journal of Lesbian and Gay Studies* 3, no. 4 (May 1997): 437–65.

22. Driskill et al., eds., *Queer Indigenous Studies*; Morgensen, *Spaces between Us*; Byrd, *The Transit of Empire*.

23. Morgensen, *Spaces between Us*, 18, emphasis in original.

24. Lee Edelman, *No Future: Queer Theory and the Death Drive* (Durham, N.C.: Duke University Press, 2004).

25. This is best demonstrated in the nineteenth century when Zulu men claimed that the ostensibly "queer" practice of polygamy as a means of shoring up traditional patriarchal power over women, lest they become known as *onindindwa* (wanderers), women of dubious moral character without a male figure to guide them. For more on this, see T.J. Tallie, "Queering Natal Settler Logics and the Disruptive Challenge of Zulu Polygamy," *GLQ: A Journal of Lesbian and Gay Studies* 19, no. 2 (2013): 167–89, https://doi.org/10.1215/1064 2684-1957195.

26. Ifi Amadiume, *Male Daughters, Female Husbands: Gender and Sex in an African Society*, illustrated ed. (London: Zed Books, 1987); Neville Hoad, *African Intimacies: Race, Homosexuality, and Globalization*, 1st ed. (Minneapolis: University of Minnesota Press, 2007); Marc Epprecht, *Heterosexual Africa? The History of an Idea from the Age of Exploration to the Age of AIDS*, New African Histories Series (Athens: Ohio University Press, 2008).

27. Cohen, "Punks, Bulldaggers, and Welfare Queens"; Rifkin, *When Did Indians Become Straight?*

28. Gayle Rubin, "Thinking Sex: Notes for a Radical Theory on the Politics of Sexuality," in *Pleasure and Danger: Exploring Female Sexuality*, ed. Carole S. Vance (London: Routledge and Kegan Paul, 1984), 267–319; Frantz Fanon, "The Fact of Blackness," in *Black Skin, White Masks*, trans. Charles L. Markmann (New York: Grove Press, 1968), 109–40.

29. Sylvia Tamale, "Researching and Theorising Sexualities," in *African Sexualities: A Reader*, ed. Sylvia Tamale (Nairobi: Pambazuka Press, 2011), 11–36.

30. Marc Epprecht, *Hungochani: The History of a Dissident Sexuality in Southern Africa*, 1st ed. (Montreal: McGill-Queen's University Press, 2004); Tamale, "Researching and Theorising Sexualities," 26–28; Epprecht, *Heterosexual Africa?*; Hoad, *African Intimacies*.

31. Andrew Spiegel, "Revealing a Popular South African Deceit: The Ethical Challenges of an Etymological Enterprise," in *The Ethics of Anthropology: Debates and Dilemmas*, ed. Pat Caplan (New York: Routledge, 2004), 213.

32. Zackie Achmat, "'Apostles of Civilised Vice': 'Immoral Practices' and 'Unnatural Vice' in South African Prisons and Compounds, 1890–1920," *Social Dynamics* 19, no. 2 (1993): 92–110.

1. "That Shameful Trade in a Person"

1. British settlers referred to *ilobolo* variously as bride price, wife-buying, and "reverse dowry," but I choose to use the isiZulu term as its translation is rather difficult to capture in English. Some settlers noticed this as well; several writers simply referred to the practice by its verb form, *ukulobola*, in English texts. I do, however, use the less precise term "polygamy" rather than polygyny or even *isithembu* as it was nearly universally rendered as such by English speakers during the period.

2. Aileen Moreton-Robinson, "Whiteness, Epistemology, and Indigenous Representation," in *Whitening Race: Essays in Social and Cultural Criticism*, ed. Aileen Moreton-Robinson (Canberra: Aboriginal Studies Press, 2004), 75–88.

3. Daniel Heath Justice, Mark Rifkin, and Bethany Schneider, "Introduction," *GLQ: A Journal of Lesbian and Gay Studies* 16, no. 1–2 (2010): 5–39, doi:10.1215/10642684-2009-011.

4. Mark Rifkin, *When Did Indians Become Straight? Kinship, the History of Sexuality, and Native Sovereignty* (New York: Oxford University Press, 2011); Cathy J. Cohen, "Punks, Bulldaggers, and Welfare Queens: The Radical Potential of Queer Politics?," *GLQ: A Journal of Lesbian and Gay Studies* 3, no. 4 (May 1997): 437–65; Scott Lauria Morgensen, *Spaces between Us: Queer Settler Colonialism and Indigenous Decolonization* (Minneapolis: University of Minnesota Press, 2011).

5. This futurity was not unidirectional; African men and women also struggled against settler attempts to challenge their own social and cultural reproduction. See Meghan Healy-Clancy, *A World of Their Own: A History of South African Women's Education* (Charlottesville: University of Virginia Press,

2014); Meghan Elisabeth Healy, "'Like a Family': Global Models, Familial Bonds, and the Making of an American School for Zulu Girls," *Safundi* 11, no. 3 (n.d.): 279–300; Benedict Carton, *Blood from Your Children: The Colonial Origins of Generational Conflict in South Africa* (Charlottesville: University of Virginia Press, 2000); Teresa A. Barnes, *We Women Worked So Hard: Gender, Urbanization, and Social Reproduction in Colonial Harare, Zimbabwe, 1930–1956* (Oxford: James Currey, 1999).

6. Eric Hobsbawm and Terence Ranger, *The Invention of Tradition* (Cambridge: Cambridge University Press, 1992).

7. Renisa Mawani, *Colonial Proximities: Crossracial Encounters and Juridical Truths in British Columbia, 1871–1921* (Vancouver: University of British Columbia Press, 2009).

8. Keletso E. Atkins, *The Moon Is Dead! Give Us Our Money! The Cultural Origins of an African Work Ethic, Natal, South Africa, 1843–1900* (Portsmouth, UK: Heinemann, 1993), 32–44; Carton, *Blood from Your Children*; Sean Hanretta, "Women, Marginality, and the Zulu State: Women's Institutions and Power in the Early Nineteenth Century," *Journal of African History* 39, no. 3 (1998): 389–415.

9. Atkins, *The Moon Is Dead!*, 42. Atkins specifically traces the ways in which *ilobolo* could be used to acknowledge investment in the labor of a new wife in an *umuzi* while acknowledging the reciprocal debt to be paid in order to provide for future *ilobolo* for the new wife's daughters.

10. See Jeff Guy, "Analysing Pre-Capitalist Societies in Southern Africa," *Journal of Southern African Studies* 14, no. 1 (1987): 18–37; Hanretta, "Women, Marginality, and the Zulu State"; Benedict Carton, John Laband, and Jabulani Sithole, *Zulu Identities: Being Zulu, Past and Present* (New York: Columbia University Press, 2009), 111–21.

11. A brief list includes David Dale Buchanan, "The Polygamy Question," *Natal Witness*, February 8, 1856; Natal Evangelical Alliance (Durban Sub-Division), *Polygamy and Woman-Slavery in Natal: Report of a Special Committee Appointed by the Durban Sub-Division of the Natal Evangelical Alliance: Adopted at the Annual Meeting of the Society, Held in the Wesleyan Chapel, Durban, May 23, 1861* (Durban: "Natal Mercury" Office, 1861); Natal (Colony), *Questions Offered by, and Replies Transmitted to, the Select Committee of the Legislative Council of Natal, Appointed 6th June, 1861, to Collect Information on the Subject of Polygamy, as Now Practiced among the Natives, and Its Attendant Evils, with a View to the Initiation of a Policy for the Suppression of the Same* (Pietermaritzburg: P. Davis and Sons, 1863); Hyman Augustine Wilder, *A Review of Dr. Colenso's Remarks on Polygamy: As Found Existing in Converts from Heathenism* (Durban: J. Cullingworth, 1856); Thomas Phipson, *Letters and Other Writings of a Natal Sheriff: Thomas Phipson, 1815–76*, ed. Ralph N. Currey (Cape Town: Oxford University Press, 1968); Josiah Tyler, *Forty Years among the Zulus* (Boston: Congregational Sunday-School and Publishing Society, 1891); James Erasmus Methley,

The New Colony of Port Natal; With Information for Emigrants. Accompanied with an Explanatory Map by the Government Official Surveyor, 3rd ed. (London: Houlston & Stoneman, 1850).

12. *Natal Mercury*, March 23, 1869.

13. Perhaps most (in)famously, Natal settler John Dunn eventually married forty-eight Zulu women and served as a counselor to the Zulu King Cetshwayo in the 1860s and 1870s, demonstrating a perhaps extreme case of settler departure from gendered/raced norms that were being developed. Henry Francis Fynn, the first British settler in Natal in 1824, married a Zulu woman and had children before eventually discarding his wife in favor of a European partner and respectable family in the 1850s. For more on British Columbia and New Zealand, see Adele Perry, *On the Edge of Empire: Gender, Race, and the Making of British Columbia, 1849–1871*, Studies in Gender and History (Toronto: University of Toronto Press, 2001); Tony Ballantyne and Antoinette Burton, *Moving Subjects: Gender, Mobility, and Intimacy in an Age of Global Empire*, illustrated ed. (Urbana: University of Illinois Press, 2008); Mawani, *Colonial Proximities*.

14. An October 13, 1848, article in the *Natal Witness* condemned the report of a white man "purchasing" an African wife, like cattle, demonstrating an ostensible failure in the raced and gendered forms of respectability that were developing in a colonial context. For more on disciplining settler marital practices in colonial Natal, see Nafisa Essop Sheik, "Colonial Rites: Custom, Marriage Law, and the Making of Difference in Natal, 1830s–c. 1910" (PhD diss., University of Michigan, 2012); Robert Morrell, *From Boys to Gentlemen: Settler Masculinity in Colonial Natal, 1880–1920* (Pretoria: UNISA, 2001); T.J. Tallie, "Racialised Masculinity and the Limits of Settlement: John Dunn and Natal, 1879–1883," *Journal of Natal and Zulu History* 30, no. 1 (2012), http://www .history.ukzn.ac.za/ojs/index.php/jnzh/article/view/1327; Charles Ballard, *John Dunn: The White Chief of Zululand* (Johannesburg: Ad. Donker, 1985).

15. Perry, *On the Edge of Empire*; Mawani, *Colonial Proximities*; Marilyn Lake and Henry Reynolds, *Drawing the Global Colour Line* (Cambridge: Cambridge University Press, 2008).

16. *Natal Mercury*, February 18, 1863. This is a consistent theme in the *Natal Mercury* and the *Natal Witness*, particularly surrounding the passage of Law 1 of 1869, which is discussed further in this chapter.

17. David John Welsh, *The Roots of Segregation: Native Policy in Colonial Natal, 1845–1910* (Oxford: Oxford University Press, 1971), 21–23.

18. Welsh, *The Roots of Segregation*, 33.

19. Shepstone was first made "agent" for the native tribes in 1845 in Natal, and officially named secretary of native affairs by the mid-1850s, a position he held until his retirement in 1877.

20. Quoted in Welsh, *Roots of Segregation*, 34.

21. Quoted in the *Natal Mercury*, February 18, 1869.

22. G. Duff, cited in Methley, *The New Colony of Port Natal*, 44–45.

23. This was not universally the case; beginning in the 1880s, a sizeable community of Trappist Catholic monks established a community near Durban. They will be discussed further in chapters 4 and 5.

24. Norman Etherington, *Preachers, Peasants, and Politics in South East Africa, 1835–1880: African Communities in Natal, Pondoland, and Zululand* (London: Royal Historical Society, 1978).

25. These years are controversial; Colenso was deposed as bishop by the bishop of Cape Town in 1863, although the Privy Council in London overturned this, and Colenso remained the legal bishop of Natal until his death in 1883. See Jeff Guy, *The Heretic: A Study of the Life of John William Colenso, 1814–1883* (Johannesburg: Ravan Press, 1983).

26. John William Colenso, *Remarks on the Proper Treatment of Cases of Polygamy: As Found Already Existing in Converts from Heathenism* (Pietermaritzburg: May & Davis, 1855), 15.

27. Wilder, *A Review of Dr. Colenso's Remarks on Polygamy*, 32–33.

28. Wilder, *A Review of Dr. Colenso's Remarks on Polygamy*, 33, emphasis in original.

29. Buchanan, "The Polygamy Question."

30. Indeed, this would be the larger series of charges brought against Bishop Colenso in the 1850s; the archbishop of Cape Town sought to remove him on the grounds of subverting the proper doctrines of the church and for acting outside of the normalizing scripts he imagined state-sanctioned Anglicanism must take.

31. Wilder, *A Review of Dr. Colenso's Remarks on Polygamy*, 29.

32. This may be somewhat ironic, given the frequently failure of missionaries to conform to these ideals themselves. See also Richard Price, *Making Empire: Colonial Encounters and the Creation of Imperial Rule in Nineteenth-Century Africa* (Cambridge: Cambridge University Press, 2008); Etherington, *Preachers, Peasants, and Politics in South East Africa, 1835–1880*; Elizabeth Elbourne, *Blood Ground: Colonialism, Missions, and the Contest for Christianity in the Cape Colony and Britain, 1799–1853* (Toronto: McGill-Queen's University Press, 2008).

33. Marc Epprecht, *Heterosexual Africa? The History of an Idea from the Age of Exploration to the Age of AIDS*, New African Histories Series (Athens: Ohio University Press, 2008).

34. *Natal Witness*, October 13, 1848.

35. *Natal Witness*, April 24, 1857.

36. *Natal Witness*, November 21, 1851.

37. Welsh, *The Roots of Segregation*, 77–81.

38. Thomas V. McClendon, *White Chief, Black Lords: Shepstone and the Colonial State in Natal, South Africa, 1845–1878* (Rochester, N.Y.: University of Rochester Press, 2010), 85.

39. M. W. Pinkerton, "Ukulobolisa," *Natal Magazine* 4, no. 14 (March 1879): 90.

40. McClendon, *White Chief, Black Lords*, 131.

41. PAR, SNA, 1/7/8, pp. 18–23. T. Shepstone, "Memorandum: Registration of Native Marriages." March 22, 1869, cited in Sheik, "Colonial Rites," 116.

42. One of the few supporters of Shepstone in this period was Bishop Colenso, who also advocated a somewhat unpopular position of limited tolerance for indigenous social customs. Guy, *The Heretic*.

43. H. E. Stainbank, "The Native Question," *Natal Mercury*, March 4, 1869.

44. Stainbank, "The Native Question."

45. "Editorial," *Natal Mercury*, March 23, 1869.

46. While David Welsh and Mahmood Mamdani argue more for an interlocking "Shepstone system" that set a model for later segregation systems throughout the continent, the ad hoc nature of his thirty-year policies remain a more convincing analysis, a viewpoint argued by Jeff Guy in his final work. See Welsh, *The Roots of Segregation*; Mahmood Mamdani, *Citizen and Subject: Contemporary Africa and the Legacy of Late Colonialism* (Princeton, N.J.: Princeton University Press, 1996); Jeff Guy, *Theophilus Shepstone and the Forging of Natal: African Autonomy and Settler Colonialism in the Making of Traditional Authority* (Scottsville, S.A.: University of Kwazulu Natal Press, 2013). For more on Shepstone's theatrical displays of authority, see Carolyn Hamilton, *Terrific Majesty: The Powers of Shaka Zulu and the Limits of Historical Invention* (Cambridge, Mass.: Harvard University Press, 1998); McClendon, *White Chief, Black Lords*.

47. I. N. Adams, "Ngokulobolisa," *Ikwezi*, February 1864. I am grateful to Mwelela Cele for his patience with my faltering translations of nineteenth-century Zulu.

48. Adams, "Ngokulobolisa." "Yitini imvelo yawo baba, ku nqala uku yi yeka into yakiti ukuti loku ukulobolisa ku vela ngamahloni, okuti intengo umuntu."

49. Pinkerton, "Ukulobolisa."

50. Pinkerton, "Ukulobolisa."

51. Natal Evangelical Alliance (Durban Sub-Division), *Polygamy and Woman-Slavery in Natal*, 14, emphasis in original.

52. Tyler, *Forty Years among the Zulus*, 129.

53. "Zulu Contact with the Civilized Races" (c. 1898), James Stuart Collection, vol. 27, p. 9, Killie Campbell Africana Library, Durban, South Africa.

54. Magema Fuze (Magwaza), "Ku Mhleli We Nkanyiso," *Inkanyiso Yase Natal*, January 17, 1891.

55. As a consequence, these *onondindwa* are queer figures from a Zulu standpoint; they represent a form of aberrant, non-normative sexuality as a consequence of the colonial encounter. I'm grateful for the insight of Meghan Healy-Clancy here.

56. Natal (Colony), *Report of the Natal Native Commission, 1881–2* (Pietermaritzburg: Vause, Slatter & Co., 1882), 20–33.

57. Natal (Colony), *Report of the Natal Native Commission, 1881–2*. For more on Edendale, see chapter 4.

58. Natal (Colony), *Report of the Natal Native Commission, 1881–2*, 90–110.

59. Guy, "An Accommodation of Patriarchs"; Carton, *Blood from Your Children*. However, this remains a far from uncontested assertion. The sharpest criticism of the patriarchal alliance theory comes from Teresa Barnes in her study of African women in colonial Zimbabwe. Barnes argues that the alliance theory is too simplistic and overinscribes patriarchy as a defining factor in African men's decisions, while negating the persuasive and collective power of women. Barnes, *We Women Worked So Hard*.

60. Natal (Colony), *Report of the Natal Native Commission, 1881–2*, 144–90.

61. Natal (Colony), *Report of the Natal Native Commission, 1881–2*, 172.

62. Natal (Colony), *Report of the Natal Native Commission, 1881–2*, 161. This reference almost certainly is directly translated from the Zulu word *onondindwa*, meaning "prostitute," but literally "one who wanders."

63. Natal (Colony), *Report of the Natal Native Commission, 1881–2*, 191.

64. Sheik, "Colonial Rites," 75–78.

65. "Editorial," *Natal Witness*, July 17, 1877.

66. "Editorial," *Natal Witness*, July 17, 1877.

67. Observer, "Matrimonial," *Natal Witness*, July 24, 1877.

68. Edelman, *No Future*, 28. This is not to argue that Nguni-speaking peoples saw themselves as queer; rather, that settlers sought to render them as discursively so for their own purposes; indigenous peoples saw their own formations as relatively normative and often made recourse to their own normative claims to challenge settlers.

69. This nonetheless created significant ambiguity within the legal record. As late as 1907, magistrates wrote to the protector of Indian immigrants inquiring about the status of mixed-faith marriages between Christians and Hindus. There is no clear answer in the record what the procedure would be. PAR, folder II 1/154 I2227/1907.

70. R. L. Hitchins and G. W. Sweeney, eds., *Statutes of Natal*, vol. 1 (Pietermaritzburg: P. Davis & Sons, 1900), 21–22.

71. Hitchins and Sweeney, *Statutes of Natal*, 1:22.

72. South African Native Affairs Commission, 1903–1905, *Minutes of Evidence*, Vol. 3: *Take in the Colony of Natal* (Cape Town: Cape Times Limited, 1904), 938–39.

73. Clipping of "Polygamy among Indians," *Natal Advertiser*, March 8, 1899, PAR, folder II I/95 I1961A/1899.

74. "Polygamy among Indians."

75. South African Native Affairs Commission, 1903–1905, *Take in the Colony of Natal*, 938–39.

76. Responsible Government refers to the establishment of self-administering institutions within a Westminster political system; under Responsible Government, executive power devolved from imperially placed governors to locally (white) elected politicians and a prime minister. This system existed in Natal from 1893 until the establishment of the Union of South Africa in 1910.

2. Sobriety and Settlement

1. The only major work covering nineteenth-century alcohol consumption in Natal is Leigh Anderson's PhD dissertation, which focuses more on criminality and the attempts of the colonial state to manage perceived antisocial activity. While useful, Anderson's work offers more of a list of crimes and crime reports than a systematic analysis of their importance to the settler colonial project. Leigh Anderson, "Society, Economy, and Criminal Activity in Colonial Natal, 1860–1893" (PhD diss., University of Natal, 1993).

2. Anne Kelk Mager, *Beer, Sociability, and Masculinity in South Africa* (Bloomington: Indiana University Press, 2010); Jonathan Crush and Charles Ambler, eds., *Liquor and Labor in Southern Africa* (Athens: Ohio University Press, 1992).

3. Benedict Carton, *Blood from Your Children: The Colonial Origins of Generational Conflict in South Africa* (Charlottesville: University of Virginia Press, 2000); Michael R. Mahoney, *The Other Zulus: The Spread of Zulu Ethnicity in Colonial South Africa* (Durham, N.C.: Duke University Press, 2012); Robert J. Houle, *Making African Christianity: Africans Reimagining Their Faith in Colonial South Africa* (Bethlehem, Pa.: Lehigh University Press, 2011); Keletso E. Atkins, *The Moon Is Dead! Give Us Our Money! The Cultural Origins of an African Work Ethic, Natal, South Africa, 1843–1900* (Portsmouth, UK: Heinemann, 1993).

4. John William Colenso, *Ten Weeks in Natal: A Journal of a First Tour of Visitation among the Colonists and Zulu Kafirs of Natal* (Oxford: Macmillan, 1855), xxvii.

5. PAR, AGO, folder 112A/1865, file 1/8/7.

6. PAR, AGO, folder 112A/1865, file 1/8/7.

7. I have found frequent mention of drunkenness reports in both the *Natal Witness* and the *Natal Mercury*; these findings are corroborated in Leigh Anderson's 1993 thesis on crime in Natal. See Anderson, "Society, Economy, and Criminal Activity in Colonial Natal."

8. PAR, CSO, folder 1200, file 1888/4627.

9. PAR, CSO, folder 1200, file 1888/4378.

10. The promotion would have required that Stransham move from coastal Durban to Pietermaritzburg, about fifty miles inland. Such a move would have at least solved the immediate problem of angry coworkers in the Durban office.

11. This move was far more significant than his initial attempt to relocate to Pietermaritzburg; Johannesburg is 350 miles northwest of Durban, and then outside of British control. PAR, CSO, folder 1200, file 1888/4627.

12. PAR, CSO, folder 1200, file1888/4096.

13. PAR, SNA, folder I/1/141, file 1891/561.

14. PAR, SNA, folder I/1/141, file 1891/561

15. PAR, SNA, folder I/1/141, file 1891/561.

16. Cathy J. Cohen, "Punks, Bulldaggers, and Welfare Queens: The Radical Potential of Queer Politics?," *GLQ: A Journal of Lesbian and Gay Studies* 3, no. 4 (May 1997): 440.

17. Anderson, "Society, Economy, and Criminal Activity in Colonial Natal," 213.

18. *Natal Mercury*, January 18, 1868. Cited in Anderson, "Society, Economy, and Criminal Activity in Colonial Natal," 171.

19. Such an assertion would have echoed well with other voices both in Parliament and in Natal's Legislative Chamber; Charles Barter and J. A. Roebuck both spoke of the decline of indigenous Africans, using Native Americans as examples of that decline. Charles Barter, *The Dorp and the Veld; or, Six Months in Natal* (London: William S. Orr and Co., 1852), 175–76; Great Britain Parliament and Thomas Curson Hansard, *Hansard's Parliamentary Debates*, vol. 116 (London: Hansard, 1851), 272–76.

20. For more on constructions of global indigeneity and global settlement, see chapter 4.

21. Natal (Colony), *Debates of the Legislative Council of the Colony of Natal: First Session—Thirteenth Council, from November 26, 1890, to February 10, 1891*, vol. 15 (Pietermaritzburg: Wm. Watson, 1891), 649.

22. Whether or not such a feat was even *possible*—given both the limited power of the colonial state and the resistance of Africans to settler interference—seems to have been debated less vigorously.

23. Mahoney, *The Other Zulus*, 98.

24. Natal (Colony), *Debates of the Legislative Council of the Colony of Natal: First Session—Twelfth Council, from September 7, 1886 to February 3, 1887*, vol. 9 (Pietermaritzburg: Natal Printing and Publishing Co., 1887), 381.

25. Mahoney, *The Other Zulus*, 99; Carton, *Blood from Your Children*, 70–72.

26. Carton, *Blood from Your Children*; Mahoney, *The Other Zulus*.

27. PAR, SNA, folder 1/1/295, file (1902) 905/1902.

28. There is a danger in investing too heavily in a narrative of patriarchal accommodation, particularly in the way that it constrains the agency of African women. Yet in this particular instance, Guy's theory is both useful and evocative. Alcohol did provide a means of both sociability and intergenerational challenge along gendered lines. Jeff Guy, "An Accommodation of Patriarchs: Theophilus Shepstone and the Foundations of the System of Native Administration in Natal" (Paper presented to the Conference on Masculinities in

Southern Africa, University of Natal, Durban, 1997); for more critical readings of "patriarchal alliances," see Elizabeth Schmidt, *Peasants, Traders, and
Wives: Shona Women in the History of Zimbabwe, 1870–1939* (Portsmouth,
N.H.: Heinemann, 1992); Teresa A. Barnes, *We Women Worked So Hard: Gender, Urbanization, and Social Reproduction in Colonial Harare, Zimbabwe, 1930–
1956* (Oxford: James Currey, 1999).

29. Natal (Colony), *Debates of the Legislative Council of the Colony of Natal:
Second Session—Thirteenth Council, from April 30 to August 7, 1891,* vol. 16 (Pietermaritzburg: Wm. Watson, 1891), 87–90.

30. Natal (Colony), *Debates of the Legislative Council 1891,* 16:14.

31. Natal (Colony), *Debates of the Legislative Council 1890–1891,* 15:14.

32. Even for legislators like Bainbridge, who advocated limited access to
alcohol for ostensibly civilized Africans, alcohol remained a privilege for
white settlers, not to be granted at large to the far more numerous indigenous
population.

33. Natal (Colony), *Debates of the Legislative Council 1891,* 16:88–89.

34. Natal (Colony), *Debates of the Legislative Council of the Colony of Natal:
First Session—Eleventh Council, from July 5 to October 24, 1883,* vol. 6 (Pietermaritzburg: P. Davis and Sons, 1883), 98.

35. Natal (Colony), *Debates of the Legislative Council of the Colony of Natal:
Sixth Session—Twelfth Council, from April 10 to July 8, 1890,* vol. 14 (Pietermaritzburg: Wm. Watson, 1890), 190.

36. "Memorial regarding the Indian Liquor Law 20 of 1890" (document 54:
1891) in PAR, CSO, folder 1451, files 1891/3362, 1891/2453, 1891/4309.

37. "Memorial regarding the Indian Liquor Law 20 of 1890."

38. Lorenzo Veracini, *Settler Colonialism: A Theoretical Overview* (New York:
Palgrave Macmillan, 2010), 26–28.

39. Veracini in particular notes the transition of Irish from racialized, degraded others in nineteenth-century American discourse to their limited and
contingent acceptance as whitened and "virtuous" others by the mid-twentieth
century.

40. "Memorial regarding the Indian Liquor Law 20 of 1890."

41. "Memorial regarding the Indian Liquor Law 20 of 1890."

42. "Memorial in favour of the Indian Liquor Law," PAR, CSO, folder 1451,
file 1891/3362.

43. "Memorial in favour of the Indian Liquor Law."

44. Natal (Colony), *Debates of the Legislative Council 1886,* 9:388.

45. Natal (Colony), *Debates of the Legislative Council 1890,* 14:295.

46. Jodi A. Byrd, *The Transit of Empire: Indigenous Critiques of Colonialism*
(Minneapolis: University of Minnesota Press, 2011).

47. Natal (Colony), *Debates of the Legislative Council of the Colony of Natal:
Third Session—Twelfth Council, from July 18 to October 12, 1888,* vol. 12 (Pietermaritzburg: Wm. Watson, "Times of Natal," 1889), 179.

48. PAR, CSO, folder 1200, file 4670/1888.

49. PAR, CSO, folder 1200, file 4670/1888.

50. PAR, CSO, folder 1200, file 4670/1888, emphasis in original.

51. "A Nasty Case," *Natal Advertiser*, September 24, 1890.

52. The 1887 case of Devon Stransham, as evidenced earlier, certainly shows in turn a measure of official pity and exasperation with an often-inebriate colonist.

53. Natal (Colony), *Debates of the Legislative Assembly of the Colony of Natal: Second Session—First Parliament, from April 25 to July 11, 1894,* vol. 22 (Pietermaritzburg: Wm. Watson, 1894), 541.

54. Natal (Colony), *Debates of the Legislative Assembly of the Colony of Natal: Third Session—First Parliament, from April 25 to August 9, 1895,* vol. 23 (Pietermaritzburg: Wm. Watson, 1895), 562.

55. Judith Butler, "Imitation and Gender Insubordination," in *Inside/Out: Lesbian Theories, Gay Theories,* ed. Diana Fuss, illustrated ed. (New York: Routledge, 1991), 21.

56. *Natal Witness*, August 19, 1881.

57. "Memorial regarding the Indian Liquor Law 20 of 1890."

58. "Memorial regarding the Indian Liquor Law 20 of 1890."

3. The Impossible Handshake

1. John William Colenso, *Ten Weeks in Natal: A Journal of a First Tour of Visitation among the Colonists and Zulu Kafirs of Natal* (Oxford: Macmillan, 1855), 45.

2. Nafisa Essop Sheik, "Customs in Common: Marriage, Law, and the Making of Difference in Colonial Natal," *Gender & History* 29, no. 3 (November 2017): 1–16.

3. The term comes from Clifton C. Crais, *White Supremacy and Black Resistance in Pre-Industrial South Africa: The Making of the Colonial Order in the Eastern Cape, 1770–1865* (Cambridge: Cambridge University Press, 1992), 11.

4. Leela Gandhi, *Affective Communities: Anticolonial Thought, Fin-de-Siècle Radicalism, and the Politics of Friendship* (Durham, N.C.: Duke University Press, 2006), 7.

5. Frank B. Wilderson III, *Red, White, and Black: Cinema and the Structure of U.S. Antagonisms* (Durham, N.C.: Duke University Press, 2010).

6. Wilderson, *Red, White, and Black*, 18, emphasis in original.

7. I am grateful for Jon Soske's phrasing here.

8. Judith Butler, "Imitation and Gender Subordination," in *Inside/Out: Lesbian Theories, Gay Theories,* ed. Diana Fuss, illustrated ed. (New York: Routledge, 1991), 313, emphasis in original.

9. Jodi A. Byrd, *The Transit of Empire: Indigenous Critiques of Colonialism* (Minneapolis: University of Minnesota Press, 2011), 38.

10. Jacques Derrida, *Given Time: 1. Counterfeit Money*, trans. Peggy Kamuf (Chicago: University of Chicago Press, 1992), 10–11.

11. Derrida, *Given Time*, 12.

12. Indeed, this was very truly the result for two generations of Colensos in Natal. The work of the Colenso family to identify with and claim solidarity with Africans against the interests of the settler government was, in many ways, a form of gift-giving. This gift was rife with power inequities, but in turn came with reciprocal claims for protection, aid, or patronage, from a variety of African peoples. This dynamic is most visible in two instances: first, in the correspondence between Colenso's daughter Harriet (1847–1932) and Dinizulu (1868–1913), the son of the Zulu monarch Cetshwayo kaMpande, who had been exiled and imprisoned following the 1906 Bambatha Rebellion. Secondly, in the reciprocal claims offered by the early African nationalist and author Sol Plaatje, who dedicated his *Native Life in South Africa* to Harriet Colenso.

13. Derrida, *Given Time*, 147, emphasis in original.

14. For more on the complexities of conversion, acculturation, and resistance, see: Jean Comaroff and John L. Comaroff, *Of Revelation and Revolution*, Vol. 1: *Christianity, Colonialism, and Consciousness in South Africa*, 1st ed. (Chicago: University of Chicago Press, 1991); Elizabeth Elbourne, *Blood Ground: Colonialism, Missions, and the Contest for Christianity in the Cape Colony and Britain, 1799–1853* (Toronto: McGill-Queen's University Press, 2008); Norman Etherington, *Preachers, Peasants, and Politics in South East Africa, 1835–1880: African Communities in Natal, Pondoland, and Zululand* (London: Royal Historical Society, 1978); Robert J. Houle, *Making African Christianity: Africans Reimagining Their Faith in Colonial South Africa* (Bethlehem, Pa.: Lehigh University Press, 2011).

15. Mimi Thi Nguyen, *The Gift of Freedom: War, Debt, and Other Refugee Passages* (Durham, N.C.: Duke University Press, 2012), 6–12.

16. Quoted in Lady Florence Dixie, *In the Land of Misfortune* (London: R. Bentley and Son, 1882), 423.

17. T.J. Tallie, "August 1882: Zulu King Cetshwayo KaMpande Visits London," in *BRANCH: Britain, Representation, and Nineteenth-Century History*, ed. Dino Franco Felluga, Romanticism and Victorianism on the Net, January 2015, http://www.branchcollective.org/?ps_articles=t-j-tallie-on-zulu-king-cetshwayo-kampandes-visit-to-london-august-1882.

18. Jeff Guy, *The Destruction of the Zulu Kingdom: Civil War in Zululand 1879–84*, 3rd ed. (Pietermaritzburg: University of KwaZulu-Natal Press, 1994); Tallie, "Cetshwayo Visits London."

19. Natal (Colony), *Debates of the Legislative Council of the Colony of Natal: Second Session—Eighth Council, from November 6, 1879 to February 19, 1880*, vol. 1 (Pietermaritzburg: Vause, Slatter & Co., 1880), 452.

20. Natal (Colony), *Report of the Natal Native Commission, 1881–2* (Pietermaritzburg: Vause, Slatter & Co., 1882), 48.

21. South African Native Affairs Commission, 1903–1905, *Minutes of Evidence*, Vol. 3, *Take in the Colony of Natal* (Cape Town: Cape Times Limited, 1904), 415.

22. Josiah Tyler, "The Jubilee Sermon," in *Jubilee of the American Mission in Natal, 1835–1855* (Pietermaritzburg: Horne Brothers, 1886), 52.

23. Tyler, "The Jubilee Sermon," 53.

24. Wilderson, *Red, White, and Black*, 12.

25. Charles Barter, *The Dorp and the Veld; or, Six Months in Natal* (London: William S. Orr and Co., 1852), 171–72.

26. Barter, *The Dorp and the Veld*, 172.

27. Great Britain Parliament and Thomas Curson Hansard, *Hansard's Parliamentary Debates*, vol. 116 (London: Hansard, 1851), 272–76.

28. W. F. Butler, "South Africa," *Natal Witness*, May 6, 1876, emphasis in original.

29. Cecil Ashley, "Notes on Native Questions, South Africa," *National Review*, June 1885, 528.

30. Ashley, "Notes on Native Questions, South Africa," 536.

31. Ashley, "Notes on Native Questions, South Africa," 536.

32. Lewis E. Hertslet, *The Native Problem: Some of Its Points and Phases* (Ntabamahlope, Natal, 1911), 12.

33. Hertslet, *The Native Problem*, 13.

34. Natal (Colony), *Debates of the Legislative Council of the Colony of Natal: Sixth Session—Twelfth Council, from April 10 to July 8, 1890*, vol. 14 (Pietermaritzburg: Wm. Watson, 1890), 295.

35. Natal (Colony) , *Debates of the Legislative Council 1890*, 14:320.

36. Butler, "Imitation and Gender Subordination," 314.

37. Wilderson, *Red, White, and Black*, 18.

4. The Mission Field

1. Clifton C. Crais, *White Supremacy and Black Resistance in Pre-Industrial South Africa: The Making of the Colonial Order in the Eastern Cape, 1770–1865* (Cambridge: Cambridge University Press, 1992), 104.

2. As well as a variety of countries; missionaries labored in Natal from Britain, France, Germany, the United States, and Norway, among other locations.

3. For more on the complex intersections of the colonial state and mission education, see Meghan Healy-Clancy, *A World of Their Own: A History of South African Women's Education* (Charlottesville: University of Virginia Press, 2014); C. G. Henning, *Indian Education in Natal, 1860–1925* (N.p.: n.p., 1992); Risimati Samuel Khandlhela, "Mariannhill Mission and African Education, 1882–1915" (MA thesis, University of Natal, 1993), Killie Campbell Africana Library; Oscar Emil Emanuelson, "A History of Native Education in Natal between 1835 and 1927" (MEd thesis, Natal University College, 1927), Killie Campbell Africana Library (T 379 EMA).

4. This is *not* to argue for a history of missions in Natal that makes missionaries the sole focus. Indeed, I would argue that an approach that over-privileges the centrality of missionaries to the larger imperial history within settler societies in southern Africa runs the risk of fundamentally missing the complex dynamics of competition and interplay between various groups that characterize such colonial regimes. This is a particular weakness in Richard Price's *Making Empire: Colonial Encounters and the Creation of Imperial Rule in Nineteenth-Century Africa* (Cambridge: Cambridge University Press, 2008).

5. Norman Etherington, *Preachers, Peasants, and Politics in South East Africa, 1835–1880: African Communities in Natal, Pondoland, and Zululand* (London: Royal Historical Society, 1978); Jeff Guy, *The Heretic: A Study of the Life of John William Colenso, 1814–1883* (Johannesburg: Ravan Press, 1983).

6. As the late British historian J. D. Y. Peel famously said of missionaries to nineteenth-century West Africa, "the redemptive sacrifice of Christ—which stood at the very heart of evangelical preaching—does not imply double-entry bookkeeping or vice versa." J. D. Y. Peel, *Religious Encounter and the Making of the Yoruba* (Bloomington: Indiana University Press, 2003), 5.

7. Mark Rifkin, *When Did Indians Become Straight? Kinship, the History of Sexuality, and Native Sovereignty* (New York: Oxford University Press, 2011), 10.

8. Such need for repetition is signaled in Judith Butler's critical dismantling of the performative nature of heterosexuality more broadly, which is entirely apt for thinking about the heteronormative ordering that accompanied missionizing. "If there is, as it were, always a compulsion to repeat, repetition never fully accomplishes identity. That there is a need for a repetition at all is a sign that identity is not self-identical." Judith Butler, "Imitation and Gender Subordination," in *Inside/Out: Lesbian Theories, Gay Theories*, ed. Diana Fuss, illustrated ed. (New York: Routledge, 1991), 315.

9. In her work on missionaries and indigenous believers in the Cape, Elizabeth Elbourne offers the most compelling and nuanced critical imperial work on missions in southern Africa to date. See Elizabeth Elbourne, *Blood Ground: Colonialism, Missions, and the Contest for Christianity in the Cape Colony and Britain, 1799–1853* (Toronto: McGill-Queen's University Press, 2008).

10. Jean Comaroff and John L. Comaroff, *Of Revelation and Revolution*, Vol. 1: *Christianity, Colonialism, and Consciousness in South Africa*, 1st ed. (Chicago: University of Chicago Press, 1991).

11. Peel, *Religious Encounter and the Making of the Yoruba*, 153. This is certainly *not* to proffer a straw man articulation of Marxist, revisionist historiography as lacking inherent nuance—Jeff Guy's work in *The Heretic* masterfully demonstrates the inherent contradictions of Bishop John Colenso's seemingly liberal approach to indigenous peoples with his equally fervent desire to fundamentally alter their lives. However, I would assert that the "conversationalist"

model has much to offer in pushing the analysis past useful, if overly broad depictions of monolithic, capitalist, accumulative settler societies (with missionaries in tow) and reluctantly affected indigenous communities.

12. The other settler colonial space that can be considered comparable to Natal in regard to racial minority rule would be the Cape Colony, but the Cape allowed limited African and mixed-race franchise in a way Natal never did in the nineteenth century.

13. Recent work by Robert Houle has effectively argued for indigenous autonomy in the adoption of Christianity, but takes an insufficiently critical approach to the vast power differential that confronted indigenous believers. Robert J. Houle, *Making African Christianity: Africans Reimagining Their Faith in Colonial South Africa* (Bethlehem, Pa.: Lehigh University Press, 2011); Michael R. Mahoney, *The Other Zulus: The Spread of Zulu Ethnicity in Colonial South Africa* (Durham, N.C.: Duke University Press, 2012).

14. G. H. Mason, *Zululand: A Mission Tour in South Africa* (London: James Nisbet & Co., 1862), 12.

15. Eliza Whigham Feilden, *My African Home; or, Bush Life in Natal When a Young Colony (1852–7)* (London: T. W. Griggs, 1887), 311.

16. Josiah Tyler, *Forty Years among the Zulus* (Boston: Congregational Sunday-School and Publishing Society, 1891), 129.

17. Feilden, *My African Home*, 16–17.

18. Esme Cleall, *Missionary Discourses of Difference: Negotiating Otherness in the British Empire, 1840–1900* (New York: Palgrave Macmillan, 2012), 49.

19. Jean Comaroff and John L. Comaroff, "Home-Made Hegemony: Modernity, Domesticity, and Colonialism in South Africa," in *African Encounters with Domesticity,* ed. Karen Tranberg Hansen (New Brunswick, N.J.: Rutgers University Press, 1992), 37–74.

20. Nancy Rose Hunt, "Colonial Fairy Tales and the Knife and Fork Doctrine in the Heart of Africa," in *African Encounters with Domesticity,* ed. Karen Tranberg Hansen (New Brunswick, N.J.: Rutgers University Press, 1992), 163.

21. Eva Jackson, "The Economic Experimentation of Nembula Duze/Ira Adams Nembula, 1845–1886," *Journal of Natal and Zulu History* 27 (2011): 9.

22. This approach was not unique to Natal. Edward Elwin, a British missionary to India, mused that "other missions, and especially those worked by dissenters, always make their children and converts wear trousers, on account of which people have sometimes sarcastically spoken of the spread of Christianity amongst the heathen as being made a matter of trousers." Edward Fenton Elwin, *Indian Jottings: From Ten Year's Experience in and around Poona City* (London: J. Murray, 1907), 43.

23. The Grouts were long-term missionaries appointed by the American Board of Commissioners for Foreign Missions (ABCFM), a predominantly Congregationalist body that also at times admitted Presbyterians, Dutch Reformed, and other mainline Protestant sects. Their station eventually grew

into a still-extant community, Groutville, located about forty miles north of Durban, near the coast.

24. Charlotte Grout, "Nomashinga," *Life and Light for Woman* (1875): 285.

25. Meghan Elizabeth Healy and Eva Jackson, "Practices of Naming and the Possibilities of Home on American Zulu Mission Stations in Colonial Natal," *Journal of Natal and Zulu History* 29 (2011): 5.

26. For more on the construction of kinship and the normativizing power of heterosexuality in relation to colonial family networks, see Cathy J. Cohen, "Punks, Bulldaggers, and Welfare Queens: The Radical Potential of Queer Politics?," *GLQ: A Journal of Lesbian and Gay Studies* 3, no. 4 (May 1997): 437–65; Rifkin, *When Did Indians Become Straight?*, 5–7.

27. Healy and Jackson, "Practices of Naming."

28. Grout, "Nomashinga," 285.

29. Grout, "Nomashinga," 285.

30. Susan W. Tyler, "The Contrast," *Life and Light for Woman* (1874): 92–93.

31. James Dube was the father of John L. Dube, who in 1912 became the first president of the organization that evolved into the African National Congress.

32. As the wife of the colonial secretary, Lady Barker and her husband, Frederick Broome, lived primarily in Pietermaritzburg.

33. Lady Mary Barker, *Colonial Memories* (London: Smith, Elder, & Co., 1904), 210.

34. Barker, *Colonial Memories*, 213.

35. Presumably, *ilobolo* (see chapter 1). Barker, *Colonial Memories*, 213.

36. Barker, *Colonial Memories*, 214.

37. Sihlobosami [A. T. Bryant], *Roman Legion on Libyan Fields; or, The Story of the Trappist Missionaries among the Zulus in Natal, South Africa: The Establishment of Their Monastery at Mariannhill and the Past and Present Condition and Prosperity of Their Missions* (Mariannhill: Mariannhill Press, 1887), 40.

38. Sihlobosami [A. T. Bryant], *Roman Legion on Libyan Fields*, 246.

39. Sihlobosami [A. T. Bryant], *Roman Legion on Libyan Fields*, 47.

40. That Africans themselves would have likely identified as heterosexual is irrelevant to the process of pathologization rendered by a white heteronormative settler society. See Cohen, "Punks, Bulldaggers, and Welfare Queens," 454–55.

41. Feilden, *My African Home*, 289.

42. Feilden, *My African Home*, 289.

43. Sihlobosami [A. T. Bryant], *Roman Legion on Libyan Fields*, 188–89.

44. Butler, "Imitation and Gender Subordination," 313, emphasis in original.

45. Butler, "Imitation and Gender Subordination," 314, emphasis in original.

46. Emma Tarlo, *Clothing Matters: Dress and Identity in India* (Chicago: University of Chicago Press, 1996), 40–42.

47. Feilden, *My African Home*, 28–29.

48. Feilden, *My African Home*, 31.
49. Feilden, *My African Home*, 32.
50. Elbourne, *Blood Ground*, 196.
51. For the use of bricolage, see Jonathan A. Draper's work in *The Eye of the Storm: Bishop John William Colenso and the Crisis of Biblical Inspiration*, illustrated ed. (New York: Continuum, 2004).
52. Barker, *Colonial Memories*, 214.
53. Esidumbini was located about fifty miles north of Durban. Tyler, *Forty Years among the Zulus*, 141.
54. I have discovered very little written on *Ikwezi* in an academic context. The newspaper merits a brief mention in Jonathan Draper's work. See Draper, *The Eye of the Storm*.
55. "Izindaba ngokuqala kwa le ncwadi," *Ikwezi*, April 1861, emphasis added. Original Zulu: "Abelungu bonke, ba na zo izincwadi. Ezinye zi cindezelwa ngemihla yonke kusasa na kusihlwa. Uma umlungu enga yamukeli incwadi, si ti umpofu lowo, uma enge mpofu, si ti, u fanele uku datyukelwa kakhulu, ngokuba u hlezi, e ngazi 'luto ngokuhamba kwabantu aba njengaye ezizweni ezinye. Po ke si nge be nayo ngani incwadi tina na? Singabafundayo abaningi kangaka Ezikoleni zonke!"
56. "Izindaba ngokuqala kwa le ncwadi." Original Zulu: "Si tanda kakulu ukuba si yi bone njalo incwadi pakathi kwezindhlu zabantu amanyama na loko'kutanda ku si rolele ukuba si yi veze le'ncwadi."
57. "Izindaba ngokuqala kwa le ncwadi." Original Zulu: "Lobanini ngemikuba yabantu ba kini nangabamhlope, ninga sabi, ni shumayezane."
58. "Izwe lase Natal li ya buswa manje," *Ikwezi*, January 1863. Original Zulu: "Izwe lase Natal li ya buswa manje. Kwenziwa amabruhu (bridges) pezu kwemifula—nemigwaqo I ya lungiswa—-izindhlu ezinhle ziyanda—umhlabati u ya linyway—umoba nekampokwe nekofi nokunye ukudhla.... Abamnyama bay a fundiswa ezikoleni, ba busa kakulu, bay a fukulwa'mpela ngezwi leNkosi."
59. For more on the very minimal progress of Christian conversion among Zulu peoples in the nineteenth century, see Etherington, *Preachers, Peasants, and Politics in South East Africa, 1835–1880*; Houle, *Making African Christianity*.
60. Of particular interest is the Zulu-language explanation of the Emancipation Proclamation in January 1863, made by Inkosi Mr. Lincoln ("Chief Mr. Lincoln"). "Izwe lase Natal li ya buswa manje," *Ikwezi*, January 1863.
61. The January 1863 article, in addition to describing the Civil War and the Emancipation Proclamation, also described how presidential elections took place and provided a brief sketch of how American politics functioned.
62. "Naso isafazana sama North American Indian!," *Ikwezi*, August 1863. Original Zulu: "Naso isifazana sama North American Indian! Si pet' ingane. Omunye umtwana waso upanyekiwe emutini. Ama Indian ezweni lase Merika ba ngabantu aba bomvu. Izinhlobo zi ningi. Abanye ba kanyisiwe. Abanye ba

sebumnyameni, ba yalway njalo. Pakati kwamaSioux, ku tiwa, intombi i yal' indoda, uma yona i nga letanga ku yo isikumba sekanda sesita sakubo."

63. Jodi A. Byrd, *The Transit of Empire: Indigenous Critiques of Colonialism* (Minneapolis: University of Minnesota Press, 2011), 27.

64. Edendale also became name to the larger apartheid-era township that developed from the original mission station, situated about six miles south of Pietermaritzburg. Sheila M. Meintjes, "Edendale 1850–1906: A Case Study of Rural Transformation and Class Formation in an African Mission in Natal" (PhD diss., University of London, School of Oriental and African Studies, 1988), 119–20; Debbie Whelan, "Whose Colony and Whose Legacy? Layers of Power and Hybrid Identities in Edendale, Pietermaritzburg, South Africa," in *Colonial Architecture and Urbanism in Africa: Intertwined and Contested Histories,* ed. Fassil Demissie (Burlington, Vt.: Ashgate, 2012), 108–9.

65. For more on the history of Edendale, see Marc Epprecht, *Welcome to Greater Edendale: Histories of Environment, Health, and Gender in an African City* (Toronto: McGill-Queen's University Press, 2016).

66. Mary Anne Barker, *A Year's Housekeeping in South Africa*, 2nd ed. (London: Macmillan, 1879), 198.

67. "Edendale," *Natal Witness*, January 11, 1876.

68. "The Native Question," *Natal Witness*, August 16, 1879.

69. "The Native Question," emphasis added.

70. Barker, *A Year's Housekeeping in South Africa*, 205.

71. Barker's reaction typifies what Homi Bhabha described as colonial mimicry's ability to serve as a "sign of the inappropriate, however, a difference or recalcitrance that coheres the dominant strategic function of colonial power, intensifies surveillance, and poses an imminent threat to both 'normalized' knowledges and disciplinary powers." Homi Bhabha, "Of Mimicry and Man: The Ambivalence of Colonial Discourse," in *Tensions of Empire: Colonial Cultures in a Bourgeois World,* ed. Frederick Cooper and Ann Laura Stoler (Berkeley: University of California Press, 1997), 153.

72. Etherington, *Preachers, Peasants, and Politics in South East Africa, 1835–1880,* 162–68.

73. "Unveiling the Monument," *Natal Witness*, February 14, 1880.

74. Esme Cleall, *Missionary Discourses of Difference: Negotiating Otherness in the British Empire, 1840–1900* (New York: Palgrave Macmillan, 2012), 57.

75. Natal (Colony), *Debates of the Legislative Council of the Colony of Natal: Second Session—Eighth Council, from November 6, 1879 to February 19, 1880,* vol. 1 (Pietermaritzburg: Vause, Slatter & Co., 1880), 200.

76. Natal (Colony), *Debates of the Legislative Council 1879–1880,* 1:149.

77. Natal (Colony), *Debates of the Legislative Council 1879–1880,* 1:200.

78. Natal (Colony), *Debates of the Legislative Council 1879–1880,* 1:149.

79. Natal (Colony), *Debates of the Legislative Council 1879–1880,* 1:49.

80. Natal (Colony), *Debates of the Legislative Council 1879–1880,* 1:151.

81. Natal (Colony), *Debates of the Legislative Council 1879–1880,* 1:151.

82. Natal (Colony), *Debates of the Legislative Council 1879–1880*, 1:151.

83. Natal (Colony), *Debates of the Legislative Council 1879–1880*, 1:282.

84. "The Performance at Edendale," *Natal Witness*, February 14, 1880.

85. Richard Price, *Making Empire: Colonial Encounters and the Creation of Imperial Rule in Nineteenth-Century Africa* (Cambridge: Cambridge University Press, 2008); Marilyn Lake and Henry Reynolds, *Drawing the Global Colour Line* (Cambridge: Cambridge University Press, 2008); Catherine Hall, *Civilising Subjects: Metropole and Colony in the English Imagination 1830–1867* (Chicago: University of Chicago Press, 2002); Crais, *White Supremacy and Black Resistance*; Dane Keith Kennedy, *Islands of White: Settler Society and Culture in Kenya and Southern Rhodesia, 1890–1939* (Durham, N.C.: Duke University Press, 1987).

86. As was certainly the case in all other settler colonies; however, Natal's settler population lacked the simple demographic majority to even *pretend* that they were the only inhabitants in the colony.

87. Cleall, *Missionary Discourses of Difference*, 163.

88. Solomon Kumalo, "Ku mhleli we nkanyiso," *Inkanyiso yaseNatal*, June 7, 1889. Original Zulu: "Indaba ezimnandi sizizwa ngekwanelelyo ezincwadini ezingcwele (religious books) nasemasontweni. Epepeni lendaba (newspaper) silindele indaba zembuso, nezinye ezimalunga nosizo lwomuntu lapa emhlabeni."

5. "To Become Useful and Patriotic Citizens"

1. Natal (Colony), *Debates of the Legislative Assembly of the Colony of Natal: Second Session—First Parliament, from April 25 to July 11, 1894*, vol. 22 (Pietermaritzburg: Wm. Watson, 1894), 103.

2. CSO, folder 1308, file 1891/4888.

3. Natal (Colony), "Part VII.—Education," in *Department Reports—1896* (Pietermaritzburg: P. Davis & Sons, 1897).

4. Natal (Colony), *Debates of the Legislative Assembly of the Colony of Natal: Second Session of the Fifth Parliament, from August 20 to October 3, 1907. Second Volume of Session*, vol. 43 (Pietermaritzburg: P. Davis & Sons, 1907), 255–57. According to Percy Barnett, the superintendent for education, in 1902, the "expenditure per head for all European schools, per pupil, in the year, was £4 7s. 4d; the expenditure for all Indian schools, per pupil, was £1 11s 1¾ d; the expenditure for all Native schools, per head, was 13s. 2¾ d." South African Native Affairs Commission, 1903–1905, *Minutes of Evidence*, vol. 3, *Take in the Colony of Natal* (Cape Town: Cape Times Limited, 1904), 237.

5. In 1911, the American Mission Board estimated "the present cost to Government for the education of each native child, reckoned on the basis of average attendance is 18/8 ($4.42), as compared with £6 10s 7d ($32.12) per European child." James Dexter Taylor, *The American Board Mission in South Africa: A Sketch of Seventy-Five Years* (Durban: John Singleton & Sons, 1911), 43.

6. "Report of the Inspector of Native Education on the Government Industrial Native School, Zwaartkop Location, for the year ending June 30, 1892," CSO, folder 1344, file 1892/4580.

7. "Petition representing the Natal Indian community, regarding regulations under Sec 9 of No. 5. 1894, re: education of Indian Children," CSO, folder 1872, file 1909/2847.

8. Oscar Emil Emanuelson, "A History of Native Education in Natal between 1835 and 1927" (MEd thesis, Natal University College, 1927), 38–39, Killie Campbell Africana Library (T 379 EMA).

9. Emanuelson, "History of Native Education," 58–59.

10. Meghan Healy-Clancy, *A World of Their Own: A History of South African Women's Education* (Charlottesville: University of Virginia Press, 2014), 71.

11. "Memorial on the Subject of Native Education," CSO, folder 726, file 1879/4976.

12. Quoted in Ernest Albert Belcher and G. Churton Collins, eds., *The Durban High School Record 1866–1906* (Durban: John Singleton & Sons, 1906), 41.

13. This is, however, not to imply that all schools for European children were undifferentiated by factors such as class. While the number of Dutch-speaking children was much smaller in proportion in Natal than in the Cape, differences in ethnic origin, socioeconomic status, and geographic location all did impact education for white students. For more on class and language differences among European children, see S. Duff, *Changing Childhoods in the Cape Colony: Dutch Reformed Church Evangelicalism and Colonial Childhood, 1860–1895* (New York: Springer, 2015).

14. It remains important to note that this was not a universal experience for white settler children, particularly the children of artisans or poor farmers. However, the prevailing power and influence wielded by these wealthy children and their descendants would shape legislation and government policy. Robert Morrell, *From Boys to Gentlemen: Settler Masculinity in Colonial Natal, 1880–1920* (Pretoria: UNISA, 2001).

15. Keletso E. Atkins, *The Moon Is Dead! Give Us Our Money! The Cultural Origins of an African Work Ethic, Natal, South Africa, 1843–1900* (Portsmouth, UK: Heinemann, 1993), 2.

16. R. E. Ridley, "Native Policy," *Natal Mercury*, March 11, 1869.

17. Natal (Colony), *Report of the Natal Native Commission, 1881–2* (Pietermaritzburg: Vause, Slatter & Co., 1882), 157–70.

18. Natal (Colony), *Report of the Natal Native Commission, 1881–2*, 157–70.

19. Emanuelson, "History of Native Education," 116.

20. Healy-Clancy, *A World of Their Own*, 72.

21. Robert Plant, "Minute on Native Education," in "Report of the Inspector of Native Education for 1890 on the Government Aided Native Schools," CSO, folder 1253, file 1890/1603.

22. Plant, "Minute on Native Education." For more on Inanda and Adams Training College/Amazimtoti, see Healy-Clancy, *A World of Their Own*, 73.

23. Emanuelson, "History of Native Education," 121–23.

24. "Report of the Inspector of Native Education on the Government Industrial Native School, Zwaartkop Location, 1889," CSO, folder 1253, file 1890/1603, p. 4.

25. "Report of the Inspector of Native Education on the Government Industrial Native School, Zwaartkop Location, 1889," CSO, folder 1253, file 1890/1603, p. 4.

26. South African Native Affairs Commission, 1903–1905, *Native Affairs Commission (Natal)*, 234.

27. "Report of the Inspector of Native Education on the Government Industrial Native School, Zwaartkop Location, for the year ending June 30, 1892," CSO, folder 1344, file 1892/4580.

28. Healy-Clancy, *A World of Their Own*, 74.

29. Indian men and women first began to arrive in Natal in the early 1860s to provide labor on sugar plantations on the coast.

30. Natal (Colony), *Report of the Coolie Commission, Appointed to Inquire into the Condition of the Indian Immigrants in the Colony of Natal; the Mode in Which They Are Employed; and Also to Inquire into the Complaints Made by Returned Immigrants to the Protector of Emigrants at Calcutta* (Pietermaritzburg: P. Davis and Sons, 1872), 18.

31. Natal (Colony), *Report of the Coolie Commission*, 22.

32. Natal (Colony), *Report of the Coolie Commission*, 27.

33. Henry David Kannemeyer, "A Critical Survey of Indian Education in Natal, 1860–1937" (MEd thesis, University of the Witwatersrand, 1943), 36, Killie Campbell Africana Library.

34. Kannemeyer, "Critical Survey of Indian Education," 48.

35. Natal (Colony), *Debates of the Legislative Council of the Colony of Natal: Second Session—Ninth Council, from October 6, to December 14, 1881*, vol. 3 (Pietermaritzburg: P. Davis and Sons, 1882), 180–81.

36. Natal (Colony), *Debates of the Legislative Council 1881*, 3:180–81, emphasis added.

37. Natal (Colony), *Debates of the Legislative Council 1881*, 3:181.

38. Natal (Colony), *Debates of the Legislative Council 1881*, 3:181.

39. Quoted in Emanuelson, "History of Native Education," 84–85.

40. Quoted in Emanuelson, "History of Native Education," 84–85.

41. Natal (Colony), *Debates of the Legislative Council 1881*, 3:181.

42. Kannemeyer, "Critical Survey of Indian Education," 150.

43. F. S. Tatham, *The Race Conflict in South Africa: An Enquiry into the General Question of Native Education* (Pietermaritzburg: Munro Bros, 1894), 6.

44. Tatham, *The Race Conflict in South Africa*, 18.

45. Tatham, *The Race Conflict in South Africa*, 20.

46. Charles Barter, *The Dorp and the Veld; or, Six Months in Natal* (London: William S. Orr and Co., 1852), 171–72.

47. Cecil Ashley, "Notes on Native Questions, South Africa," *National Review*, June 1885, 528.

48. Frederick Tucker, *On Native Education* (Pietermaritzburg: P. Davis & Sons, 1895), 1.

49. Tucker, *On Native Education*, 2.

50. Natal (Colony), *Debates of the Legislative Assembly 1894*, 22:104–5.

51. The invocation, however, is somewhat inconsistent, as the Morant Bay Rebellion linked to Gordon led to inter-imperial outrage and resulted in the revoking of the authority of the white-dominated House Assembly in Jamaica. As a consequence, Jamaica became a Crown colony, the exact opposite position of the newly won Responsible Government of Natal's settler minority government.

52. Natal (Colony), *Debates of the Legislative Assembly 1894*, 22:155.

53. Natal (Colony), *Debates of the Legislative Assembly of the Colony of Natal: Fourth Session—First Parliament, from April 8 to July 1, 1896*, vol. 24 (Pietermaritzburg: Wm. Watson, 1896), 168–69.

54. Natal (Colony), *Debates of the Legislative Assembly 1896*, 24:174.

55. Natal (Colony), *Debates of the Legislative Assembly 1894*, 22:105.

56. Natal (Colony), *Debates of the Legislative Council of the Colony of Natal: Third Session—Twelfth Council, from July 18 to October 12, 1888*, vol. 12 (Pietermaritzburg: Wm. Watson, "Times of Natal," 1889), 203.

57. South African Native Affairs Commission, 1903–1905, *Native Affairs Commission (Natal)*, 213.

58. South African Native Affairs Commission, *Native Affairs Commission (Natal)*, 537.

59. Ernest Albert Belcher, ed., *Teachers in Council: Being a Record of the Natal Teachers' Convention, 1903* (Durban: J. C. Juta & Company, 1904), 11–12.

60. Belcher, ed., *Teachers in Council 1903*, 11–12.

61. Belcher, ed., *Teachers in Council 1903*, 32–34.

62. Morrell, *From Boys to Gentlemen*, 60–61.

63. Belcher, ed., *Teachers in Council 1903*, 32.

64. Belcher, ed., *Teachers in Council 1903*, 104–11.

65. Belcher, ed., *Teachers in Council 1903*, 104–11.

66. Belcher, ed., *Teachers in Council 1903*, 34–36.

67. Belcher, ed., *Teachers in Council 1903*, 11.

68. Belcher, ed., *Teachers in Council 1903*, 35–36.

69. Healy-Clancy, *A World of Their Own*, 60–70.

70. Healy-Clancy, *A World of Their Own*, 73–74.

71. Healy-Clancy, *A World of Their Own*, 73–74.

72. Robert Plant, "Annual Report of Native Schools for 1891," CSO, folder 1308, file 1891/4888.

73. Jeff Guy, "An Accommodation of Patriarchs: Theophilus Shepstone and the Foundations of the System of Native Administration in Natal" (Paper presented to the Conference on Masculinities in Southern Africa, University of Natal, Durban, 1997); Healy-Clancy, *A World of Their Own*, 60–70.

74. Michael R. Mahoney, *The Other Zulus: The Spread of Zulu Ethnicity in Colonial South Africa* (Durham, N.C.: Duke University Press, 2012).

75. Emanuelson, "History of Native Education," 157.

76. Quoted in Risimati Samuel Khandlhela, "Mariannhill Mission and African Education, 1882–1915" (MA thesis, University of Natal, 1993), 106, Killie Campbell Africana Library.

77. Belcher, ed., *Teachers in Council 1903*, 119–20.

Conclusion

1. Mrinalini Sinha, *Colonial Masculinity: The "Manly Englishman" and the "Effeminate Bengali" in the Late Nineteenth Century* (Manchester: Manchester University Press, 1995); Tony Ballantyne, *Orientalism and Race: Aryanism in the British Empire*, Cambridge Imperial and Post-Colonial Studies Series (Houndmills, UK: Palgrave, 2002); Tony Ballantyne and Antoinette Burton, *Moving Subjects: Gender, Mobility, and Intimacy in an Age of Global Empire*, illustrated ed. (Urbana: University of Illinois Press, 2008); Antoinette Burton, *At the Heart of the Empire: Indians and the Colonial Encounter in Late-Victorian Britain*, 1st ed. (Berkeley: University of California Press, 1998); Antoinette Burton, *Bodies in Contact: Rethinking Colonial Encounters in World History* (Durham, N.C.: Duke University Press, 2005); Catherine Hall, *Civilising Subjects: Metropole and Colony in the English Imagination 1830–1867* (Chicago: University of Chicago Press, 2002).

2. Andrew Duminy and Bill Guest, *Natal and Zululand from Earliest Times to 1910: A New History* (Pietermaritzburg: University of Natal Press, 1989).

3. Bernard Porter, *The Absent-Minded Imperialists: Empire, Society, and Culture in Britain* (Oxford: Oxford University Press, 2004); Richard Price, *Making Empire: Colonial Encounters and the Creation of Imperial Rule in Nineteenth-Century Africa* (Cambridge: Cambridge University Press, 2008); David Cannadine, *Ornamentalism: How the British Saw Their Empire* (Oxford: Oxford University Press, 2002).

4. This is more in keeping with the weblike, refractory, and multifaceted views of imperial connections argued best by Ballantyne, Burton, Mawani, and Perry. Ballantyne, *Orientalism and Race*; Ballantyne and Burton, *Moving Subjects*; Renisa Mawani, *Colonial Proximities: Crossracial Encounters and Juridical Truths in British Columbia, 1871–1921* (Vancouver: University of British Columbia Press, 2009); Adele Perry, *On the Edge of Empire: Gender, Race, and the Making of British Columbia, 1849–1871*, Studies in Gender and History (Toronto: University of Toronto Press, 2001).

5. For this insight I am indebted to Jean Y. Lee.

6. Natal (Colony), *Debates of the Legislative Assembly of the Colony of Natal: Second Session—First Parliament, from April 25 to July 11, 1894,* vol. 22 (Pietermaritzburg: Wm. Watson, 1894), 576.

7. Natal (Colony), *Debates of the Legislative Council of the Colony of Natal: Second Session—Eighth Council, from November 6, 1879 to February 19, 1880,* vol. 1 (Pietermaritzburg: Vause, Slatter & Co., 1880), 308–9.

8. Michael R. Mahoney, *The Other Zulus: The Spread of Zulu Ethnicity in Colonial South Africa* (Durham, N.C.: Duke University Press, 2012); Robert Morrell, *From Boys to Gentlemen: Settler Masculinity in Colonial Natal, 1880–1920* (Pretoria: UNISA, 2001).

9. Judith Butler, "Merely Cultural," *Social Text,* no. 52–53 (1997): 265–77.

10. Keletso E. Atkins, *The Moon Is Dead! Give Us Our Money! The Cultural Origins of an African Work Ethic, Natal, South Africa, 1843–1900* (Portsmouth, UK: Heinemann, 1993), 2–4.

11. Butler, "Merely Cultural," 272, emphasis in original.

12. Stuart Hall, "Race, Culture, and Communications: Looking Backward and Forward at Cultural Studies," *Rethinking Marxism* 5, no. 1 (1992): 10–18, https://doi.org/10.1080/08935699208657998; Eric Williams, *Capitalism and Slavery* (New York: Capricorn, 1966).

13. Sumaya Ismail and SAPA, "Mixed Reaction to Zuma Apology," *Mail & Guardian,* September 28, 2006, http://mg.co.za/article/2006-09-28-mixed-reaction-to-zuma-apology.

14. "Zwelithini: Gays Are 'Rotten,'" *Mail & Guardian Online,* http://mg.co.za/article/2012-01-23-zwelithini-gays-are-rotten/.

15. Puleng Mashabane, "'Gay Slur': Zulu Fundi Hears Audio," *The Citizen,* January 24, 2012, http://www.citizen.co.za/citizen/content/en/citizen/local-news?oid=253975&sn=Detail&pid=146849&%E2%80%98Gay-slur%E2%80%99—-Zulu-fundi-hears-audio.

16. This is contrasted with *isishimane,* a man deemed too timid to interact with women properly. See Mark Hunter, *Love in the Time of AIDS: Inequality, Gender, and Rights in South Africa* (Bloomington: Indiana University Press, 2010).

17. Neville Hoad, *African Intimacies: Race, Homosexuality, and Globalization,* 1st ed. (Minneapolis: University of Minnesota Press, 2007), xvi.

18. Scott Lauria Morgensen, "Settler Homonationalism: Theorizing Settler Colonialism within Queer Modernities." *GLQ* 16, no. 1–2 (April 2010): 106.

19. Raewyn Connell, "Rethinking Gender from the South," *Feminist Studies* 40, no. 3 (2014): 518–39; Marc Epprecht, *Heterosexual Africa? The History of an Idea from the Age of Exploration to the Age of AIDS,* New African Histories Series (Athens: Ohio University Press, 2008), 14.

Index

Achmat, Zackie, 10
Afghanistan, 147
Ahmed, Sara
alcohol: and belonging, 55, 57–58, 63–64, 68, 73, 76–77, 79–80, 82, 108; brandy, 59, 90; and citizenship, 50, 53, 57, 60, 72–74, 76–77, 82–83, 86; as commodity, 53, 55, 79–80; drunkenness, 55–56, 58–67, 76, 79, 83–85, 88–89; and gender normativity, 54, 56, 58, 64, 83–87; gin, 59, 85; indigenous beer, 11, 54–55, 58, 68–70, 75 (see also *utshwala*); laws against, 58, 70–76, 79, 82, 86–90, 185, 187, 191 (*see also* 1890 Liquor Law); and morality, 54, 56, 72, 79, 81, 83, 85–89; and race, 11, 53–55, 57, 60, 62, 64–65, 68, 72–75, 79–80, 83, 85–90, 187, 191; and resistance, 54–55; and sobriety, 11, 56, 58–59, 61, 89–90; and threat of sexual violence, 83–86
amakholwa, 35, 37–38, 47, 63, 65, 113, 115, 118, 121, 123, 132, 134, 136, 139, 142, 148–49, 155, 159, 165, 177–79. *See also* Christianity; mission field

Anglican, 11, 25, 37, 44. *See also* Christianity
Anglo-Zulu War, 34, 56–57, 99, 101, 116, 138, 140–42, 148, 155, 157–59, 183
anxiety, 3, 20, 27, 45, 129, 152
Atkins, Keletso, 158
Australia, 2–3, 6, 43, 57, 153

Barker, Lady Mary Anne, 2, 123–24, 132, 137, 139, 148
Basotho, 137
bodies: control of, 1, 11, 16–17, 21, 27, 34, 39–42, 49, 55–56, 71–72, 88, 90, 95, 111, 119, 122, 136, 145, 191; as corrupt/aberrant/queer, 7–8, 16, 23, 47, 65, 72, 88, 117, 128, 145, 190; sites of conflict, 28, 72, 88, 94, 111, 122, 167, 184–85
Boer, 22, 62, 137
Boer War, 183–84
Boshoff, J. C., 143
bridewealth (*ilobolo*), 8, 10, 15–44, 47, 51, 54, 148, 187
British Empire, 1, 4, 11, 20, 43, 73, 99, 124, 146, 184–86, 191. *See also* colonialism